FOCUS ON SURVIVAL

A young family's struggle to survive World War II

JULIE BAYL

Copyright © 2019 by Julie Bayl

All rights reserved. No part of this book may be reproduced, scanned, or distributed in any printed or electronic form without permission.

First Edition: January 2019
Printed in the United States of America

ISBN-10: 164254082X
ISBN-13: 781642540826

To the memory of Gerard Bernard Heinrich Bijl (Ben Bijl),
Maggeltje Bijl-Flach (Em), and their children, Gerda,

Charles, Louis, Marjolein, Paul, Walter, and Selma,
and Ben's children from a previous marriage,

Ben and Hans, and also Johanna.

For my children, Anita, Paul, and David, and
my grandchildren, Lennon and Banjo.

Wisdom is for protection, the same as money is for protection: but the advantage of knowledge is this: Wisdom preserves the lives of its owners.

—Ecclesiastes 7:12 (NWT)

For everything there is an appointed time: a time for … love … war … peace.

—Ecclesiastes 3:1, 8 (NWT)

I would like to express thanks to the following people
who helped me in the writing of this book:

Mum and Dad, you were my inspiration, Mum for sharing
with me the details that make this story come alive.

AnIta, David, Gerda, Charles, Ada and Marjo, thank
you for proofreading and for your input.

Also, Paul and David, Gerda and Debbie, thank you for your
great assistance with the photos that paint the picture.

Table of Contents

1. Zeist, Province of Utrecht during Nazi Occupation in The Netherlands, late 1943 1
2. Chaam, Province of North Brabant, The Netherlands, 1926 10
3. Her Heartfelt Wish 19
4. The Meeting in Baarn, 1934 29
5. Love, 1935 43
6. The Move to Zeist in 1936 57
7. The World at War, 1939 64
8. A Son with Haemophilia 74
9. Forging Passports for the Underground 80
10. Apprehended by the Nazis 87
11. The Masquerade 97
12. The Game of Cat and Mouse Continues 110
13. Survival the Paramount Issue 117
14. A Death and a Birth 125
15. Manpower Called up in Zeist 140
16. A People Betrayed 151
17. A Joyful Wedding 154
18. Trouble Comes in Threes 165
19. Hungry and Pregnant Again 171
20. The Ride to Zwolle 181
21. Em's Courage and a Man with a Kind Heart 199
22. Living with Haemophilia 216
23. The Desperate Winter 1944-45 224
24. Liberation Day Arrives! 231

PROLOGUE

The creation of any family is the melding of two unique family trees and backgrounds. This true story is about Em Flach and Ben Bijl. Following is a brief history of their two families.

Em

Em's parents were Johan Flach and Anna van der Waal, who were born in The Netherlands in the last quarter of the nineteenth century. To Anna's parents, Em's grandparents, marrying Johan was absolutely taboo! The prejudice of 1900 Dutch society was very much akin to the Indian caste system. "The twain shall never meet," as the saying goes, and to Anna's family—the wealthy van der Waals and van der Giessens —Anna was marrying beneath herself. Although Johan Flach's parents made a comfortable living, owning a haberdashery business and they were also travelling tailors, Anna's parents still did not approve. As a result, Anna's father at first forbade the marriage. However, on his deathbed, her father (who died very young due to a fall from a horse) gave his consent, but her mother, Maggeltje, continued to oppose it.

Em was named after her grandmother, who was an extremely good businesswoman. She won fame, awards, and wealth throughout her home province for her amazing cheeses. She also owned much property and set her sons up for life on beautiful farms. Although opposing her only daughter, Anna, in her determination to marry Johan, in the end she allowed the young couple to marry, out of respect for her late husband, Cornelius' wishes.

Anna though had a price to pay. The penalty was to be cut out of her wealthy family's will.

In the early years of their marriage, Anna and Johan lived in Ridderkerk. Anna gave birth to seven daughters and one son. During this time, Anna's mother came to the aid of Anna and Johan, helping them survive the German Occupation over The Netherlands during the Great War.

Johan searched for a farm of his own, so he sold his lucrative haberdashery business in Ridderkerk and looked for land suitable for mixed farming. Finally, he purchased land in the south of The Netherlands in the small town of Chaam. The family rented a house until their traditionally built farmhouse and barns were erected on the virgin land. To own his own farm had always been the passion of her father, but Em, the third daughter, detested the rigorous farm life, as she and her sisters worked like men with their father in the fields and cared for the menagerie of animals. Why didn't her brother, Gerrit, work with his father? He had a very delicate constitution. So as Em grew into her teens, she vowed she would never marry a farmer. Life on the land was just too hard. She could never understand why a man with eight children—all girls but one—would take on such a challenge. The girls were encouraged to become tailoresses like their father, but Em had other ideas.

Ben

In the little village of St Maartensbrug in North Holland there is a monument built in the shape of a camera to commemorate the work of W.D. Niestadt and Sons. He is called the Father of Photography in The Netherlands. Today there is a museum which is presently setting up 1000's of photos taken by W.D. Niestadt and his descendants for public exhibition.

Ben's grandfather was Gerard Bernard Heinrich, the elder of William Diederich's sons. He was born in 1842 in Berge in Germany. His younger brother was also called Wilhelm, after his father. The boys' father Wilhelm, along with his twin brother, decided to move to The Netherlands after the boys' mother, Wilhelm's wife, died. It was around 1850 when they moved to St. Maartensbrug.

Ben's parents, GBH Niestadt and wife, one of WD Niestadt's sons.

The Monument in St Maartensbrug honouring the Niestadt family for pioneering Photography since 1869.

Inscription at the bottom of the Monument to Ben's family in St Maartensbrug, Nth Holland.

Wilhelm, GBH's father, had heard about this amazing way of creating pictures with light, and he played around with it. Wilhelm taught his fascinated sons all he knew. GBH was about sixteen when he began his own serious experiments with lenses and light. His results instilled a desire to perfect this mind-boggling magic, today known as photography. He used the glass from a cheap pair of binoculars he had bought at a country fair as his first lens. For the chemical solution to develop these early photos he had made on glass sheets, he melted down gold and silver coins. These glass sheets became his first primitive negatives.

GBH and his brother, Wilhelm, opened their first photography shop, calling it Gebr. Niestadt St. Maartensbrug. Realizing the interest their work engendered, in 1867 the brothers separated, and Wilhelm set up his own business in another town some distance away.

When GBH married in 1870, he moved to Dirkshorn. In 1891, he moved with his growing family to Delft, partway between the city of Rotterdam and Amsterdam. During the years that followed, both Wilhelm and GBH's offspring set up a chain of studios in the country. Around 1900, there were possibly eight or more photography shops throughout the country, and the deep-seated human desire to preserve the past made it a very successful business indeed. Even GBH's daughters became professional photographers— although "women in business" was almost unheard of at that time. They paved the way for women's liberation.

Toward the end of the nineteenth century, a young man from the northern province of Drenthe arrived at the GBH Niestadt Photographie shop in Delft looking for employment. Adriannus Anselmus Antonius Bijl was born in 1874 in the town of Assen, a farming community. But farming was not for Adrian—he had a brilliant mathematical mind and was already an extremely talented photographer in his own right when he came to Delft. GBH was impressed with Adrian's work and his friendly and cooperative disposition, which led him to employ Adrian. Before long, Adrian had fallen in love with the boss' lovely daughter, Catherina. They were married in December 1900 in Delft. Adrian and Catherina were forward-thinking, and within a year after their marriage they set up their own photography business, Photographie Bijl, in Amsterdam, working together from home at the Hoofdweg 88, five blocks or so from the central business district. In those early years, five children—three sons and two daughters—came along in fast succession.

After growing up, one of Adrian and Catherina's sons worked with his parents as a photographer in Amsterdam. He was Bernard Gerard Heinrich (Ben), named after his famous grandfather. Ben was an accomplished gymnast and violinist, but his real desire was to become an actor. Really World War I forced him to discontinue his drama studies. Photography was the only other alternative he had at that time. So that is what he pursued. Later, Jack, his younger brother, also went into photography.

The Map of The Netherlands

CHAPTER 1

Zeist, Province of Utrecht during Nazi Occupation in The Netherlands, late 1943

An almost continuous knocking at the door blasted away what was left of the pleasant tranquility of that crisp, autumn morning. Em's young heart beat faster, and a rising feeling of dread enveloped her. (Maggeltje Bijl was affectionately known by the nickname Em.) This day was something she would never forget. Her arms and legs trembled as fear of answering the door fought with the logic of her mind.

I must answer it; I must! She hesitated. But how? I must stay calm.

"I hear knocking, Mama. Mama? Can't you hear it? There's someone here." Gerda's inquisitive voice urged her to see to it.

But she could not answer.

Beautiful Em

Gerda ran from Em's bedroom to the landing and back again, the little girl tugging at her mother's hand. "Mama! What's wrong? Can't you hear it? There it goes again, that loud knocking. Aren't you going to answer the door?"

Gerda was Em's firstborn child and Ben's only daughter. To her parents, she was pure joy and stunningly beautiful with her fair skin, grey-green eyes, and golden curls. She had her father's colouring, but her features were more delicate, like her mother's. She had just commenced kindergarten this year.

Em was about to brush and comb Gerda's long hair and braid it into two plaits when the ominous knocking began. Em forced her mind back to reality. The door—yes, I must answer the door. Please, please, dear God, protect my Ben. Please, protect all of us this day!

Em and Ben were all too aware of the purpose of this visit because during the early morning, trucks had driven up and down the streets, loudspeakers crackling. Their message had been loud and clear. "All men between the age of eighteen and forty-five are to be on the street with a knapsack at 11.00 am."

Baby Louis was down for his morning sleep. He was jerked awake by this barrage on the door, his cries adding to the din. Em still held the red ribbons and Gerda's hairbrush, which she had grabbed off the cluttered dresser.

Turning away from the dresser, Em stepped through the bedroom door, leaving the soft warm accents of her favourite perfume, Maja, the bottle almost empty now, lingering in the bedroom. She grasped Gerda's hand as they hurried along the hall toward the stairwell. She finally began to descend very slowly down the stairs, each foot being drawn, as if by a magnet, almost to a stop on every tread.

If only we were somewhere else. Anywhere but here, she thought, bracing herself, taking a deep breath to settle her nerves.

Softly yet hurriedly she said to Gerda, "Not a word now, sweetheart. Remember what Mama has told you." Finally approaching the entry, she unbolted the heavy timber front door.

Standing before Em, their right arms raised in greeting, were two German soldiers. "Heil Hitler!" they barked, nodding their heads and clicking their shiny, black leather boot heels with practised precision.

Em raised her eyes upward, taking in the grey-blue uniform common to the enemy.

One was a sergeant, while his companion was a young, newly enlisted man, a private. The sergeant, she imagined, would have been fifty; although he wasn't so tall, his solid stature was enhanced by the flattering colour of his uniform. His face, perhaps once quite handsome, had a hard look about it indicating this man was not to be trifled with. In contrast, the young private tall and fair. Quite striking really, especially the blue eyes darting from beneath his cap.

Em felt her knees knocking together, but now more than ever before in her life, she told herself, Em stay calm. You have to maintain your composure.

"Good day," Em finally responded. "What can I do for you?" her voice appeared quite calm as she pulled the door behind her. She sensed he resented her failure to respond with the Hilter salute.

He ignored that slight and immediately got to the point "Madam, you have no doubt heard the loudspeakers on our trucks, which have been driving up and down all morning. The Nazi occupation headquarters has ordered that all men between eighteen and forty-five be ready, on the street, in front of their homes, with a knapsack and blanket, at eleven this morning. It is in your family's best interests to cooperate with the Nazi cause. Why then is your husband not waiting at the front for us as ordered?"

She looked at him almost blankly and shrugged, but as he waited, words failed her.

"Well?" His eyes rested on her child. He again paused and then almost spat out the words, "You do have a husband, madam!" She nodded, her eyes still averted. "And just where is your husband?"

"Gone," Em replied simply.

The sergeant looked irritated at her lack of information. "I can see you are married. So, tell me. Just where has your husband gone?"

The young private stood looking subserviently from his superior's face to the genteel person standing in front of him. Then Em noticed his gaze slowly moving down from her face until his eyes, with a look of admiration, alighted on her daughter nestling beside her protectively. Her eyes were oozing with childlike curiosity. The private continued gazing at Gerda until his testy sergeant spoke again.

"So then, madam, I'm waiting. Where is he?" His foot tapped impatiently.

Em sighed deeply. "It is true. I am married as you can see." Her eyes moved from her right hand where there was a gold band and then in the direction of her daughter. "But my husband, the miserable creep, left me not long after our youngest son's birth." Em radiated amazing calm despite the fact she was never a good liar.

"Then it won't worry you at all if we conduct a search. You and half the neighbourhood have been mysteriously left without husbands!" The sergeant's smirk sickened her, whilst he quickly added, "I trust you understand the gravity of this situation if you are lying, madam? Our instructions are to shoot on sight anyone who refuses to appear today as a volunteer for the Third Reich!"

"I told you already. He is not here!" Em replied indignantly, heart pounding.

"Then of course we will search your property because frankly, madam, we don't believe you." The sergeant stepped forward menacingly. Pushing Em aside brusquely, he and his protégée rushed into their house and commenced a thorough search, looking for hiding places in which there may be concealed another "volunteer" for the mighty Fuhrer.

Initially they marched into the living room, where Em's eldest son had been playing with his wooden blocks. The little boy, Charles, not yet in school, stood stunned, but as they moved closer, he panicked, running to his mother's side. "Mama! Mama!"

Em bent forward, picking him up reassuringly. The sound of the soldiers' boots was ominous on the timber floors throughout the downstairs areas of their house.

"W-who, who are they, Mama?"

"Never mind, sweetheart, never mind," she said softly, running her fingers through his hair. "It's all right, Charles, Mama's here." His crying abated.

The two soldiers continued. "Kurt! Check the laundry first," the older man ordered, "while I check the yard."

The laundry was bursting to the seams with clothing waiting to be washed. When the war began, one of the first things to become unprocurable was soap. It was hard enough to wash ordinary clothes without washing powder and hot water, let alone soiled nappies. With absolute disdain, the young soldier picked through the mountain-like pile of laundry, looking for evidence of an adult male's presence in the house. The sergeant joined him shortly thereafter, eager to find evidence that indeed there was a husband still living at Veldheimlaan 20.

"Die Mongrels haben sogar genommen, alle Menschen die Kleidung!" ("The mongrels have even taken away all the men's clothing!") The sergeant's countenance began to fall. His cheeks coloured, as he had to admit even in the laundry, which would often give his victims away, there proved to be no evidence of the man of the house. "But we haven't finished yet."

"Let's check out the coal bin," the private said hopefully, but it was as empty as an upturned pail. "No luck here either."

"Nothing! Absolutely nothing!" the sergeant rasped in exasperation. His face was getting redder.

Kurt just nodded and continued to look thoughtful.

They returned inside, stopping at the cellar door underneath the upstairs stairwell.

"We'll make a search down there before we head upstairs," the sergeant mumbled, reaching for the door handle.

They turned sharply to the right, off the landing into the stairwell and the dark depths below. They spent a great deal of time searching in the cellar, doubtlessly because many people had hidden in this part of their homes in the past.

After some time searching, they returned empty handed and ran upstairs to further their investigation. Negotiating the carpeted stairs, missing two and three treads at a time, they looked perfunctorily into the tiny toilet at the top of the stairs.

"Empty, of course. You couldn't swing a cat in here!" The private sniggered. They moved on to the bedrooms.

Em's baby, Louis, had settled down after the knocking ceased, but now when two uniformed strangers with guns peered down upon him, he cried out in fear. They did not take too long in the bedrooms, just checking under beds and in wardrobes and then, finding nothing, moved on.

However, they were really intrigued with one of the upstairs rooms because they walked in expecting to see another bedroom. All Dutch homes have bedrooms upstairs.

"Himmeldonnerwetter!" the sergeant hissed. "What'n the hell is this? I'll bet he's in here, Kurt. Come on!"

The room was painted stark black all over—the floors, the walls, the ceiling. "Wow! You said it, Serge. What is it? Looks like a witch's haven. Maybe that woman's one!" The young man laughed heartily, but one withering look from his superior resulted in an abrupt halt to his humour.

"My, what have we here?" the sergeant asked excitedly as he shined his flashlight over the lead-lined tubs and equipment. "A dark room! Well, my guess is, Kurt, that our volunteer could be up to more than hiding. What do you think?"

"Could well be, Sergeant, could well be!" The private, suddenly giving him his rapt attention, began diving into the cupboards that lined the room, pulling boxes and papers from the shelves into a heap on the floor. They proceeded to examine the contents of the cupboards with great care.

"Nothing! Nothing incriminating at all!" The sergeant knocked over a row of jars filled with chemicals, and they smashed against the leaded tub as he flung open one of the cupboard doors. "Himmeldonnerwetter!" He cursed again.

Then his eyes lit upon dozens of neatly wound rolls of negatives. "What have we here?" He shined his flashlight on the negatives he unrolled and hung them from the many pegs over the tub. "Could be something interesting on these."

He squinted but was unable to see them well enough, so he moved to the door and held them up to the bright light coming through the doorway. The hall was always lit due to the large glass-tiled walls of the stairwell landing. His examination revealed nothing suspicious.

When they finished, roll after roll of film, as well as other photographic paraphernalia, lay in a tangled mess on the floor. Finally, they came out of the darkroom, the over-conscientious sergeant visibly annoyed.

The last stage of their intense search was upstairs in the attic. The private opened the door along the first-floor hall. Beyond the door was the stairway that led to the attic. They clattered noisily in their heavy boots up the flight of wooden steps leading up.

Em imagined each thud of their boots as clods of dirt falling on the coffin of her beloved Ben. The attic is used in most Dutch households for storage, or if the family is very large, it may be used for a bedroom or a maid's room.

The soldiers stepped away from the balustrade edging the stairwell, which surfaced in the middle of the spacious attic area. To the left of the stairwell were two skylights facing Veldheimlaan. The attic was painted a pale green. From about hip-height, there was vertical wood panelling running the perimeter of the attic, pleasantly breaking up the expanse.

"Let's check what's outside those windows," the sergeant said as he climbed up on a rickety old stool to look out the dormer window and ascertain whether someone was lying along the roof.

"No-one to be seen out there, but there are hidden spots behind the dormers. Indeed, one cannot be sure," he mumbled almost to himself as he dropped down to the floor again, extremely miffed over their fruitless efforts.

His companion had shot past him earlier. There, near the wall, on the floor directly opposite the balustrade, were several old Hessian bags. Spread out on top of these dusty old bags, so that the air could circulate easily, was a small armful of patchy, bright red and green apples, which Em had been guarding for her family.

"Wow, where did she get these?" the boyish soldier asked, enviously eyeing off the apples. He wiped his lips. They weren't very big, but in these days of scarcity, oh so inviting! He determined one would be his before they left the attic.

In the other corners of the sprawling area were pieces of broken furniture. An old cane armchair with a broken armrest and an ancient looking rocker whose spindles had all but come adrift stood out prominently amongst all the other items, which the family used occasionally, as well as a couple of enormous old seafarer's trunks.

The sergeant bent down and wrested one of the larger trunks open, saying, "What's in here, I wonder?"

"Nothing in these trunks but old trash and—pooh! The smell of camphor!" He gasped, pinching his nose and turning away quickly to avoid the pungent odour.

Em kept linen and woollen blankets in it.

"A-gah! Yuk!" He emphatically cast the contents aside, leaving the floor strewn with old clothing, with no thought to the chaos he was causing.

Kurt looked questioningly at him. The sergeant reluctantly shrugged. "Looks as if we've met a stalemate."

"There's nothing up here, Sergeant. Let's call it a day, eh?" he suggested hopefully.

"Okay. Let's go then, Kurt." The sergeant ceded defeat. He stepped to the top of the stairwell and turned to see his junior companion bend forward and whisk up two apples.

"Mmm, mmm!" He bit into one and handed his sergeant the other.

He sniffed the fragrant offering with a curt nod, grabbing it as he strode past the private and descended the narrow stairs.

The young soldier followed. They descended, rechecking each room until they were back in the hall at the main bedroom doorway, facing Em.

Em had stared back defiantly, saying nothing when the soldiers had begun their search. However, when they went upstairs, she and Gerda had followed and waited in the main bedroom on the pretence of checking on the baby. After calming the infant, to keep her composure, Em began to comb and plait Gerda's hair. All the while she strained to hear what was happening, fear pounding in her heart and brain. With each twist of the child's hair, Em held her breath; stopping expectantly; waiting; fearing the worst, wondering will they find him?

Em continued weaving Gerda's hair into plaits, but each time she sensed something was amiss, she stopped, fingers rigid and still, until she heard the voices of the soldiers again. Each time she stopped plaiting, Gerda became agitated, possibly sensing the tension her mother was feeling.

Suddenly Em's intense concentration was diverted.

"Look, Mama!" Gerda pointed excitedly toward the dormer window on the neighbour's house behind theirs.

Em peered in the direction to which the little hand pointed. There she noticed in absolute horror Bert Pubben, their neighbour's eighteen-year old son, climbing out his dormer window and proceeding to lie flat on the roof behind the opening. He quickly disappeared from sight, and doubtlessly began to pray.

She focused on her daughter's eyes. "Gerda, are you listening? Not a word, sweetheart, and whatever you do—listen to me—do not look out the window if the soldiers come back into this room. Understand?"

"Y-yes, Mama," she whispered, nodding, wide-eyed. "But—"

"Shh! Shh now! They're coming!"

The soldiers re-entered the bedroom again, and again a frustrated sergeant addressed Em. She noted that he had white rings around the perimeter of his irises. She knew through her nursing knowledge that this was a sign of significant health issues. His hard eyes seemed to see right into her heart. "Madam, if we return and find a man in this house, I warn you again. There will be no mercy. He will be shot on sight as a traitor to the cause!" His icy gaze met hers as he raised his hand and pointed his finger defiantly into her face. "Do you understand?" Em nodded without meeting his gaze.

"Heil Hitler!" He clicked his heels together and marched out of the room, nodding to his companion to follow. They marched down the next flight of stairs to the ground floor and strode through the open front door. The friendly garden that once had adorned their home along the front pathway was all but gone now. There were too many other things occupying their minds at that time to tend it.

When the heel of the private disappeared over the threshold, Gerda shrieked in unrestrained delight, "They didn't find him! They didn't find him, Mama!"

Em dropped the brush to the floor as she clamped her hand over her child's mouth, pulling her close. "Shhh! Shhh!" Em whispered in her daughter's ear.

Her own heart pounded, intense fear gripping her. Had they heard?

CHAPTER 2

Chaam, Province of North Brabant, The Netherlands, 1926

It really was a family of contrasts. The last of the poorer friends and distant relatives had boarded their farm wagons, about to leave. The wealthy van der Waals and van der Giessens, in their showy new horse and carriages, rode off ahead of the commoners, disappearing down the murky track that had been the road. For the past week, the unusually early winter snows blanketed the Chaam district like a white damask quilt. Today was no exception. Only the lane out of town to the little Protestant cemetery was muddy, and a myriad of broad, solid footprints, both large and small, made by the wooden clogs of the poorer relatives led from the roadside into the cemetery. These footprints, interspersed with finer, more delicate imprints from the elite, finally came to an end surrounding the grave. A small grave strewn with jonquils in profusion and just a touch of colour to lift the monotony of white, yellow, and green was the focal point of the scene. A darkhaired young woman was the last to leave the graveside.

Weeping silently, she stooped down and dropped a single purple flower on top of the floral tribute below. She whispered, "Good-bye, my dearest brother, Gerrit. May you rest in peace at last."

She slowly joined the grieving family. They stood, viewing the raised mound of enshrouded earth, glistening tears running silently down wind-chafed cheeks, nine people embracing one another. Johan stood beside his lovely wife, Anna, their children huddled around—all young women and girls, arms entwined, trying to find solace. There they lingered, every heart broken, staring at the grave of their only son and only brother.

The white-haired pastor stood back a little from the sorrowful group, giving them their space, sadness written on his lined old face. He had known Gerrit since the Flach family arrived in Chaam not long after the end of the Great War. Gerrit was a little fellow of about eight when this family from the north first appeared in his church. Though of a tender age, the boy had always walked with a stick, his knees swollen like an old man with arthritis. He never attended the nearby school, although it was close. This family from Ridderkerk had squeezed into the tiny home next to the local schoolhouse because it had more ground attached to it, and the owner allowed Johan Flach to build a barn to house his dairy cattle and pigs while he was having a new home and barn designed and built under the supervision of an architect. The new house was just a little out of town on a forty-acre plot of ground, off the Meerleseweg.

The parcel of land he had purchased was called "heath land." That meant it was virtually virgin ground, and the government tax on profits from such land that needed to be nurtured and enriched over the years was lower. It had only had one previous owner, who had worked it for twenty-eight years. The original owner had called the property "Bleke Hei" (meaning White Heather). There were many problems, and the project took a lot longer than Johan had envisioned, but finally they moved in. Then tragedy struck.

Even the man of the cloth wondered why. Why? Why Lord? Gerrit was only fifteen! He had suffered so much in his short life. After some minutes, the minister walked up to Johan and, commencing with him, embraced them all, one by one. "I am so sorry! So sorry!" He whispered, "May God grant you all strength to cope with your great loss." Ever so slowly he moved away from the heartbroken family. He was unable to do anything more, so he mounted his wagon and slipped away. The wind was whipping up. It was mid-afternoon. Probably it would take away the snowfall, but nothing would take away the heavy pain in the hearts of the Flach family as they took their leave of their precious Gerrit in his final resting place.

*

Anna forced herself out of bed early the next morning, although her older daughters had urged her to stay in. Wrapping herself in her dressing gown, she walked to the bedroom window and pulled the drapes aside. She had hoped the sun would be shining, but the lack of brilliance in the crack between the curtains told her it was not. Peering out of the colonial panes, she saw the earth blanketed in snow for yet another day. What she saw transported her to the fateful day that ultimately led to Gerrit's death. Never again would she view snow in the same way. Her mind rushed back to the day of the first snowfall of the year…

It was early winter in 1926, and the Flach family had awoken greeted by the magnificent display of snowflakes falling so delicately, so silently on the farmlands of Chaam. The morning was quite still, snow blanketing the landscape in a fairyland of glistening white.

"Gerrit, wake up, son, and look outside your window," Anna had said, drawing the heavy drapes back and then placing a porcelain mug of warm milk on his bedside table.

"Oh, Mama, do I have to? Can't I sleep a bit longer?" he mumbled sleepily as he sat halfway up and rubbed his eyes, still heavy with sleep. "Gerrit, I know it's quite early, but look outside—it's snowing!" she added more forcefully. "I thought they were snow clouds gathering last night."

"Did you say it's snowing, Mama?" Gerrit started up with unusual speed, diving out of bed, grappling with his crutch for balance, and clip-clopped over to the window. The many tiny panes were edged with white icy flakes, and there, as he looked out into the garden, was a winter wonderland. Trees adorned with little icy tentacles running down toward the ground and the midnight blue tinge of dawn gradually began its chameleon change to pristine white as a new day dawned. Together mother and son stood gazing at a scene that never ceased to move them in absolute awe.

"This is my favourite time of the year, Mama," the lad exclaimed excitedly. "If it stops snowing early in the day and it stays calm, I'm going for a ride on the sled."

"Gerrit, do you think that's a good idea? It's only a few weeks since you had a bad knee, perhaps it is too soon, and you may set off the bleeding again and end up worse than you were before."

The boy laughed almost bitterly. "Mama, you worry too much!"

"Son, that's what mothers are for," Anna retorted, shaking her head.

"Well, you can't coddle me all the time. I want a life too, Mama, you know how much I love the snow and sledding. It's so exhilarating! Don't say no! Because there are so few things I can do—but this is one of them!"

"All right, Gerrit. But please be careful. I'll help you dress early today because I have to go visiting with Papa in town this morning," she said as she gathered his clothes from the drawer and assisted him putting them on. Dressing was difficult since his joints had become stiff and arthritic from so many bleeding episodes.

"So where are you off to?"

"Mr. and Mrs. Schroon have invited us for morning tea. They have something amazing to show us."

"Yes? And what is it?" he asked rather nonchalantly.

"It's called a 'radio,' Ger. It's a box and voices and music come out of it. It's amazing what clever people have been able to give us, don't you agree?"

"I'd say that would be pretty amazing all right. Maybe if Papa likes it, he'll let us get one too."

She nodded. "Maybe he will, son; maybe he will." Anna turned to leave the room but stopped and faced the boy again. "I'm going to get breakfast now, so come in when you hear the bell."

Anna bustled out of Gerrit's bedroom and left him still studying the dream world outside his window.

At half-past seven, Johan and Anna left on the daily milk pickup from the farmers in the district. He had contracted to take all the farmers' milk to the milk factory daily. Anna usually didn't go with Johan, but today she was excited because today's ride would be particularly beautiful. Besides, they had been invited to the Schroons' house for "elevenses" (morning coffee) and to see their wonderful "new invention." Em, who was almost seventeen, would make sure the younger girls were not too late getting to school.

Hector responded immediately to his master's gentle but firm voice: "Gee up, Hector. Let's go now." Johan lightly slapped Hector's rump with his whip. The roads going out of town were slippery, and the tracks left by the wagons, horses, and people trudging along in wooden clogs through the snow-covered terrain quickly became murky and tricky to navigate.

At the third farm along the route, one can of milk tipped over when Johan slipped sideways on the track as he bent down to load it onto the wagon. "What in the name of …!" He decided against the expletive.

Shrieks of laughter came from his normally subdued wife as she witnessed the can rolling sideways. Then Johan lost his sure footing and slipped down onto one knee to steady himself. Milk poured out one side of the large, stainless-steel milk can, spraying spots of white and froth all over him.

"Papa, you should see yourself," Anna said, almost choking on the words, still in peals of laughter. "You do look funny!"

Tall and lean, Johan looked down at his suit and yes, his wife had spoken the truth—he looked like a spotted giraffe! "Well, I can't see anything funny about it at all." Johan's voice was sharp and his face a frown. "It's certainly not funny when you have to pay for spilt milk. Not at all!"

In time the milk cart had done all its pickups along the route to town, and now the cart was full of jangling milk cans. Fortunately, that was the only incident for the morning. The snow had stopped, and it turned out sunny despite the cold weather. So, when they arrived at Mr. and Mrs. Schroons' for coffee, Anna was pleased indeed.

"Welcome, Anna and Johan. Do come in and warm your feet in front of the fire," Mrs. Schroon greeted them. "Now what would you like to drink, coffee or chocolate? Henk will be here in a minute. He's playing with his new toy. Go through to him in the living room, Johan."

*

Back at the farm, under Cor's supervision, seeing Mama was away, Gerrit finished his school work for the day and proudly announced over morning tea, "I'm going out on the sled for a spin through the snow."

He noticed Cor's questioning look and added hastily, "It's okay, Sis. I've finished my lessons for today, and Mama knows. Here! Have a look if you don't believe me." He offered his book. "And do you like this sketch?"

It was a picture of a windmill in the distance and the lovely white flakes, half-melted, falling from the mill's arms. In the middle of the page, he had sketched the view outside their house. Icy white snowflakes hung like stalactites from the branches of the deciduous trees in the forefront, the paddock bedecked with various farm animals—pigs, goats, cows, ducks, and geese. Gerrit was a natural artist, especially with pencil sketching. It just slipped from his pencil like lightning.

"Wow, Gerrit, I love it! Great work. When did you sketch this?"

"Oh, just now."

"I wish I could draw like that, Brother. To me, it's not easy." She looked at his work, and all seemed in order. "All right, boy, I'll help you carry the sled down to the slope," Cor called as she watched him limping off to the barn. It was a rare occasion to see him so active.

They got the sled out of the barn and dragged it down the paddock until they came to a little hill on the corner of the property. From that spot, you could see the old windmill at close quarters, its stately arms just turning as the wind was low.

"This'll do, Cor, stop here," Gerrit said enthusiastically.

"Now, boy, be careful. Do you hear me?" she added somewhat apprehensively.

"Always, Sis, always," Gerrit said, winking at her, thinking, Cor is getting more and more like Mama and Cien every day.

"Well, Gerrit, just remember—"

But he interrupted and mimicked kindly and firmly, "I know, Cor, 'Don't overdo it!'"

She nodded, smiling as she turned back toward the house and the sewing machine. She was nineteen now and an accomplished seamstress like her older sister and her father's family.

As she walked back to the house, Gerrit called out, "Thanks!" Gerrit didn't ride the sled like most people because his right leg was so stiff. That did not stop him heading down the incline. He yelled in sheer delight as he slid along. Having reached the flat at the bottom of the hill, he struggled back up the gentle slope with great difficulty, but if he fell, it didn't usually matter, because the snow was soft. It was a very slow affair, and quite demanding for a youth who lacked stamina, but he had been sledding every winter for as long as he cared to remember with no ill effects—that is, as long as he didn't overdo it!

*

After Gerrit persisted and had the time of his life for about an hour, Cor came from inside the house and yelled out, "Gerrit, you'd better stop for a while. You don't want to start another bleed now."

But he just laughed and ignored her warnings. She didn't have the heart to insist he stop there and then. However, Cor jumped up with a start when she heard the clippity-clop of Hector pulling the old wagon into the paddock. She looked at the clock on the kitchen hearth and realised in horror that it was almost one o'clock! Her parents had arrived back home, and Gerrit was still out whooping everytime he slipped down the snow-covered hill on the sled.

She raced outside to greet her parents. "Hello, Mama, Papa. How did it go?"

"Cor! You won't believe it! Can you imagine a box with voices and music coming out of it—just like you were listening to someone singing or talking in the living room. It's called a 'radio,' isn't it, Johan?"

A puff of smoke rose from his pipe. Johan nodded amused. "That means the sounds travel without wires through the air waves and are picked up by the radio's aerial. The result is the sounds you hear from the radio."

"Sounds out of this world." Cor was intrigued.

Anna turned toward the hillock and smiled. "Well, isn't Gerrit having such a wonderful time? How long has he been out there, Cor?"

"Too long I'd say. I've already called him several times to stop now, but he just laughed and kept going. I don't think I've seen Gerrit having such a great time for ages."

Anna said, "I think we should entice him back inside before he regrets it. Some of that mouth-watering soup I put on the wood stove before I left should do the trick. You have kept an eye on it, haven't you?"

"Of course. Don't I always, Mama?"

*

Meanwhile, Johan strode down the hillside to join his son. He derived much pleasure just being able to see him doing something he liked without anyone helping him. The snow looked well-worn on the hillock that Gerrit had been negotiating and was getting sloppy.

"Hi, Papa. I've had a great time!" Gerrit yelled out as his father approached.

"I'm very pleased, son, but can I entice you inside for some delicious chicken soup? You must be starving by now."

"Oh no, it couldn't be that long. I just got started and I'm not hungry."

"Anyway, I'll pull the sled back up the hill, and you come in now. Mama will have lunch ready by the time you wash up. You know how she hates us to be late for dinner."

"Okay, Papa." The boy's expression changed from jubilant to weary. He reluctantly relinquished the sled to his father and tried to keep up with him as his father hauled the sled with ease back up the slope.

The gnawing in his stomach told him Papa was right—he was hungry. "Mama, I'm starving!" He washed his hands at the water pump in the kitchen.

Anna laughed, happy to see the smiling expression on her son's face. His cheeks, normally pale, were rosy, and his eyes looked bluer than she had ever noticed before. Now one metre-seventy, he was becoming a real young man. Her heart welled up with pride and pleasure. It wasn't often Gerrit looked like he did today—really well!

Johan led the family in prayer, and they commenced the meal.

"I think the fresh air has worked wonders on our boy, Johan," Anna said. A nod said he agreed.

Halfway through his second bowl of soup, Gerrit suddenly coughed, and soup splashed all over the damask tablecloth around his bowl. "Excuse me ..." Before he could finish his apology, he coughed again, the blood suddenly draining out of his face. He slumped in his chair and said, "Mama, I'm sorry, but I have a sudden pain in my stomach ... I think I'm going to be sick."

Anna jumped up to assist him. Before she could get him a bowl, he had slumped to the floor. "Gerrit! Gerrit!" Anna was scared as she saw him vomit blood all over the tiled floor.

He screamed, "Get the doctor! Quickly, the doctor!" He continued to vomit.

His parents put him to bed, but the pain and vomited blood continued. They kept a vigil, but in those days, people, even the doctors, did not know how to stop internal bleeding, so his parents were resigned to pray that it would stop before it was too late. Cold compresses were applied and various tinctures applied topically as well as internally to try to stop the bleeding, to no avail.

"I'm scared, Johan!" Anna's eyes welled up with tears.

Her husband was also alarmed. He looked at his wife as if trying to read her mind. Anna's eyes searched her husband's.

Johan stood, wringing his hands. "It must have been all that bumping up and down on the sled! But he has often done it before. Unless something happened that he hasn't told us about. I will drive across to Dr. Blumsheim and see whether he can come out. Now don't worry. We've had some close calls before, and he has always pulled through."

"But the doctor said if this happens and the blood keeps coming, there is nothing he can do that we aren't already doing." Johan sadly agreed. Feeling helpless, they waited, praying.

Throughout the following morning, the boy continued to deteriorate. The sad thing was, Gerrit had fallen into unconsciousness for some time. His mother was distraught.

Anna walked sadly into the kitchen, almost in a trance. In her mind, she was telling herself, "It's a dreadful dream! Tomorrow it will be all right."

Em was trying to prepare food for the family. No-one was hungry.

In the early hours of the morning, December 12, 1926, their dear Gerrit finally took his last breath.

*

Suddenly her mental journey came to an end. She was not dreaming; it was real; her only son had gone. Anna searched for her handkerchief as she brushed away the tears rolling down her delicate cheeks. She dragged herself away from the window. The hall clock was chiming. It was nine o'clock. But Anna fell onto her bed and wept helplessly. Her own mother had lost three sons in childhood as well, and nobody knew why. One thing they all had in common though—they all bruised easily and had curious swellings in their knees or ankles, or other joints, often bleeding for prolonged periods. And they all died very young, some even in infancy.

CHAPTER 3

Her Heartfelt Wish

Francien, the eldest of Johan and Anna's daughters, was nearly twenty-one when Gerrit died. She had been apprenticed to become a tailoress, which she loved immensely, like many of her forebears. This pleased her papa. He had already set Cien on the task of teaching Cor the tailoring business. Despite Cien's uncooperative spirit in teaching her the arts of sewing, Cor also was doing well in that line of work.

About the time of Gerrit's death, Johan suggested, "It's time you learnt a trade, Em. Why don't you follow in your sisters' footsteps and become a tailoress as well?"

"But, Papa, I don't want to be a tailoress." Em had a look of determination in her eyes.

"Maggeltje," (usually the family called Em - Ma, short for her name) her father said sternly, "it's a necessary service and an honest way to earn a living. It will also be inexpensive for us, since Cien can apprentice you. God knows with the expense of the funeral now, it would be an ideal way to teach you a means of living, like your sisters, without burdening us down with more debts."

"Papa, I know what you're saying, but I really want to become a nurse, you know—but not just a nurse, a midwife!" Em persisted. "I always enjoy looking after people and well, that's my heart's desire. You of all people, you and Mama must know how I loved looking after Gerrit when he was ill—which was almost all the time. Mama has often said, 'Ma, you are a wonderful nurse.'"

"Maggeltje, your mother and I agree you have been a wonderful help during the difficult times with your brother, but this is different! You were always under the watchful eye of your mother, and you were safe caring for Gerrit. But midwifery—I'll not be having a daughter of mine gallivanting around the country on a horse or a bike in the middle of the night delivering babies in strangers' homes. It is far too dangerous and it's just not proper. Do you hear? It's men's work. I tell you."

"Papa, is this your final word?" Em asked boldly. She fought to hold back the tears of disappointment.

"Yes, child, it is. I will not allow it."

Em continued to rein in her flood of tears but then persisted respectfully, "Well, could I please not be a tailoress? I could do something else that is useful. Perhaps a housemaid for someone in the district. I'd rather do that any day than tailoring."

"Ah, girl. You push me!" Johan's temper was about to burst forth. "All right! See if you and Mama can find someone - first of all - who is willing and perhaps, just perhaps, if the people are decent, I may consider it."

Em's blue eyes suddenly danced with anticipation, helping dry up her pressing tears. It wasn't her heart's desire; she was deeply disappointed, but this second choice was preferable to sewing for a living.

"Thank you, Papa. I'm sure we'll find something."

"I need you to work in the fields today raking hay, Ma. Please hurry!"

"Yes, Papa, I'm coming." She shuddered at the task ahead.

As her father walked out of the house to face another day of laborious work, Em stood looking after him, Oh my dear Papa, she thought. You look so tired and sad these days. If only you had kept the haberdashery business in Ridderkerk, we girls would have had plenty of good jobs to occupy us and contribute to the family's income. But now, here we are—struggling with mountains of work, endless work—with only one man out of nine souls to do the heavy work!

With that mental observation, Em picked up her hat and coat and walked out to help her father. As she worked alongside him, she couldn't get the thought out of her mind, I would still love to do nursing, and one day when I'm older, she vowed, I swear to God, I will.

*

About two months later, Johan came home to his family after visiting his brother-in-law, Aart, and his wife, Leintje, Johan's sister. He sat down to the evening meal in unusually good spirits.

"How was your visit to Aart and Leintje, dear?" Anna asked as she passed her husband a bowl of piping-hot mashed potatoes.

Ignoring her question, Johan said, "Mmm! Potatoes! The best food there is!" He hesitated further as he ladled a huge helping onto his plate.

"Said like a true Dutchman, Papa!" Cor couldn't resist saying.

Finally, Johan looked up and smiled at Anna. "They are all well and send their love and greetings, Anna, but I do have some really good news for Maggeltje." He turned to look at Em's surprised face. "Ma, Auntie Leintje and Uncle Aart would like you to come and work for them as a housemaid. Well, girl? What do you think?"

Em jumped up and threw her arms around his neck. "Oh, that's great news, Papa. Thank you! Thank you! So when can I start, Papa?" Despite her smiling countenance, inside Em was still smarting over not being able to do the nurses' course. "This at least is better than sewing all day long."

"They said as soon as you wish. So, let's say—well." Her father stopped short as he mentally surveyed his schedule of work. "Let's say after we finish harvesting. Monday fortnight should just about do it." Uncle Aart and Auntie Leintje had a large farm not too far from Johan's property. It was what people today would call a "sheltered workshop." All in all, there were about a dozen working for Uncle Aart while Em worked there. Em's uncle and aunt were kind to her and looked after her very well, but the desire to reach out into the nursing field was still there, eating away at her. Em yearned for change.

*

Sometime passed. One Sunday she was visiting her family as usual, going to church and then spending the afternoon catching up on all the news. During the midday meal, Johan mentioned something that made Em's ears tingle. "My cousin Piet is looking for someone to manage the house on the estate he just purchased in the old Princenhage Village."

Em hung on his every word. "And …?"

"He was wondering if you might be interested in a trial period, say for a month, to see if you would like working for him and his Indonesian wife, Miron. What do you reckon, Ma?" Johan's face broke into a wide grin waiting for her response.

"Sounds much better than what I'm doing at the moment, but what exactly would I be doing?" Em asked.

"Well, he said housework and cooking for a start. If you work well, perhaps a more interesting and responsible position."

"Sounds great! Has to be better than the dairy farm."

Anna gently reminded Em of her obligations. "No doubt it is, Ma, but we must not forget your uncle and aunt's generosity in offering you a position."

"Oh course, Mama, but these people are rich, so I think it will be a more pleasant job, with much nicer surroundings—that I will enjoy!"

Johan puffed on his pipe, nodding. "And that you will, Ma; that you will."

So, Em left her uncle and aunt's employ and went to work for her father's wealthy cousin at the stately mansion called Princenhage, named after the old village. Her second cousin was a retired tea merchant who had gone to Indonesia when he was young and worked for a tea grower. In time, he built up his own tea plantation and exported the teas to The Netherlands and other European countries. He took an Indonesian wife, whom he brought back to The Netherlands when he retired.

The mansion was ornately decorated with many carved Indonesian artefacts and finely carved furniture. Em's new mistress also taught her fine Indonesian cuisine, such as nasi goreng, satays, and curries. This young nineteen-year-old girl had great organizational skills and a good "money" head. Instead of just cleaning and cooking, she was soon given some responsibility doing all the family's buying. This was to be a permanent position. Em enjoyed being able to go into town each week to do the shopping and the freedom from the mundane work she had up until that time been confined to doing.

After another year, Em proved herself so thrifty and efficient that her cousin gave her "the purse" for the entire household. Being the manager of the household, she immensely enjoyed the pleasure of purchasing and making informed and responsible decisions. She was proving to be a good businesswoman. She was determined, like her grandmother, after whom she was named. Still though, the old ache would resurface, and her dream to become a nurse continued unabated. Eventually, after her twentieth birthday, although Em was quite happy with her achievements and very successful as a house manager, she resolved to venture into the world of nursing. With enthusiasm, she set out to carry out her plan. To do so, she needed to confront her father once again. Thus, the next Sunday she set off for her home, mentally rehearsing what she would say to her father.

Over a cup of tea, Em quickly got to the point of her visit. "Papa, there is something I wish to speak to you about. I'm still as keen as ever to do the course, and I have come to tell you I have enrolled in the nursing school. I will commence in July, doing the course by correspondence."

"Maggeltje, you know I do not approve of your doing this course. Why must you defy me?"

"Papa, I am not doing this to defy you. Please understand that all my life I have wished to do this, and as I'm of age, I'm going to carry it out."

"Maggeltje, it's not the work itself I'm against, it's the circumstances which arise in order for you to do such work. You will be moving from place to place and staying with people you do not know. God knows where you'll end up, girl! Your mother and I are only concerned for your welfare." Johan restated his view calmly and, to Em's surprise, he did not tell her she was forbidden to do it.

"Am I to understand it's okay?" she asked excitedly.

"Maggeltje, it's like this: you are old enough now and do not live at home anymore. Hence, we, your parents, cannot categorically stop you. However, we do have serious reservations, as I have just said. And just how will you survive whilst you do this course?"

"I have discussed it with cousin Piet, and he and Miron agree that I should do it. I have one day off a week and evenings, so I will have time to study. You see?"

Johan rolled his tobacco and tipped it into the pipe. It was time for contemplation.

Em threw her arms around her father's neck and hugged him. "Thank you for being so understanding, Papa. I understand your concerns, but I will be careful, and if I have any doubts about a certain position, I will refuse." She looked at her father and gave a little giggle. "You should know me by now, Papa. I don't do things I don't want to do."

"You always were headstrong, Maggeltje! Too much of your Opoe (the name given to her grandmother) in you." She bristled. "I'm not hard like Opoe!"

"No, my dear, that's true, but you do have grandmother's determination, my girl. But, fortunately, you have usually done the right thing in your life. Godspeed if it is to be."

She left the following day ecstatic, to return to Princenhage.

*

The years passed quickly, with Em absorbed in her work. Excitedly she wrote to her parents, "I have just received my papers. I have passed my basic nursing training with honours! I am now determined to add to my knowledge and ability by doing a midwifery course as well."

Although they were proud of Em's accomplishments, Johan and Anna continued to despair, but the die had been cast. During the following months, Maggeltje excitedly struck out on the midwifery course, anxious to fulfil her life long dream.

On Em's next day off, she labored on her final monthly exam in the midwifery course. Em paused, staring into space. An enormous frown engulfed her face as a fearful scenario opened before her. "Wouldn't it be dreadful if you were helping a poor mother in childbirth—and it suddenly all went wrong? What if the baby died? What if the mother haemorrhaged so badly that she bled to death?" Em felt her heart pumping faster. Beads of perspiration broke out across her forehead. Her fountain pen, dangling from her fingertips slipped through them, falling onto the answer sheet. A great splotch of black Indian ink rippled across the neatly written page.

"Oh no!" Em screwed up her face in frustration. "And I only had two lines to finish the page! Bother!" A less delicate word instantly popped into her mind, but true to herself, she was, afterall, a lady, and moulded by the discipline of her strict Protestant family, she withheld it. Em displayed remarkable self-control. She never raised her voice, even when under the surface she was seething. You'd never know it. With a long, drawn-out sigh, she reached for another clean, white sheet to commence the arduous script again.

Em carefully lay down her pen and surveyed the newly written replacement sheet. She was happy with her answers. Next month she would sit for her final exams in order to complete her midwifery course. Then she would commence working with an experienced midwife at the beginning of July.

"And I can't wait!" Em said as she contemplated her future. "It's been four long years! But I'm finally here." She stood up, taking a deep breath. It was time for a well-earned break.

Slowly she removed her spectacles, plain and simple orbs rimmed in tortoiseshell. She rubbed her eyes, a little strained after three hours of study. Em's dark eyes suddenly came to life, illuminating her face like midnight-blue sapphires. Her gaze was drawn to tiny streams of water running silently down the window panes. It had been an overcast day, and she hadn't noticed the rain had begun to fall. In reality it was never far away. It was light, fine rain, leaving the world outside misty and romantic on this mid-spring afternoon. The meandering driveway made of neatly laid cobblestones edged with magnificent cedar deodars led from the commanding brick and wrought iron gateway to the mansion on the rise—Princenhage.

Compared to anything in her previous life, it was like living in a virtual paradise. "Why would anyone want to leave this delightful estate?" this determined farmer's daughter mused. Lush parkland, constantly changing deciduous beauties—oaks, elms, liquid ambers, ashes, chestnuts, and more—dotted the gently undulating slopes throughout the wealthy estate. A palette of pale-green leaves adorned the delightful branches of trees scattered over the rich green carpet carefully mown by hand.

Princenhage was one of the district's most stately mansions in the beautiful province of North Brabant. Princenhage was once a small medieval village, now abandoned. It was just the right distance to drive by sulky to Em's family home, "Bleke Hei," in Chaam. (Chaam had a population of only about three thousand and it was a little nearer to Breda in the north east but twelve kilometres southwest of Tilburg, in The Netherlands.)

Piet had come up the hard way. He understood their family's predicament. Piet also knew Em's mama had been excluded from the family fortune because of her marriage to an ordinary tradesman—a man like himself, who had done well for himself despite humble beginnings. Em's father had done well enough to purchase a farm and build his own home on it, but of course that was insignificant compared to Piet's good fortune.

Over the years they had corresponded, and he had always visited Anna and Johan when he returned to The Netherlands for business or vacations from Indonesia. Piet knew their seven daughters well too, and he liked what he saw. The Flach's had done a good job with their children—not only their behaviour, but they had been taught to work. Therefore, when he, the wealthy tea merchant, returned to retire and enjoy his wealth, it was only natural, he decided, that one or two of them would live in as housemaids or perhaps a cook. He wanted a girl he could trust and who was genteel as well to work for his Indonesian wife, Miron.

Miron, with her jet-black hair, straighter than anything Em had ever seen before, had been delightful to work for; she always treated Em as an equal, not just a servant. Miron's almond eyes, like pools of dark chocolate, and her light-brown skin drew people to her, but it was her genuine sweetness and sincerity that made any request she made a pleasure to fulfil. Working for Miron never made Em feel apprehensive, as Piet's wife lacked the ingrained Dutch aristocracy's snobby airs and graces.

Em's mind wandered to thoughts of her dear mother's family. They were totally unbending rich and proud landowners from Zwolle, the capital of OverIJssel Province in the northeast of The Netherlands - proud Zwolle with a history that stretched back to Roman times.

Hence, by contrast, Miron was a saint as opposed to Opoe, who sat like a queen on her ornately carved chair and barked orders to her maids—as well as her granddaughters, Em and her sisters, when they were solicited to work for her while growing into their teens. Em always felt inferior to her imperious grandmother during her visits.

Opoe's favourite job was to get Em and Cor to clean and polish all the silver in her huge house. The upside, however, was Opoe's fetish for fine perfume. She had given Em the most delicate and lingering perfume, called Maja, produced by the House of Myrurgia. Em had loved the flowery feminine fragrance from the first moment her nostrils inhaled it. This was to be her favourite fragrance for life, and she determined to never be without it, even if Papa thought it an extravagance.

What a difference! Em had started off merely as a cook for cousins Piet and Miron, but she was soon promoted from a servant to household manager. Her position also meant a much higher salary, which allowed Em to save and pay for all her nursing and midwifery lessons.

Em Flach, you certainly have come a long way since since Gerrit's passing—my poor dear brother. It's already seven years since you left. Em swallowed hard. She still felt the pangs in her heart when she thought about Gerrit. She knew leaving Princenhage would be hard but felt she would not regret it.

There was a knock on the door of Em's room, which brought Em's thoughts back to the present. "Miss Flach," the young maid said, "Master and mistress await you in the large living room. Afternoon tea is ready."

"Thank you, Leina." Em stole a look at her face in the mirror as she hurried out of the room, nodding to herself. "You'll pass, Ma. Now for tea."

The fire was burning brightly in the winter lounge. Piet and Miron sat at a round mahogany table with beautifully carved legs.

"Come in, Ma. Sit down." Piet looked approvingly at her. He laid down his pipe, and a wisp of smoke trailed away from it. The strong smell of tobacco filled the room. It reminded Em of her father. "We were just saying, Ma, you must be sick of studying after all these years! How long is it now?"

Smiling, she said, "No, Piet, not really, although it is almost four years since I began. I have a thirst for knowledge. It's time now I put it all into practice."

Piet and Miron looked at each other disappointed but resigned. Miron spoke first. "We will miss you, Ma."

"But of course, Ma, you must follow your heart. That is what I did." Piet patted Em on the shoulder. "I left The Netherlands a poor lad and after forty years returned with a delightful wife and a fortune. Life has been good to me. And yes, I followed my heart. In time you would regret it if you didn't follow yours."

Em smiled. "Thank you, Piet. I guess it's time for you to seek a new household manager."

In 1933, Em left Princenhage and commenced midwifery in Amsterdam. In a city of perhaps half a million people, she soon accompanied her mentor on dozens of births. Em was a natural; she had great aptitude, was attentive, and was willing to do anything asked of her. Her mentor soon agreed she was qualified to work alone.

Em rented a room from an old lady, Mrs Aspen. Amsterdam, the ancient city of canals on the Markermeer was like its sister city Venice, on the Adriatic. The canals and roads radiating from the city's Central Station were like spokes in a wheel. In writing to her parents, she excitedly described her new surroundings.

"It's so different from sleepy Chaam. It has a unique beauty, with its picturesque, tall, thin houses and delightfully different gables in many different colours and designs. There are so many quaint little bridges of varying shapes and sizes crisscrossing over the canals too. Daily the barges slip along with their milk, cheeses and vegetables to sell at the market. Life is so busy here and I must say I love it."

Em, graduated with honours, midwife circa 1933.

Em Flach, taken during her midwifery work, circa 1935.

CHAPTER 4

The Meeting in Baarn, 1934

It was a pleasant Saturday morning during the height of the Dutch summer when Em received a phone call from a Mrs. van der Laan. She asked if Em could attend her daughter's confinement (the time of giving birth) a few months later in October. Picking up her diary, Em verified she would be available at that time. "Now what is your daughter's address, madam?"

Mrs. van der Laan answered, "The address of my son-in-law's business is Photographie Bijl, Laanstraat 52, Baarn. He will direct you from there to their home above his shop."

Some weeks later, Em set out to Baarn. She soon found directions to Laanstraat, and there at number 52 was the sign in the window, Photographie Bijl. Em hopped off her bicycle and leaned it against the sidewalk. She approached the shop in search of Maria Bijl. As she stepped across the threshold, a bell tinkled in the back. Presently a smiling man came out of a darkened room off the main body of the shop.

Ben the photographer.

He immediately identified Em by her brown, nun-like uniform. "Sister, what can I do for you?"

"Mr. Bijl?" Em asked politely.

"Yes Sister. Ben Bijl, guilty as charged. And who are you?" he replied with a chuckle. The shadowy haze in which he first observed Em as his eyes became accustomed to the light had hidden her youthful beauty. But her voice indicated she was not an older woman, as midwives are often expected to be.

"My name is Sister Flach—Maggeltje Flach. Your wife's parents no doubt told you I would be in contact. They said you would like my services for your wife's upcoming confinement. Is that right?"

"Yes, that's right." His eyes, now accustomed to the light, studied her carefully. She would be a good subject to photograph as she had finely balanced features—beautiful dark-blue eyes, dark-brown hair that was mostly hidden by her brown, white-edged veil. She wore no makeup. Yes, Ben always had an eye for a pretty woman.

"I was expecting to hear from you, Sister. What did you say your name was again?" Ben's eyes were rippling pools of amusement.

"Sister Mag—" Em stopped abruptly. She guessed what he was thinking—everybody did!

"Sister Mag…" Ben laughed again. "If you don't mind, I'll call you Em for short. That's easier, isn't it? Yes, Sister Em sounds much nicer."

"Yes, I'd have to agree, Sir. Well now." She paused to gather her thoughts. "Is it possible to speak with your wife about her confinement?"

"But of course. Yes, Sister Em, we live in the apartment directly above the shop here. My wife, Miep, is up there now." He gestured with his arm. "There are two—ours is on the right at the top of the stairs."

"Thank you very much, Mr. Bijl." She offered her hand. He shook it enthusiastically.

"I'll be off then. Good-bye for now." Em sped up the stairs. Her mind was distracted with thoughts of the man she had just met. He was a funny little man—a bit of a character really, but still … quite nice. But what funny eyes he has! she thought. Like frogs' eyes. He's very short too. Ben Bijl…mmm.

Try though as she did to put these ideas aside, the man she had just met kept occupying her thoughts. She had always liked fair men, but his eyes—they were full of conviction, and he was striking, in an unusual sort of way. He looked like a man of purpose. His eyes had strength few men show. There was definitely something about Ben Bijl she liked—despite the eyes.

Having ascended the stairs, she knocked on the door to the right.

No-one came. She used the bronze knocker again.

A friendly and possibly curious neighbour opened her door opposite and greeted Em cheerfully, "Good day, Sister." Then, turning to her neighbour's door, she added, rolling her eyes, "She's home. Just keep knocking."

"Thank you, madam," Em replied, knocking again. Finally, after a lot of shuffling, the repetitive sound of a child's voice, and the pattering of little feet, Em realised someone was coming.

Shortly thereafter the door opened. A round-faced young woman with big sad eyes stood there, in slippers and dressing gown, by her side a fair-haired boy. He is obviously Ben's son; I can see it in his eyes, Em observed. The likeness is strong. Those eyes!

His mother had light-brown hair, which was a little unkempt. In fact, her whole appearance looked like someone who had just been aroused from sleep.

Strange, Em thought. It is almost eleven o'clock in the morning. Perhaps she is sick. And this child looks old enough to be at school.

Her thoughts were quickly interrupted by a pleasant voice. "Good day, Sister."

"Good day, madam. My name is Sister Flach, and I am the midwife your mother contacted. But I am sure you knew that."

"Yes, I guessed as much, your nurse's uniform gives you away, Sister. Please excuse me," she said, looking down at her rather dishevelled dress. "Do come into the living room and sit down. I haven't felt so well of late."

Mrs. Bijl held out her arm in welcome. Em followed the young mother and child into the house. The cute young boy looked about five or six, but he still clung to his mother's gown —like a younger child would, she thought—as they progressed down the hall. She motioned to Em to sit on the window seat in view of the street.

The window was a picture with its lace curtains. In the middle of the room was a contrasting Persian rug in royal blues, golds, and reds. In the room was an expensive Edwardian lounge suite covered in gold brocade material. Quite lovely! The room was finished to perfection with a matching dresser. It was a pleasant, well-furnished room, but it felt like it needed a breath of fresh air and a thorough dusting.

"My name is Maria Bijl," she said, smiling, "But please call me Miep."

"Miep it is. And this is?"

"This is our little Bennie," Miep said, cuddling the child.

Initially shy, Bennie soon relaxed. Em asked how old he was. The little fellow looked at his mother.

She prompted, "Tell Sister Flach how old you are, Bennie."

He held up one hand, and another little finger hovered up and down beside it.

"So young man, you are six! I guess you go to school now. Yes?" He nodded, his bright eyes blinking.

"No, Bennie, you need to put up another finger because you turned..." Miep said, coaxing him.

"I forgot! I'm seven now! Aren't I, Mama?"

She smiled approvingly at him. "But he had a sore throat this morning, so he's having a rest with Mama at home today, aren't you, Bennie? But it's school tomorrow."

"And I see, Bennie, you are like your papa," Em added.

Bennie said he was going to be a photographer like his papa when he grew up.

Em turned her attention to his mother. "Now Miep, getting back to your needs. I will need some details from you in order to ensure everything goes well and I will be available for your coming confinement. when is baby due?"

"According to the doctor, the baby is due on the eleventh of October," she said, gently touching her bulging belly. "But I think I am not so far ahead, perhaps the end of the month would be more likely. I would like you to come and live in for the month before my confinement date, if that is at all possible. We would of course pay for your extra services and provide you with a room of your own."

"Yes Miep, that will be fine. I would like to do an examination before I go today to get a more accurate picture of where you are in the pregnancy."

After the examination Em smiled and said, "I think you may be right Miep, baby seems like it won't be long in coming. Now, could I please see the room I will be occupying while I am with you?"

"Oh yes, of course. Come along. It's upstairs. I'll show you now." Miep led the way.

The two women, along with Bennie in hot pursuit, walked up the narrow stairs in single file. It was two flights, so Em guessed it would probably be the attic. It was.

Miep stopped at the door, puffing a little, and turning to Em, said, "Well, this is to be your room, Sister. I hope you like it."

Em looked inside the door. The room was tiny, but she had expected that. However, it was well appointed and comfortable, and clean enough although a little untidy at present. A single bed and matching wardrobe and dresser with fine inlaid timber highlights occupied the room. The room also had a large deep-blue padded armchair, which looked very inviting, on one side of the bed.

A stream of sunlight fell through the dormer window, and that in itself, made the room suddenly appear brilliant, warm, and inviting. She knew she would love staying there.

She looked at Miep with a smile of satisfaction. "This will be fine." Over the previous months since she had begun midwifery, she had stayed at numerous homes, and although this wasn't the best of them, it was quite high on the list by comparison to some of the others.

On returning to the living room, Miep suggested, "Now, Sister, how about a cup of tea before you go?"

"Many thanks for the invitation, but I must be going as I have some other appointments to see to today, but I thank you for asking. I think we have done everything we can at this stage."

Em picked up her medical bag and papers and then, as they approached the door, she shook Miep's hand. "It was lovely meeting you, Miep—and you too, Bennie. I'll be here on Monday, September 17 as agreed unless I hear from you earlier. Here is my phone number in that event. All right?"

"Thank you. Good-bye for now."

"Bye Miep. Bye Bennie."

During the next few weeks, she couldn't help but think about Miep and her husband, Ben, who had cheekily called her "Sister Em"—yet for some strange reason she liked it.

*

Monday morning on the appointed day in September, Em pedalled her way to Baarn. The ride from Amsterdam was busy as usual with hundreds of people on bikes pedalling to only God knew where. It may seem strange to modern society, but cycling was the most accepted way of travel in The Netherlands during the 1930s. For a fact even in this, the twenty-first century, cycling still is normal in The Netherlands. People were healthy, and riding kept them that way. The Netherlands is not a large country, so most towns are within riding distance, especially if a rider is not faint hearted.

The prevailing wind was chilling, and Em's brown midwife's great-coat, made of the heaviest wool, was a blessing indeed. She had a deep contralto voice and often sang along the way to pass the time more quickly. Harmony was Em's forte, but most of her repertoire centred on hymns, "Rock of Ages" being one of her favourites. In her work, she was always looking forward to the challenge of assisting the doctor in safely delivering infants. She also helped with feeding problems or with postpartum depression (which we have come to know as the "baby blues") and in general adjusting to the new little member of their family. Each birth was unique. She had no regrets over leaving Princenhage.

As she approached the outskirts of Baarn, Em looked at her watch. It was a little after half-past one. She had made good time. She heard the town hall clock strike two as she got off her cycle in front of the photographer's shop.

Ben rushed out to assist her up the flight of stairs with her suitcase. He knocked impatiently. Miep promptly answered the door. Bennie was not yet home from school. Em stood at her door with her medical bag in hand, her cheeks flushed from the cutting wind along the way.

"Miep, the midwife is here," Ben called.

"Come in, Sister." Miep pointed upstairs and said to her husband, "Please take Sister's luggage to the attic, Ben." Turning to Em, she added, "Have you come far today, Sister?"

"Thank you, Miep. My last confinement was in Amsterdam, so yes, it is quite a distance to Utrecht Province. I enjoy riding, but today it was cold." She removed her overcoat, happy that Ben had carried the heavy suitcase up the two flights of steps.

"Then I'm sure you won't say no to a cup of tea and something to eat."

"That would be lovely. Thank you, Miep."

As Ben emerged from the stairwell, Miep called out, "Ben, would you like tea?"

He smiled but excused himself. "Sorry, ladies, but I am a busy man today. Tea shall have to wait. Bye for now." He disappeared, closing the front door.

Em relaxed on the lounge, sipping tea and enjoying toasted currant bread. "That was a wonderful pick-me-up, Miep. Now, if you'll excuse me, I'll just go upstairs and unpack. In the meantime, you might think of what I can do to help you when I return."

"All right, Sister. I will. You know the way—two flights of stairs, I'm afraid."

"Never you mind about that. I'm used to stairs and attics!" Em spoke in a refined manner, but she also moved in a very elegant way as she walked out of the living room. Her stature added to her elegance, she being around 175 centimetres tall. She was definitely a lady!

*

In those few weeks before the infant's arrival, Em did her best to help Miep. This included final preparations, cleaning, washing, ironing, and child minding when needed.

"Come on, Bennie, let's go for a walk to the park and let Mama have a little rest. After we have some fun on the slippery dip and the swings, we'll come back home, and Sister Em will read you a story. Would you like that?"

"Oh yes, I would! I would!" Bennie responded. "I love going to the park where the pond is—you know, near the school?"

"Well, if it's not too far from home, we'll go there."

"I love to feed the ducks that come to the pond."

"I see! Let's hurry then; otherwise we will be late for dinner!" Em took his hand.

*

As the weeks slipped by, a friendship blossomed. Bennie was a dear little boy. Since she was staying in the home of a man who made photography his life, and Ben's living room wall was alive with wonderful examples of his work, Em asked while they were preparing the evening meal, "Miep, are you a photographer yourself?"

"No, I'm afraid that's not me, but I am a pianist. I love it! However, Ben's family has been in photography since its infancy here in The Netherlands."

"Tell me more. What do you mean 'since its infancy'?"

Miep asserted proudly, "Ben's grandfather was known as the one of the Fathers of Photography here in The Netherlands. Ben's family on his mother's side emigrated from Berge in Germany to The Netherlands around 1850. Ben's grandfather, after whom he is named, Gerard Bernard Heinrich Niestadt, or GBH, as the family called him—that's a mouthful, isn't it?—began dabbling in early photographic experiments when he was just a lad. His father had also introduced the possibilities and some basic ideas to his sons earlier."

"I often wondered how they did it. That's amazing, isn't it?"

"I guess it is really. Anyway, by the time GBH was eighteen, he had his own cottage industry taking photos. Ben has some of his early photos—one I recall was taken in front of their house there. Shortly afterward, his brother, Wilhelm, joined him, and they were soon doing so well that they left their bakery business entirely for photography, possibly around 1865, Ben tells me."

"I can imagine that people would be amazed. I am still—even today, Miep."

Miep, obviously proud of Ben's achievements, continued. "A few years later, Wilhelm moved to Vlaardingen, which is north of Rotterdam and not too far from Delft. You know Delft, of course? Anyway, Wilhelm set up his own atelier (studio) there while GBH stayed at St. Maartensbrug. Both of the Niestadt brothers did very well."

Em's interest was obvious. "And what better way than photos! Everyone you meet loves to see themselves in a picture! It certainly was a great stride forward—I suppose the artists guilds would have been gnashing their teeth when the Niestadt brothers' fame began to spread across The Netherlands."

"Yes, that's certain, because for centuries the artists had the unique privilege of painting people to preserve their image. They were always sought after and paid well by the aristocracy for their services. Photography made an impact throughout all of Europe. Suddenly these photographers were on the scene stealing the artists' bread and butter. Anyhow, as I was saying, after some years, GBH married and moved with his growing family to Delft. He set up—not just a cottage industry but eventually he did so well, he set up his own atelier, like Wilhelm, in the town. All his four children took up professional photography, including Ben's mother, Catherina, the elder daughter. This was sometime around the 1890s—so GBH's daughters were really way ahead of their time, don't you agree?"

"I couldn't agree with you more, Miep. I know how much my parents disagreed with me doing this midwifery course. My father felt it just isn't proper for women to be roaming the countryside. Fifty years ago it would have been far worse. So, I gather Ben grew up with this strong influence to go beyond the norms."

"Yes, he did, but it didn't only come from Ben's mother, Em. You see, his father, Adrian, was an excellent photographer in his own right."

"Really? Both his parents were professional photographers?"

"Yes, but when I explain how they met, it will be quite obvious. You see, Adrian came to Delft to seek GBH out since he had heard of his fame. Adrian came from the north, from the province of Drenthe. His family were just humble farming people, but Adrian turned out to be a brilliant mathematician and extremely interested in all the new sciences. Along the way, photography caught his attention too."

"He must have had a very keen mind. So how did he meet Ben's mother?"

Since he had worked with other fledgling photographers in the north, he determined to seek training from the very best in The Netherlands— and trail-blazer GBH Niestadt proved to be the man! It would have been around the turn of the century, perhaps 1898, because Adrian and Catherina were married in December 1900 in Delft. Ben was born in Schiedam near Delft in October 1902, but his parents later opened a business in Amsterdam where he and his brothers and sisters grew up."

"Are all of them in photography today?"

"Actually, Ben is the only one who has joined his father so far," Miep said.

The animated conversation was interrupted when Ben bounced in the door. "Hello, ladies!" He clowned around, kissing their hands, smiling from ear to ear. "Dinner ready?"

"My goodness, Ben! Is it that late already? And we still haven't finished the preparations for the evening meal," Miep said.

"So, Miep. How do you feel?" he asked.

"I'm, fine Ben, just tired, as usual. But fine." She turned toward the hallway, calling, "Bennie, Papa's home."

Footsteps running down the stairwell heralded his son's arrival. Ben rushed toward his son, arms outstretched.

"Papa! Papa!" Bennie exuberantly jumped across the room and landed in his dad's outstretched arms. They tumbled and rolled and tussled for a couple of minutes, all the while Bennie chattering, "Guess what, Papa? Sister and I went to the pond today and fed the ducks! And one of the ducks almost ate my finger."

His father examined it sympathetically.

"Ben, I've just been telling Em about your family," Miep said.

His eyes twinkled. "Oh yes, my wonderful family. Such perfect specimens! So very handsome and such perfect manners!" Ben's voice broke into a naughty laugh.

Em added, "No, something far more interesting, Ben—your family's history of photography! I'm fascinated."

"In my family, it wasn't at all like Miep's—she was born with a silver spoon in her mouth, being the only child, but in our family, we were born with a camera in our hands."

"Ben, you're always joking," Miep said, almost censuring him.

"Your grandfather was a clever fellow!" Em insisted, trying to get onto neutral ground.

"I guess he was. In 1900 he had his own travelling studio built onto the back of a truck and went all over the country provinces offering his services. That was very much ahead of his time, I think."

"Certainly was, I'd have to agree," Em ceded.

"But so was my father. Did Miep tell you about Papa's work for the Rijks -museum? He had quite a go-ahead business mind."

"What do you mean, Ben?" Em asked.

"After my parents moved to Amsterdam and established their own independent business, Papa approached the Rijksmuseum and offered his services as a photographer. Once he demonstrated how clearly he could photograph priceless works of art, they were sold on him."

"Why would museums want his services?" Em asked. "Wouldn't they think he would be competing against them and a threat to their artworks? It was true photographers were stealing their livelihood by providing photos instead of paintings of their clients."

"Well even back then museums would send their paintings to other museums for exhibitions, say from Amsterdam to London or somewhere else. In order to determine which paintings would be sent for exhibition, a curator would have to travel personally to each museum and decide through direct viewing of the art which ones he would use. My father suggested to the curator of the Rijksmuseum that his photos would be so clear that it would no longer be necessary for the curators to travel back and forth from one place to another to secure desirable exhibitive works. My father said his photos would be good enough—clear enough to choose which ones they would want to have transported on loan. Until that time, photography was only used for preserving memories really, but Papa demonstrated there are many uses for it."

"I think we might have to interrupt this conversation because dinner is finally ready," Miep said as she placed the last bowl on the table. "Would you all please come to dinner?"

After a hearty meal, Em asked, "Could you recommend a suitable camera for me? I would love to learn how to take photos."

"Em, come down to the shop in the morning and I'll show you what is available," Ben replied enthusiastically.

The next morning Em went down to the shop. Above the shop window was a sign advertising Photographie Bijl, and once again she wondered about Ben. She saw that he had indeed established a good business with people bustling in and out. Whilst waiting for Ben to finish serving a man, she studied the equipment in his front window display. The man had brought in photos to be developed, and after Ben finally located his account, the man paid and left. Em was amused. Ben was clearly a little disorganized in the accounts department.

He certainly could do with an office girl in here, she observed.

Ben turned his attention now to Em, and after a thorough investigation of what was available, she decided on a very expensive camera called a Zeiss IKon.

"Now let me show you how it works," he added, oh so confidently.

*

October 17, 1934 was the day Miep and Ben's second son, another healthy baby, was born. The confinement was only four hours, and she had no complications in the delivery. Em took the tiny baby and wrapped him in a cosy blanket and handed him to his mother. The infant immediately snuggled against his mother's breast. Em's heart leapt with appreciation. "Just look at him, Miep!"

Miep smiled. "A playmate for Bennie. I would have liked a little girl though." She studied the tiny bundle.

Em said excitedly, "Maybe a little girl next time. Would you like me to tell your husband?" Miep nodded. Em hurried down the stairs to the living room where Ben sat with his sister Guda, who was cuddling her young nephew.

"Ben! Great news! You have another son!"

"A-ha! Another son!" He immediately got up to go to his wife and child.

It was difficult for Em to hold the family back until the doctor finished his work. The father and older son were thrilled to see the new arrival.

"At last I have a little brother to play with me!" little Bennie said as he leaned over his mama to examine the tiny being in her arms. "He's very little though, isn't he, Mama?"

"Yes, Bennie. You will have to wait until your new baby can walk. That will be in about a year. Then he will be able to play a little," Miep said reassuringly. "Now's the time to enjoy him and watch him grow."

"He'll grow like a mushroom, Bennie, you'll see!" Auntie Guda added.

"What are we going to call our baby, Papa?" Bennie suddenly asked as he gazed at the infant feeding peacefully.

"Your mama and I decided before he arrived if it was a boy his name would be Johannes Augustus Schieding Bijl. What do you think of that, Bennie?"

"Wow! That's a long, long name, Papa! Johannes Aug…what was it?"

Miep aided his memory. "Augustus Schieding Bijl."

"That's right. Johannes Augustus whatever Bijl." Bennie finally got the mouthful out. "Yes, Mama. I like it!"

"We'll call him Hans for short," Miep added.

"That's good. I can remember Hans easily."

Em returned to the bedroom with a tray of tea just as Guda had them pose. "Come, now all together for a family photo." Later, friends and family were sent one of these delightful photos. She thought, How nice.

Miep's recovery was good, but a few days after her confinement, she fell into a state of deep depression that revealed itself in a lack of interest in her newborn son and, in fact, everything in life. Nurses were alerted to the fact that women are often very emotional following the birth of a child (though why was not fully understood). What Em had not realized was that there had always been a problem, or at least from early in the marriage. Miep and Ben had little in common to start with, and Miep suffering from depression made problems worse. Ignorance led to frustration and eventually disinterest in each other's lives.

He was an artist, a fitness fanatic, and an advocate of plain fresh food, and she was a pampered little girl who thought nothing was better than burying her head in a love story and enjoying a box of chocolates! Her heaven was whiling away the day oblivious of the dishes in the sink and all the soiled nappies waiting to be washed in the laundry. Miep was an only child from a wealthy Jewish family, and to her that was maid's work.

Sometime later, as Em got to know them well, Guda and Leni, Ben's two spinster sisters, explained Ben and Miep's situation.

Leni explained to Em, "Within twelve months of Bennie's birth, we saw that their marriage was in decline. It was considerably less than two years since their wedding. It was a fairy-tale wedding—you know everything was perfect and ornate! They often had differences. When they had a difference, Miep would up and take off to her parents' home in Amsterdam, leaving our tiny Bennie with his father to look after him. You can imagine how difficult that was while at the same time trying to run his business. Miep had grown up expecting everything to be one way—her way. In the end, they separated for quite some months, and eventually because Ben was concerned about the seriousness of the situation for their son, he agreed to reconciliation. They moved in together again about a year before Hans was conceived, and it wasn't long before Miep was pregnant with another child on the way."

The marriage however, seemed just as shaky as ever. The fighting and arguing resumed as it had before the long separation, so Ben decided to stay with her until the child was born—and then another decision had to be made.

CHAPTER 5

Love, 1935

Occasionally Em would call into the shop in Baarn to pick up film or have more photos developed. Em was greatly distressed to see Ben's sadness. His world was falling apart around him.

Sadness clouded his eyes. The usual clowning was gone. "Ben, how are things for you and your family?"

"Em," he hesitated, "I am going to get a divorce."

She was stunned. "But divorce is…is so final, Ben. Surely there is something you two can do to revive your marriage."

"I've tried so hard, Em. It's ten years since we married. Perhaps it was doomed from the start. Maybe both of us married for the wrong reasons. Be that as it may, the fact is I've tried over and over and can't run a business and a home. In fact, things have gotten to the stage where whatever we had, we lost—long ago."

"I'm so sorry, Ben," she said, seeing the pain in his eyes. Her heart went out to this sad man and his two little sons and his wife. In Em's family, it was generally considered "as you make your bed, so you lie upon it." Divorce was almost always an improper decision.

Since the first day Ben met Em, he had always called her "Em" and so it continued. Em became a petname although her family had always called her Ma—short of course for the dreaded Maggeltje. Each time Em visited Photographie Bijl over the months that followed, Ben's eyes would brighten up, and he would joke around and pretend to be a real gentleman, tipping his imaginary hat and kissing her hand. She felt her presence sparked some happiness in him.

"Well, Em, good morning. How is my budding photographer? How nice to see you again."

She felt his piercing eyes could almost read her thoughts, and she became uncomfortable with her own feelings…yet she was irresistibly drawn to this unusually attractive man.

The next time she went to his shop, her mind was in a dilemma. But why? Why am I attracted to him? He's not tall, his eyes are more piercing than attractive…but I do like his fine physique—all that gymnastics and swimming—why wouldn't he be fit? Ohh, but he's a divorcee! She gritted her teeth. What on earth will Mama and Papa say? Yet despite all this, I keep bringing my films back to him—I could easily get them developed by his father in Amsterdam and avoid seeing him at all. But Em, be honest— you like him.

After paying for her latest photos, she was about to leave, but Ben suggested, "Look, it's almost one o'clock. I'll close the shop for a couple of hours. I was wondering, would you please have lunch with me?"

Em shook her head, but as she looked into Ben's compelling, almost pleading eyes, something inside her heart was urging her in the opposite direction. There was a long silence.

Finally, he said ever so softly, "Em, please say yes."

"Ben, thank you, but I—I don't think I should." Em swallowed hard. She felt colour rushing to her cheeks while deep down a thrill in her heart. "It just wouldn't work out, you and me. I couldn't …" She stopped.

"How do you know that, Em? Anyway, just have lunch and let's have a talk about how we feel."

"I, I don't know …"

"Please, please say yes," he urged, taking her hands in his. Ben's steely grey-green eyes looked imploringly into hers.

Em told herself, Don't be a fool! You are going to get hurt—or worse, hurt someone else. Leave now! You know he's getting divorced. Yet something about Ben Bijl had always drawn her to him in her heart, although until this point, she had never completely admitted that to either him or herself.

Amazingly, before she knew what she was saying, her heart spoke. "All right, Ben, I will."

They stood smiling at each other, transfixed, and she wished the moment would never end.

Ben broke the spell and whispered, "Thank you, Em, for trusting me." Em's heart raced. "So, Em, where would you like to go for lunch?" She could hear the excitement in his voice.

Her reply was, "Anywhere."

Hand in hand they walked out of the shop, but on reaching the street, they let go and walked casually down the cobblestones to a quiet little café.

One lunch together opened the door to another lunch, and then dinner for two, and quickly their feelings grew into full-blown love. In 1936, Ben and Em became secretly engaged, waiting until his divorce came through. That was with the exception of Ben's family in Amsterdam, where Ben would regularly take Em on the back of his highly prized Saralaya motorbike to visit. Guda had come home after baby Hans' birth, speaking highly of Em, the lovely midwife. She and Leni immediately loved Em as did Ben's father and mother, and many a quiet Saturday and Sunday afternoon was spent with them during their courtship.

Ben and Em secretly engaged in early 1936.

Often Ben would sit on the lounge and Em would curl up at his feet, with her arms resting on his lap, whilst Leni, a conservatorium trained music teacher, played the piano and Guda, a wonderful cook, served delightful treats. On still other occasions, Ben would take out his violin, and he and Leni would play classical duets. Ben and Em would sing together, both loving music and singing, their common interests drawing them even closer to each other and his family. The Bijl family had instantly taken Em into their heart. She had never felt happier or more fulfilled, feeling that at last she had found her soul-mate, a man with whom she could happily spend the rest of her life.

During the months that followed, Em wanted desperately to share her news with her family in Chaam too. Each week though she put off the trip back home. In her letters to her family, she never once mentioned Ben. Em wrangled with herself, "How do I tell them I've met the man of my dreams—let alone falling in love with someone who God forbid has been married before—even though he is now divorced!" Ben realized her family's reaction would no doubt be one of intense disapproval, given their strong Protestant religious background. He had grown up in a family intensely involved in religion and knew what bigotry could wield. Unlike his family, who were free thinkers, and not impressed by the mainstream religions, Em's family were traditionally deeply religious Dutch Reformists.

"But, Em schatje (darling, treasure), we must talk to your parents about how we feel. We must talk to them soon. You know I want to marry you. Of course, I would not like to deprive you of your family's blessing."

Em's eyes filled with tears, and her heart ached as Ben tried to reason with her. "I love you, Ben, and yes, I want to marry you, my schatje, but will my parents give their approval to our union knowing you are a divorced man?" She hesitated. "I don't think so!" The tears flowed as Ben took her into his arms, comforting her.

"You know how much I love you, don't you?"

"Yes, my dearest heart." He breathed the words into her ears, kissing her tenderly.

"It doesn't matter what I say to Papa and Mama. I know already what their reaction will be. They will never hear of any daughter of theirs marrying a divorced man; I know it! I've seen their reaction when others dared to do it."

"Well, schatje, as hard as it is, you must make a decision. It may come down to them or me. I'm so sorry that it has to come to this, but there is no other way. Having said that, we should not decide for them.

You must go and visit them and pour your heart out—tell them all. Who knows? Perhaps they will see the genuineness of our love. What do you think, my sweet?"

"I have no work scheduled next month, perhaps I should take the opportunity to go and visit them for a couple of weeks and gradually reveal what is in my heart."

"You go for a few days and lay the ground work, acquainting them with our news and then I will ride out on the weekend and you can introduce me personally." He looked into her eyes waiting for her approval. She nodded. Reluctantly Ben prepared to leave. They embraced at her door.

Again, Ben hesitated to leave, although it was a cold night.

"You must go now, schatje. It's late. I love you." She held out her hand for one more touch. "Go now, my Ben."

He walked slowly down the steps to his motorbike. He hesitated and turned to look at her again.

Em waved him forward. "Go!"

Ben pulled on his leather jacket and gloves. He smiled at her again. Soon the engine roared and he stole one more look at his prize, blowing her a kiss. "Good night, precious schatje."

"Good night, Ben." She waved. The Saralaya shot forward, and he soon turned the corner and disappeared out of sight. Only then did Em—chilled by the icy Dutch winds although it was summer— unlatch the door and walk inside.

The day came when Em left for her parents' home in Chaam. The long bike ride was not arduous since it is mile after mile of monotonous flat roads with low hills as she got closer to the Belgian border. The heaviness in her heart became more and more burdensome with each mile. Memories of her childhood flooded into her mind as she turned into Meerleseweg on the south edge of Chaam, where her parents' farm lay. The sound of the wheels scratching on the graveled pathway leading toward the family farm house heralded her presence.

This is it! Em thought as she stepped off the bicycle. "Mama! Papa! Mama! Papa! Are you there?"

Almost instantly she heard her mama calling from within, "Come, Johan, our Maggeltje's home! Come quickly!" They ran out the front door to welcome their daughter, whom they had not seen since Christmas. It was now mid-June 1936.

Reunion with Em's parents, Johan and Anna Flach
after the birth of their first two children.

"It's so lovely to see you, Maggeltje." Her Papa hugged her and kissed her on both cheeks. "You look so well. Very well! Doesn't she look great, Mama?"

"Yes, yes. Let me look at you. You do look fine, girl. What a wonderful surprise to see you. Can you stay for long?" her mother asked. She was hugging her now and pulling her back and scrutinising her, then hugging her again. "Do I detect that there's a man in your life? Tell me dearest, have you a boyfriend?"

"What makes you ask such a silly question, Mama?" Em parried, buying time.

"I don't know, there's something about the way you look. I've not seen it in you before, but I have seen it in others." Anna was beaming, her face almost a question mark, she was in such suspense. "Tell me. Tell me! Who is he?"

"First of all, let's go inside for coffee, girls." Papa interrupted, laughing, with a knowing little smile under his moustache at this exchange between his intuitive females.

"That's a great idea, Papa. I'm starving!" Em said as she grabbed her father's arm and stepped into the kitchen of her childhood home.

Her senses tingled at each and every sensation—fond memories springing to mind. "I have forgotten how much there is to love in this place, Mama."

"Oh, girl it's so good to see you again." Her mother laughed, turning to her husband. "Johan, can you believe it? This is the girl who hated living on the farm speaking."

Em's father chuckled. "Funny thing about growing up, isn't it? We often see things so differently from what we did when we were children." Em smiled, acknowledging the truthfulness of her father's words.

Anna prepared a large tray. "Coffee's ready!" There was constant chatter as they caught up. Again, came Anna's leading question, "Well, who is the lucky young man? Tell us!"

"Ma, how lovely to see you. Are you engaged? Who is it, please tell?" Annie, one of her sisters, asked excitedly. She had just arrived home from work and heard her mother's question.

"His name is Gerard Bernard Heinrich Bijl, but we call him Ben for short. He is in his thirties and he's a photographer. And yes, we are engaged and going to get married soon."

"See! I told you, Johan, she's in love." Em's mother clasped her hands with great satisfaction, an expression of relief and happiness written across her soft features. It was obvious looking at Em's mother where Em inherited her refined and ladylike features.

"And you say he's a photographer, is that right?" asked her Papa almost matter-of-factly as he lit up his pipe, no doubt to aid him in assimilating this pleasing revelation of his independent-thinking daughter's life. "At last you've decided to do what normal young women do: settle down and have a family. No more gallivanting around the countryside with this midwifery then."

Em pretended not to hear her father's latter comments.

"You do have a photo of him to show us, seeing he's a photographer?" her father asked dryly.

"Why, yes, of course I do."

"Show us the photos, girl," Anna said impatiently. Em brought out some good shots of Ben. Her mother looked shocked, "Oh but Maggeltje he looks so much older!"

"Perhaps Mama but that isn't really important now, is it?"

"So? Have you two set the date for your wedding, or are you going to bring him here so he can officially ask me for your hand in marriage, like all good boys do?" Johan puffed on his pipe.

"Well, not exactly, Papa. Ben will come and ask you shortly though." Em was suddenly very uncomfortable. She still hadn't told the most important detail. The evening meal finished and still Em had said nothing of the fact that Ben was a divorced man.

The longer she waited, the harder it became. After a few days with her parents and sisters, Em became physically sick; the emotion she kept bottled up inside her was taking its toll.

"Maggeltje, if I didn't know better, dear, I'd say you were worried about something. But you must be happier now than you have ever been. Tell me what's wrong, dear? When will Ben come down to visit us?"

"He's riding over on Saturday afternoon Mama."

"So, what's worrying you my dear?"

Em turned to her mama, eyes downcast. "Mama, you're closer to the truth than you realize."

"Maggeltje, what do you mean?"

"I'm afraid there is one thing that I haven't told you about myself yet." She hesitated.

"Whatever is wrong, Maggeltje? You're not pregnant?" Anna searched her eyes for truth.

"No."

"Well then, God forbid. He isn't a married man, is he?"

"Well, he is divorced now, and I am going to marry him. I love him very much, and he's a good man. Please, Mama, say it's all right!"

"Maggeltje, he is a Christian, isn't he?" Anna looked sad.

"No, Mama he is not! But he is a good man, and he does believe in God!"

"It goes against all we have taught you, child. Not a Christian and divorced!" her mother said so sadly, so disappointed. "And besides he looks so much older than you say. Are you sure he's only in his mid-thirties girl?"

"He is only in his thirties Mama, just losing his hair more quickly than Papa has, that's all." Em looked into her mother's eyes; silent yet pleading for understanding.

Anna walked away from her daughter crying, and Em in turn threw herself on her childhood bed and cried until she thought her heart would break.

Em's father was not so kind. He was a good man, but this was more than any man could accept peacefully. "Maggeltje, you must not do this bad thing. He is already married in God's eyes. This is sin! Your mama and I can never give our approval to such a union. Please, Maggeltje, you must reconsider. You just must."

"I'm sorry, Papa, but I will marry Ben. I hate to go against you and Mama, but we love each other. He's a good man whether he's divorced or not. And he is coming on the weekend to meet you all."

Ben arrived in the late afternoon on the Saturday as arranged, whilst Em was helping her father milk the cows. Johanna called her, saying, "Come quickly, Maggeltje. He is here!"

Em ran to Ben, hugging him. Together they walked to the farmhouse door and knocked.

Anna came out and invited Ben and Em into the living room, where they waited until her father had finished the milking and came into the house. Em introduced Ben, and the situation was explosive.

Ben put his hand out to shake Johan's hand. Johan refused. Hence, Ben quickly got to the point. "Mr. and Mrs. Flach, I came here today to ask you both a question. I would like to marry Em. I've come to ask for your consent."

Johan spoke for the family. "You are both adults, Ben, and we are not able to prevent this marriage, but we do not approve. I am sorry, Maggeltje, but your mama and I and your sisters will not be able to attend this wedding, and we can never give this marriage our blessing. It is against all we believe in and hold dear."

Em cried as she searched her father's eyes for sympathy. There was absolutely none. Likewise determined, not for one moment did she waver in her decision. No matter what happened, she would marry Ben. She had given her heart to him, and there would never be another. "Please, please, Papa, won't you reconsider? There were extenuating circumstances…"

"No, Maggeltje. Hear me? No! The answer is no!" All her pleadings did not win a change of heart in her Papa.

*

Ben and Em took leave of her parents and sisters the next morning. All stood tearfully at the front of her family home. If she married Ben, it would be as she had suspected all along—without the presence of her beloved family and without their so much desired blessing.

She determined, "Well, my parents may not come, but it's my guess we'll get some of my older sisters to attend. After all, Cien's married now, and her husband may not be so harsh in his judgments. Cor and Sjaan being engaged already—may stand against my parents." A few tears fell down Em's cheeks as she pictured the day, but as sad as it was, nothing was going to stop her marriage to Ben Bijl! The long journey back to Baarn with Em riding her bicycle and Ben riding at a snail's pace to keep her company, was one with feelings running from one end of the spectrum to the other.

Eventually they reached Em's flat. They spoke at the door for some time until finally Em said, almost guiltily, "For goodness sake, come inside, Ben."

He didn't need a second invitation. Later they decided to discuss their future over dinner in a secluded little nook of the classy French restaurant in Baarn.

"The conversation I had with my parents, although for a different reason, was akin to the one they had with Mama's parents thirty years or so ago." Em looked out the restaurant window into a small garden.

There was such a far away look in her eyes.

"Please tell me what happened to them, Em?" he asked softly.

"I told you, didn't I? Mama married Papa against her parents' wishes. Funny isn't it? History repeating itself."

"Why are people so unreasonable?" Ben's eyes smouldered, trying to control his indignation. Then he looked sad. "I have put you in this position, sweetheart. So sorry!"

"It's all right, schatje. It's all right with me." She patted his hand empathetically.

Ben looked up, tears in his usually smiling eyes. He forced them back. "Schatje, I so wish it wasn't this way, but it is, and I cannot turn back the hands of time! Young people lack experience, and sometimes they make huge mistakes, as Miep and I did."

Em leaned forward across the table and dusted his forehead with a tender and understanding kiss.

"Are you sure you've made the right decision, Em? I want to be sure you're sure." His piercing eyes looked into hers, intensely seeking to lay bare her heart and mind.

"I am twenty-six years old now, and I know what I want. This is not a decision I have taken lightly. I have never been surer of anything in my life, Ben. I believe our marriage will turn out to be a lasting union, just as my parents believed theirs would."

Ben smiled, for he knew by her eyes and words she spoke the truth he so desperately needed to hear. "Thank you for trusting me and giving me another chance to enjoy life. Believe me, I have learnt a lot through the mistakes of my youth. I am almost thirty-four years old, my sweet, and I really know what I want."

She gazed at him with eyes brimming with love. "So do I, my dearest Ben. And I am not going to let you slip through my fingers."

"Let's set the date for our wedding tonight, sweetheart," Ben said, his eyes suddenly twinkling again.

"When would you like to get married?" Em teased. "Tonight!" Ben's eyes twinkled mischievously.

"Oh, Ben, you're incorrigible!" Em's eyes danced too.

"Well, as you can see, I think as soon as possible."

"It would be nice when the weather isn't too cold," she said.

"How about in the autumn then? How about September?"

"September is only two months away! I was thinking about early spring next year. That will give me time to prepare."

"Well, it appears we won't be having a large wedding, so what's the problem? Can't you organize your work around it? All you need is a lovely dress. It's not as if we must wait until we're old enough. You're twenty-six already and, well." He laughed. "I'm an old man. Come on, Em." He drew her lips to his.

Em's objections melted away with that kiss. "Two months! I suppose, I could try."

"How about the end of September—the twenty-fourth?"

Em studied her work schedule for the next couple of months and came to the pleasant conclusion that that particular period was not very booked out, therefore it would probably be a good date as long as someone didn't go over or under time in their confinement. That was always a consideration in midwifery.

"All right, Ben. September 24 it is."

"Great! All I want is you, Em."

Em smiled, eyes shining. "So, dearest, I'm curious. When did you first start to fall in love with me?"

"Instantly the moment you walked into my shop, Em, I was attracted to you."

She smiled. "You're joking, Ben Bijl. Seriously."

"I swear to God, Em, I was attracted to you at that very moment. I've loved you ever since." His eyes softened again. "Em, thanks so much for loving me in return."

"I do, Ben," she said simply. "You know I do."

"Here comes our poulet bon femme casserole." He smiled. Together they celebrated with a delightful meal.

The next evening, Em responded to a knock on her front door. It was Ben. He darted in the door and swept her into his arms. "I don't know how I'm going to wait until September, Em."

She chuckled. "Of course, you will, Ben. I'll see to that!"

He laughed, drew Em toward him, and quickly pulled a little parcel from his pocket. "I have something special for you, dearest."

She gazed at the tiny little package—she guessed what it might be. Yes, it was an engagement ring. On their wedding day this ring would be transferred to the other hand and as was the custom, it became the wedding ring.

*

The wedding invitations were sent out to all members of the families both his and hers.

The wedding day arrived on a mild, sunny day, hardly a cloud in the sky. Em and her older sisters, who chose to defy their father and attend the wedding, spent the morning preparing the bride. She chose a fine white satin gown with a V-neck white lace bodice over a satin under-bodice. The lace neckline was achieved with a deep plunging cowl from the shoulder. The sleeves were soft and slightly billowing but became tight-fitting lace from elbow to wrist. The satin skirt fell smoothly to the floor in gentle folds. A pair of white, satin-covered low-heel shoes complemented the beautiful gown.

"Ben will love you, Em," Annie said reassuringly, surveying her older sister.

At the arranged hour, the marriage party arrived at the town hall for the registration of the marriage. (In The Netherlands, all marriages must first be registered legally, and then the group may progress to a Church if desired.) Ben and Em chose to be married only in the civil ceremony at the Zeist Town Hall.

Ben, in his morning suit and top hat, looked dapper indeed. Em was radiant as always, the epitome of elegance!

The celebrant asked, "Do you take this man to be your lawfully wedded husband?" Em looked straight into Ben's eyes and said, "I do!" As twilight lingered, the happy couple rode away on his Saralaya motorbike to a secret destination to begin married life together.

*

A few weeks later, after they had settled into the tiny apartment as a married couple, Ben asked, "How did you feel on our wedding day?"

"It was bitter sweet, but I knew I could not live my life without you being part of it. I'm twenty-six years old and I know what I want. And you, Ben—you are what I want!" She snuggled into his arms. "Happy?" His playful eyes spoke better than any word she could have uttered. The passion of his kiss was his fervent reply. He grabbed her by the hand and together they ran up the stairs to their bed.

Ben and Em's wedding day, 24 September 1936.

CHAPTER 6

The Move to Zeist in 1936

"With the divorce settlement," Ben explained. "I am forced to close the business in Baarn, at least for the present. So, I am going to work from home until we get back on our feet financially. But I am afraid we will need more room than we have here."

"That's fine, Ben. I'm willing to do anything to make things easier for us."

"Then come with me, Em, and I will show you another place in Zeist, that may be suitable for us to live in and also have a temporary dark room setup in one of the bedrooms." Zeist was a short drive from Baarn. The house had a shop-front in the middle of the town.

"Wow Ben. This is a pretty place. Oh, and what is that imposing old tower up ahead?"

"That's the old water tower for the town but the clock tower at the Town Hall, where we were married is much older. This town goes back to the eighth century AD. Wait till you see the ancient "Slot Zeist" – it's such a magnificent old castle with a moat around it."

"It's so lovely here Ben. I like the forests we drove through to get here. It's really hilly too, so nice. I'm sure I'll love it here."

"Yes, I agree. And there are lots of spots great for picnics and bush walks as well, in the forests around here. The rich people from Utrecht often have homes here because it is so lovely, which also means we will be able to make a good living from their clientele."

"Sounds good." Em said contentedly.

Em the budding photographer.

"Weddings will have to be our specialty for a while, since we will have no shopfront to attract customers."

During the two years he had known Em, she had developed into a very able photographer, having an eye for beauty. She had an aptitude for placing people well in situations, to take a photo to the best advantage.

"Em, your skills will be a boon now. Would you like to work with me? Together we can make a good living, I'm sure."

"I would love to, Ben, but am I good enough yet? I don't really think so." Em's brow furrowed, a little concerned.

"Oh course! You're getting better all the time. And I'll be with you. Anyway, together we should be able to manage it. Besides, we have to bring along a lot of lights for nightshots, and someone needs to arrange and help carry them from "a" to "b." I'll be able to help you develop your skills even further in Zeist. You wait until I take you to one of my favourite spots in the forest along the river. We'll have lunch there. I love it because it has so many different photogenic spots."

"Can't wait!" she said.

Presently they pulled up at the tranquil spot Ben had described. A little stream meandered through leafy trees, the water rippling across its surface as the gentle breeze blew and lovely wild ducks swam, babies following in a triangular parade after them.

"Ben, you're absolutely right. I love it!" Em gasped. "We should come here often. It's magic!"

"So it is, my sweet. And great for photographers." He already had his camera out.

*

After a thorough inspection of the apartment on the Steinlaan 70, Ben and Em decided to take it. They busily set about making the unit a cosy love nest. Em could sew well, which was a bonus, since she could make all the curtains, tablecloths, and other material items for a fraction of the cost to purchase ready-made.

Ben set up his darkroom in the second bedroom. The next thing he did was run ads in the Zeister Chronicle, the local paper. She and Ben also decided to give their new venture a new name too. Short and eye catching – "Foto Bijl." It quickly yielded results, bringing in many calls for weddings in the coming year since Ben's name was already well known in the Utrecht district.

Meanwhile, Em was learning the ropes working with Ben. She still practised midwifery in the local area.

About six months after the wedding, Em found she was pregnant. She was ecstatic and Ben, no stranger to the idea of children, was happy although somewhat concerned. He had already gone into debt to buy out his ex-wife's share in the original business. The baby was due in late November. "Happy, my sweet?" Their eyes met.

"Couldn't be happier, my Ben!" Em hugged him. "I've seen many miracles in the course of my work, but the most exciting will be the birth of our own child. By the way, I would like you to be my midwife for the confinement."

"Who, me?" Ben looked at her, astonished. "But I'm not capable. I don't know enough about such things—"

"That's true, schatje, but I do, and I'll tell you what to do. It will be fine!" There wasn't much she had seen faze Ben Bijl.

Weekends were hectic since on Sundays, Ben's son Bennie would stay over, and later so did Hans, when he was a little older. Bennie was about nine by then, and Em loved him very much. In truth, she grew attached to both boys, but Bennie was never as close to her since he remembered his life with his parents before the divorce and understandably felt resentment toward her. When their family expanded, the boys, especially Hans, continued to visit regularly, sharing an occasional day at the beach during the summer months or other physical activities, such as skating or skiing, in the winter months.

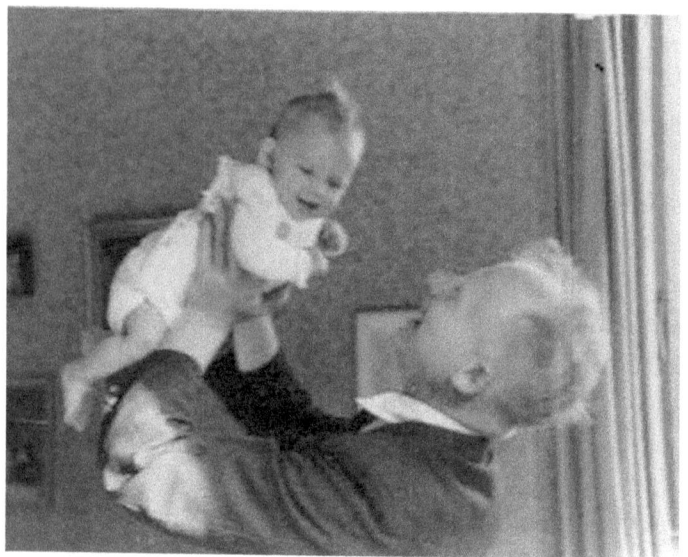

The birth of Gerda in November 1937.

The little girl was born on November 19, 1937, as the autumn leaves fell and the cold icy winds of winter set in. The doctor delivered their beautiful little baby girl. Ben followed Em's instructions, and everything went like clockwork. He assisted, spellbound!

"Well, Em, how did I do?" Ben asked proudly as he held her in his arms, offering her to her mother to hold for the first time. Her heart leapt as her husband handed the precious little bundle to her. "Ben! She's beautiful! A healthy child. And you were wonderful, Ben. I knew you could do it."

He laughed, beaming at the bundle of joy in her arms. "Said like a true midwife, I suspect." Em nodded. He took some photos, and then they discussed the newborn's name.

"We will call her Gerda Heindrika after her father. Yes?" Em looked at her husband's expression. His smile grew, spreading from ear to ear.

"After her father? What about her lovely mother?"

"No, Ben, she is your first daughter. Let's name her after her father. Besides, I love the name Gerda."

"Well it's settled then—Gerda Heindrika it is! I had better make some phone calls to let my family know all is well—and we have a little angel." Em wrote to her mother since she had no telephone.

Gerda was indeed angelic to look upon, but what a determined little girl she proved to be! "Can't" was not in Gerda's vocabulary, and independence went hand in glove with her determination. Although she had a softer look in her eyes than her father, she was nonetheless like him in her obvious desire to do her own thing. Her mother wasn't lacking in that department either.

Angelic? Ben soon found out he was wrong about that. Even before Gerda could talk fluently, she would grit her teeth and say, "Zelf Doen" (which means "I'll do it myself!") She was delightful not only to her parents but her grandparents and her two maiden aunts on the Bijl side as she was the second granddaughter to Ben's parents.

She had the distinction of being the first granddaughter on Em's family side—that is if they would recognize her. Thankfully the letter Em and Ben posted along with the photos won their hearts, and soon a letter and welcoming gift arrived from the Flach fold.

Gerda thrived and was soon crawling and babbling away contentedly. Em was a natural mother and enjoyed her role wholeheartedly. No regrets. One morning in early 1939, she received a letter from Annie, her younger sister, announcing her engagement to Gerrit de Graaff. "Listen Ben, Annie says they're getting married in April – but not until April 1941. How exciting!"

"That's good news indeed. Your mother seems to really like him."

"Yes, she does. I have some good news for us too, which I'm sure she'll like as well."

"And what's that?" Ben asked, looking surprised.

"We're going to have another baby! I suppose we'll have to look for a bigger house—although there's plenty of time to find something suitable."

"Another pregnancy! How exciting Em." Ben took her in his arms.

"Yes Em, Gerda needs a little play-mate doesn't she? But yes, it does create a problem."

Ben's brow furrowed. "That means another upheaval for our business too. But I'm sure you'll love it, Em. Another opportunity to put your decorating panache into action! I hope we have plenty of weddings booked in the next few months. It'll be a costly affair, this moving."

"Don't worry, everything will be fine. I'm a good organizer and budget well. My years as money manager at Princenhage weren't for nothing."

A few weeks later they arranged to spend a Saturday searching for a larger place to live. Not far from their Steinlaan apartment in Zeist, in Veldheimlaan, they found exactly what they were looking for—not a tenement but a lovely suburban three-storey duplex in a relatively up market estate. Built in the twenties, it was still quite new. The streets were lined with chestnut trees. These trees originally formed a beautiful border on either side of the long driveway to the gates of the property known as The Veldheim Slot. Sometime, possibly after World War I, the owners sold this land for housing. This street on the original drive to the Slot was named Veldheimlaan after the original property. It being almost summer, the trees were donning their first delicate green shoots, which would gradually unfurl into long spiky leaves. The effect of the sunlight, dappling in and out of those leaves, was lovely. The house was built with attention to aspect, facing south, which enabled one to get the most out of the winter sunshine. Ben wanted a room he could use as a darkroom, and this house was big enough for that as well.

The Veldheim Slot where the Nazi Headquarters
was set up in Zeist during World War II.

They found out their neighbour was a Mrs. de Rue, a widow, and she said the neighbours on the other side of the duplex were a brother and two sisters, none of whom had ever married. Dijkstra was their name.

Ben said, "I like this location. Besides its beauty, it is very central. I can either ride my bicycle on warmer days or my Saralaya in freezing weather. Then when I need a car for special occasions or on Saturdays to take weddings, I can hire one from Mr. Van der Toom up on the next corner. It's so close and convenient. All in all, I think we couldn't have found a better location, and it's fairly new—what more could a man ask for? Only problem is, it's not available until February next year."

"Well, there is another place we can rent for a couple of months in Kritzingerlaan until it comes available."

They moved into the Kritzingerlaan flat in March 1939.

CHAPTER 7

The World at War, 1939

One evening Ben came roaring in on his motorbike, the Telegraaf newspaper rolled up under his arm. It was the mid-September 1939 issue. The largest bold headlines Em had ever seen announced blood-chilling news: WAR!

"Look, Em! Germany has invaded Poland. The world is at war! I knew it was coming. Anyone could see the signs—Germany has been pouring all their resources into defence and armaments for the past several years, but this soon! It has taken us by surprise. Britain and France have now declared war on Germany. And it won't finish there— you wait and see!"

"Oh, Ben, the thought of war frightens me! What are we to do?"

"The paper says The Netherlands will remain neutral at all costs. But I doubt if that will really be possible." Ben shook his head.

They looked at each other for a moment in stunned silence. Then he took Em into his arms and said quietly, "we have to do whatever it takes to survive. In the meantime, we must anticipate our needs and try to provide solutions that will work, even if The Netherlands is overrun by the Nazis. It's pretty likely. Look what they did in the Great War. Our poor country was the filling in that sandwich, and it may well be again!"

"No, Ben, surely not! Not again!" There was fear in Em's voice.

"Let's be realistic. Germany needs seaports and outlets to get at other nations. Don't put your head in the sand like the proverbial ostrich! We must be affected! It's better to prepare for the worst and at least we'll cope better than people who won't face reality and in a desperate situation have no idea what to do."

"But Ben, how do you prepare for war?"

"There is always a shortage of food and other important commodities during conflicts, Em, so I am going to start buying things I'll be able to exchange for food on the black market or barter with farmers when things get tough. Things like cigarettes, soap, and butter are some of the most sought after. I remember clearly what it was like during the end of the 1914–18 war here."

"I guess you're right, Ben." She looked at her husband, wanting to trust him. "I'm so glad I'm married to you." Em nestled protectively in Ben's arms. They felt the magic of their child kick against him from within the warm cocoon of her belly.

"I love you too, little one," Ben said as he bent down and kissed Em's belly and patted where he felt the kick. A sudden little jerk appeared again, as the infant in her womb seemed to react to the emotion his parents were clearly displaying on that fateful day.

December 6, St. Nicholas Day, finally came, and Gerda squealed with excitement to find the presents he and his helper friend Zwarte Piet delivered.

*

On December 19, 1939, in the early afternoon, Em's water broke. "Ben, it's time. We'd better get ready, honey."

Ben smiled and gently patted her belly. Em went into full-blown labour within two hours. The doctor arrived just in time to deliver the baby without any complications, and shortly thereafter he handed into Ben's open arms another healthy-looking newborn. Ben scrutinized the infant looking for faults, but he was perfect!

He held the rosy, screaming little mass up to his mother. "Look, Em! This one is a boy!"

"I can see. I can see—a son!" Em's face was ecstatic, belying all her efforts seconds earlier. "We have a girl and a boy!"

Ben, satisfied his third son was intact, held him lovingly and swaddled the infant in a soft knitted blanket and passed him into his mother's outstretched arms.

Baby Charles born 19th December 1939.

"Oh, Ben, he's beautiful, isn't he? We'll call him Charles." Em looked lovingly at him. He was a true Aryan baby, with a smooth, round, little head covered only with white down. His little body was robust and chubby. He had a broad chest and long torso, although in contrast, his limbs were not lanky like his torso. Charles' eyes were pale blue-grey in colour, and like his sister Gerda, he too was a healthy and beautiful child.

Ben took delightful pictures of Charles and his older sister, sending a photo to all members of their family and friends to announce baby Charles' safe arrival. It was an announcement and a photo all in one.

Extremely modern for 1939!

The home in Zeist, Veldheimlaan 20 that the family moved into in early 1940.

Then on February 20, 1940, the big move occurred. Ben and Em were extremely excited. It was a happy day when they all sat down with Adrian and Ben's two sisters after the move was completed.

They had great plans to furnish this rather large house. Ben often went around to auctions looking for bargains on cameras and photographic equipment, and this time he looked for a dining set, lounge chairs—and of course no Dutch home would be gezellig (warm and cosy) without a lamp and coffee table. These he found. The following Monday afternoon a delivery truck pulled up out the front of their house.

"Ben, it must be the furniture you bought last weekend!" Em said as she checked, looking out the front window. She quickly opened the front door.

Two men began unloading many articles of finely crafted furniture, which Ben had successfully sniffed out at the auction.

"Oh, Ben, this really is fine furniture! I hope it was cheaper than it looks!" Em laughed.

The deliverymen looked at her in surprise. "Did you get all this at one auction, madam?"

Ben answered. "Yes, as a matter of fact, it was my lucky day. These were all water damaged when fire broke out in the shop where they were for sale. I checked them carefully, and they were not badly damaged, just a few water stains, which I believe some good oil will remove."

*

The weeks sped through winter into spring until one afternoon, Em opened the front door to answer a knock. Ben was busy developing in the darkroom upstairs.

A deliveryman was at the door, asking for Mrs. M. Bijl-Flach. He had a piano for her. Em was astounded because she had not ordered a piano, although she would have loved to have one. The man reassured her the docket stated, "Delivery for Mrs. M. Bijl-Flach." It was an early birthday present for Em from Ben.

She was delighted, and Ben was thrilled because he wanted her to have something very special—the sound of music in their home.

The days flew by! Em and Ben clung to the joy of a happy family knowing it could end all too soon. There was a fragile peace in the country for a time. By April, the writing was on the wall.

Newspaper reports indicated there was a build-up of German troops and army equipment on the eastern borders of The Netherlands! The government called up all soldiers and reserves and cancelled all leave.

On May 9, 1940, the people of The Netherlands went to bed as normal but awoke to the heart-wrenching news that overnight, Hitler's forces had bombed the enormous seaport and businesss sector. Rotterdam was bombed to the ground. Hitler knew that by crippling Rotterdam on the mighty estuary of the Rhine River, he could put a stranglehold on the economy of all the nations of Europe, thus giving him a strategic and financial superiority over all the countries he wished to vanquish. The Dutch army fought boldly but received many casualties, and many people were killed in the conflict that followed over the following week. Hitler then threatened to bomb the ancient city of Utrecht with its many educational and cultural treasures. Utrecht was also the Dutch Railways central rail junction and vital for transportation throughout the whole country. Fortunately, the Nazis wanted to preserve the Railway network in tact for their own use.

The Dutch government gathered to make a decision. The only conclusion they could reach was to capitulate to the Germans, as they could not hope to win. Their army had not kept up with the latest battle equipment, and they were so small compared to Hitler's army. The signing of the surrender took place on May 15, 1940.

Ben's family woke to the news that The Netherlands had officially become the buffer state between the Nazis and the Allies. The war was burgeoning. Nazi Germany occupied their homeland within hours. The Royal family had escaped to England overnight. To protect the heirs to the Dutch throne, Queen Wilhelmina fled with her daughters to Canada while Prince Bernard stayed on in Britain where he could keep contact with his people via the clandestine radiowaves.

Em was most upset when she saw that the beautiful old castle at the end of Veldheimlaan had been forcibly taken over by the Nazis as their headquarters. Swastikas blew everywhere in the wind, reminding the Dutch that they had lost their freedom. However, for the first two years following, things went along reasonably well—with a good amount of normality, if you will. It was the lull before the full force of the storm broke forth.

The new Nazi government tried to be benefactors to the Dutch people, initially encouraging them to oust the "House of Orange," the Dutch royal family, and align themselves with Germany and Austria as part of the Greater Third Reich. Hitler expressed the opinion that the Dutch nation was primarily of Aryan stock and worthy to be counted among the "super race" that he advocated.

Until that time, the Jews in The Netherlands had superb protection under the arms of the Dutch government. According to the scrupulous Dutch records, about one hundred forty thousand Jewish people were living in the nation. A goodly number of Jewish people may have already fled Germany, seeking refuge in The Netherlands, a benevolent country.

Within a few short months though, the new Nazi government had accessed all the Dutch census records and saw that finding the Jews in The Netherlands would be much easier than in other places where they had been persecuting them. (The Dutch government, unlike Hitler, had taken this action in order to collect church taxes for the various religions in The Netherlands, including the Jews.) What the Dutch government had done with a good motive became a tool for the Nazis to identify Jews.

Even in 1940, the Nazi rule started influencing people's anti-Semitic feelings with much propaganda. Then they pressured businesses throughout The Netherlands to put up signs saying, "Jews not welcome here." Soon those who were in favour of the Nazi philosophy, although a minority, started to openly persecute the poor Jewish people, raiding their businesses and destroying their possessions, much like the Krystallnacht ("night of broken glass") atrocities in Germany.

The first people to begin a resistance movement in The Netherlands were the Social Democrats and the Communists. They immediately set up small cells and were actively anti-Nazi, but by and large they tried to make their point through strikes in the business sectors and utilities throughout the country. They were focused on guerrilla warfare, not violence. They were willing to disrupt the enemy at every turn. One way they did this was setting up escape lines for the Jewish people, who had become one of the Nazis' primary targets.

Ben was a member of the Communist Party before the war. He identified with the right of every person to have equality and freedom, which the party in theory advocated. As things heated up in The Netherlands during 1941, Ben observed, and learnt through one secret journal distributed by the Orthodox Protestant Resistance, namely Trouw (meaning loyalty, faithfulness, fidelity), that the Nazis had actually begun a systematic deportation of any Jewish families they could find.

He also saw how sneakily they had tried to infiltrate the private lives of all people in the country but especially Jews. Initially they were sent to an interim concentration camp at Mauthausen-Gusen. Later, as the war continued, there were concentration camps erected at Vught and Amersfoort, two towns very close to Zeist.

Now, toward the end of 1941, he was seeing similar ominous signs of change as the German war machine keep eroding his homeland's economy and food supplies for the Nazi war effort. Everywhere downtown, even in Zeist shops, displayed signs: "Jews not welcome here."

Gradually the covert methods used to seek out the Jews became overt. It was a daily occurrence in large cities like Amsterdam to see the SS dragging away men, women, and children, herding them into trucks and off to the railway station to be shipped in cattle trucks without any dignity to the concentration camps. Even in Zeist, Ben had seen this happen and it made his blood boil!

Out of fear of the Nazis, many Dutch people buckled under pressure from the local government, now controlled by the Occupation. If a business did not cooperate with the Nazi regime, they were boycotted, their businesses often having to close down. Others openly supported the Nazi philosophy and joined in, seeking out anyone of Semitic origin in their communities. Or if they detected their neighbours were harbouring Jews, they would report this to the local police. Notably, anyone who applied for positions in authority, such as public servants, police chiefs, mayors, and the like were given an ultimatum: sign the document, which was called the "Aryan Attestation," or go home. This document had to state their religious, ethnic ancestry, and political bias. Understandably some felt for the sake of their positions or incomes they had to agree to the terms of the Nazi rule. Those who did often leaned toward fascism, so a political group known as the Nationaal Socialistische Bewegning (called by most NSBers) became synonymous with those who sided with Hitler's Third Reich. However, because the police stations were largely manned by men who were Nazi sympathisers, the Jewish people had nowhere to turn to for protection.

Seeing this happening made Ben feel incensed at the injustices of life. His earlier observations on the hypocrisy of most religions in times of war caused him to look elsewhere for justice. It was these observations that led him to become an advocate of communist socialism for some years because he felt in principal the ideals of sharing and equality of man were good. His hatred for Nazism grew every day as he saw innocent people carted off by the Occupation forces to concentration camps and in most cases execution. One hundred and seven thousand Jewish people were deported to Germany from The Netherlands during World War II, and only five thousand survived the concentration camps. And what crime did they commit? Nothing, except they were not Aryans. The look of terror in the eyes of fathers and mothers as they saw their little ones wrenched away from them burned in his heart. Perhaps he thought of his own two sons, Ben and Hans, whose mother's family were of Jewish descent although they did not look typically Jewish. They fortunately were outside the fourth-generation demarcation that Hitler had made as to who actually qualified to be called Jewish.

Many Jewish people did not identify themselves as Jewish in the census, but that did not protect them. If a family or person even had Jewish features and colouring, he would be closely checked out—just on suspicion.

Those who were not Jewish and caught harbouring Jewish people were also punished. Therefore, fear governed people's every breath. Day by day the search for Dutch Jews was heightened. Ben's sense of justice continued to boil. His communist associates agreed with his sentiments and like Ben were eager to assist the poor innocents. Many brave men and women became involved in assisting Jewish people, particularly to escape the Nazi clutches. Ben became intensely interested in doing his part to help too.

*

Whilst sharing their morning coffee together, Ben broached the subject with his wife. He held a copy of the Telegraaf. "Em, I know you realize where all this is leading. Within a few short months, not only all Jewish business will have been closed down, but all our businesses will have to close, and food will be almost unprocurable."

"Y-yes," Em said, wincing in anguish. "It terrifies me! Especially now. What are we bringing our precious children into? Surely it won't be the same or as bad as before. Surely!"

Ben drew Em into his arms and said, "I'm sorry, but I believe it will. Rest assured though, my schatje, I'll never leave you or our children. I promise. I have been thinking about this at great length, and I have some ideas that may help us survive."

"Oh, Ben, how can you fight against the mighty swastika and win?"

"Well for one thing, we will not starve. I have spent all the money I could get my hands on buying up cigarettes, soap, and butter. You know some people would even barter their food rations for filthy cigarettes! Can you believe that? Anyway, I'm sure I'll find people who will want to buy them off me in return for food—food that will help us survive!"

Each night as Em went to her bed, she prayed, "Dear Lord, what do we do? Every day things are getting worse. What will happen to us during the coming weeks, months, and years? How will we find enough to feed our children?"

Ben operating his business from home during the Occupation.

Ben working in his darkroom.

CHAPTER 8

A Son with Haemophilia

"Hello, Oudje!" Ben would often pinch Em on the rump when he came home. It was just a light-hearted, yet affectionate, physical greeting to his wife.

"Why, Ben, you surprised me!" Em countered, having a bit of a giggle, reflecting on the expression. "What's this 'oldie'? I'm not old yet, Ben Bijl!"

"Just funning, sweetheart! However, I couldn't help but notice downtown this morning how many businesses are closing their doors or at least laying off staff even here in Zeist. It's a worry!"

"Yes, and I'll bet the only ones still doing well are the NSBers. Right?"

"Too right I fear, Em! Ever since dear old Queen Emma died, the fascists have been gaining power here in The Netherlands. Mussert and his followers are playing right into Hitler's hands; they agree with his sentiments. Hence even though many people now can see through them, they are in favour of the Germans. So many businesses are secretly supporting the NSBers in order to get supplies and keep making money. Just about all the mayors in each town are also NSBers, put there by that rotten chancellor Seyss-Inquart, so that they are more than willing to cooperate with the Germans. I don't understand how anyone could collaborate with the Nazis after what they've done to our homeland!"

The military takeover of all vehicles—trucks, cars, vans, motorbikes, and even bicycles and the railways—hastened the collapse of the Dutch economy.

Anyone who had a mode of transportation had to make a special application for exemption. If the regime considered their application an essential service, they were allowed to keep their vehicle. Others like Ben carefully preserved their vehicle, if at all possible in a safe hiding place, but many vehicles could not be easily spirited away from the authorities.

Anyone driving any means of transport would be pulled over. If he did not produce his exemption papers, his vehicle was immediately confiscated. In the beginning, Ben, who frequented the main street, saw many people ignoring the new legislation. Within a short time though he saw even in sleepy Zeist, the vehicles being regularly apprehended. He was glad he had been proactive with his Saralaya.

Em made application to keep her midwife's bicycle. Thankfully she was granted exemption.

Suddenly people in general had to walk everywhere. Since the Nazis had commandeered the railways, utilising them to transport troops and then the Jews, many of the trains were cancelled on certain routes not considered essential by them. Then the essential food services were confiscated for feeding the Nazi army. Beautiful farms, large and small on the polders (low-lying fertile farmlands, especially in the south of The Netherlands, protected by the dykes from the sea) were taken over. Nothing was left for the Dutch people to survive on. They had precious little left.

"It won't be long before they cut off the electricity supply as well—you wait and see, Em!" Ben saw the expression of absolute disbelief on his wife's face. "Yes, schatje, even the electricity will go soon."

"Oh, Ben, how are we to cope?"

"I guess we'll just have to, if it happens, dear. But don't worry yet; when it happens, it will be time enough to worry." Ben kissed his alarmed wife reassuringly. "Other people have had to face far worse—just remember that."

"Yes, I'm trying Ben, I'm trying."

One evening Em was preparing the evening meal, but because she was running late, she asked Ben to assist with the children's baths. He found Gerda drawing, one of her favourite pastimes. She was reluctant to stop in the middle of her masterpiece, so Ben went off to rouse Charles from his afternoon nap to bathe him first.

Ben walked with the kettle into the main bedroom, where there stood a galvanized tin, oval-shaped bathtub. He poured the hot water into it and then added cold water from the tap over the hand wash basin in the room.

Charles was stirring in his room as Ben bounced in and took him hastily for the bath. The little fellow splashed and sailed his toy boat, enjoying himself immensely. As Ben walked to the cupboard to get the towel to dry him, Charles stood up and leaned forward, lost his balance, and fell face-first on the hard metal edge of the tub. Blood gushed from the thin lip skin. Charles screamed in pain. Ben rushed to him with the towel and gathered the screaming child in his arms and rushed him down the stairs to Em. They met on the stairwell.

"What happened, Ben?" One look at Charles' swollen lip and the oozing blood answered Em's question. "Quick, I'll get the Witch Hazel." She raced off to the medicine chest while Ben soothed his son. Gerda came running in from her bedroom having heard the commotion. Em returned with the naturopathic liquid. She dabbed it on his lip and then added a cold compress. The bleeding slowed and finally stopped. During dinner, everytime Charles tried to eat, his mouth would bleed again.

Em spent a long time trying to settle the little boy that night, but in the morning his pillow and the towel he had slept on were covered in blood. Em began to worry.

"Ben, remember, I told you my brother, Gerrit, died at age fifteen. He was a bleeder."

"Oh, Em, dear, you worry too much. Lips always bleed a lot. I'm sure he will be fine. Nothing out of the way, I'm sure!" Because of the constantly moist conditions in the mouth, it was very hard to curtail bleeding in this area. The bleeding continued—although slowly over the next day and night. Fear finally urged Em to further action. Her son lay listlessly on the couch in the living room.

Em studied her little son, thinking, It's two full days of constantly seeping bleeding. I think we should take him to hospital.

Ben rang the local doctor, who recommended they see a Dr. Meyer, a paediatrician in Utrecht. They were able to see her the next morning. After an examination of Charles, she said, "Mr. and Mrs. Bijl, I believe your son has the condition now known as Haemophilia—a serious bleeding condition. It is almost certainly so since your brother also had the same thing, as you say, Em. It is curious really, but it is passed on to sons from the mother only. That means your brother would have inherited it from your mother, and you have passed it on to your son. Now Mrs. Bijl, please do not blame yourself. These things are out of our control. Having said that, Mr. and Mrs. Bijl, to be on the safe side, I feel it would be a good idea if you go immediately to the Zeist Hospital with Charles."

Charles was signed into the Zeist Hospital's care, but that night, when the nursing staff could see Em was not about to leave her son, the sister-in-charge said, "Mrs. Bijl, you must go home now. It's nine o'clock, and our rules are that all visitors leave by eight-thirty."

"I'm sorry, but I am not going home. My son needs me," Em replied firmly.

"Madam, our rules are that all visitors go home. That means you too."

"My son Charles has never been left alone without someone he knows and trusts to care for him, and I will not go home and leave him alone."

The starchy-uniformed sister-in-charge bristled at the thought of Em's impudence. "We'll see about that!" she snapped, turning on her heel and leaving the room. After some few minutes, there was the sound of footsteps rattling down the long hospital corridor, disturbing the relative quiet of the ward.

In the door bustled the matron of the Zeist Hospital, a formidable figure indeed. "Mrs. Bijl, you must leave immediately!"

"My son needs me, madam. I cannot! I will speak with his paediatrician Dr. Meyer about this tomorrow."

The matron moved swiftly forward, gathering up Em's coat and bag, and began shunting her toward the door of the children's ward. "Be that as it may, in the meantime, Mrs. Bijl, you must leave the hospital now!"

Tears sprang into Em's eyes. Charles quickly raised himself from the pillow and reached his small arms out of the cot toward his mother. Then his cries became fearful screams, and in moments, the whole ward came to life crying in sympathy.

The matron continued to torpedo the way to the door, and finally in pain and frustration, Em gave way to the steel-like authority figure whom she was physically unable to withstand.

The next morning, Ben and Em arrived very early in order to be at the hospital to speak with the youthful Dr. Meyer.

Presently, Dr. Meyer arrived on her rounds and thoughtfully examined their little boy. She looked very concerned. "We have to consider other options, Mr. and Mrs. Bijl—perhaps blood transfusions. This is a totally new treatment that has been pioneered by doctors in the Armed Forces and has been found to be very successful in saving lives in cases of extreme blood loss, provided his blood group can be matched. Now we have tested Charles for his blood type, and he is A-positive. We would like to test you two, and if one of you is the same, perhaps we can do a transfusion."

Having gained their permission, Dr. Meyer set about organising the transfusion. Meantime, Ben and Em requested Dr. Meyer give permission for Em to stay at his bedside during the night. They felt he would otherwise feel abandoned.

Dr. Meyer smiled sadly, shaking her head in sympathy. "I fully agree with your views, but the matron is the head of this hospital, and even I am unable to overturn the rules of such a stringent establishment!" Charles sobbed himself to sleep that night too.

Em was frightened for her only son. Ben's blood was transfused directly from his vein to his son's, but not without incredible difficulty. Unfortunately, the transfusion did not appear to help greatly. It appeared to do little toward improving the problem. The bleeding from the lip kept slowly oozing.

Charles' condition deteriorated further, and despite his being in the hospital, he became weaker and paler and less vocal when his parents were forced to leave his side each evening. What really upset Em was that each morning, she would find him in nothing but a singlet and a nappy under a cold fan—his little body blue from exposure to the cold. It was supposed to slow the bleeding, but it didn't seem to make any difference. What could be done? The hospital's interns said they were doing all that could be done.

"Ben," Em said seeking reassurance, "I really believe, after observing what the hospital has done during the past week, that we should never have brought him to the hospital."

"I would hazard a guess that they have never or rarely if ever had a child with Haemophilia in their care. Yes! Yes, I say we go and get him right now and bring him home!"

In desperation, Em rang Dr. Meyer, asking if she was willing to help them by coming every day to monitor his progress at home.

Dr. Meyer quickly responded with, "I agree wholeheartedly. Go and get your son." It was a cold night as they were driven by taxi to the hospital in the centre of the town. At least it wasn't freezing winds from the North Sea to contend with. The hospital officials would be difficult enough to persuade without having to deal with an ill wind!

Em shuddered as she and Ben walked into the heart of the hospital. Ben informed the sister at the nurse's station. "What do we need to sign to release him from the hospital's care?"

"Excuse me, Mr. Bijl, but you must not take this little boy home; he will die without proper care!"

"Yes, and he will die if we leave him here, madam!" Em countered without hesitation.

"Now wait. I'll get the matron. Wait a moment, please."

As the sister strode off in search of her superior, Ben and Em scooped up their son in the blanket Em had brought with them and raced out the door and down the corridor, toward the exit.

The matron and the sister could be heard by this time. "Mr. and Mrs. Bijl! What do you think you are doing? You just can't take your son out of the hospital without our permission. Stop this minute! Do you hear me? Stop! Stop, I say!" But this time the matron's steely authority did not weaken their resolve.

"Come on, Em, hurry," Ben whispered as they rushed down the corridors to the main entrance. They were not going to be intimidated. The waiting taxi sped off, and Ben clutched his wan and fragile child, praying, "Please God, may we in fact have done the right thing and it is not too late!"

From the moment Charles came home, his spirits rose and he began to improve physically and mentally. The visits of Dr. Meyer and Em's constant care and attention brought great results.

Dr. Meyer said after one of her visits, "The pale little cheeks are beginning to glow again with colour, and his strength is returning. I think your decision to bring Charles home was very wise."

Em beamed. "Yes, Doctor, so do I … and … thank you."

CHAPTER 9

Forging Passports for the Underground

As the months rolled by, news reports of many Jewish families having to flee for their lives filtered through the community. Tales of the Nazis in cooperation with the NSBers raiding people's homes looking for Jews became common place.

"This is just the last straw, Em." Ben spat out the words. "Fancy sinking so low as to help Hitler in his anti-Semitism debauchery! We can't purchase from those businesses on principal; think of all the innocent blood they are helping Hitler shed." But he was also thinking, I have to offer my services and actively help the Jewish people escape.

Ben often went out at night for a game of billiards. Em disapproved. Usually, he said he was off to billiards, but Ben had been for some time attending clandestine meetings of the Communist Party. He was fearful for his family, but he was also being driven by his conscience to do something to contribute to the great work the Resistance were doing.

Another member of the cell Ben was attending was a high-profile public servant in the town of Zeist. Publicly this high-profile figure was becoming known as an NSBer (Nazi sympathiser). Due to his apparent support of the Nazi ideology he was appointed police chief of the Zeist Police Station. This subterfuge allowed him "a listening ear" into the plans of the enemy and the ability to pass on vital information to the Resistance. It was a risky business to say the least, but he was a man of great conviction and courage. Ben spoke to him at one meeting and expressed his desire to be of assistance. Ben offered to photograph escapees and forge new identities for them. He was asked to wait for further instruction. It was not too long in coming, because having a local with Ben's expertise simplified things a great deal for their work. Shortly thereafter Ben received a phone call from a local, a lady in Zeist.

"Mr. Bijl, I hear you are a fine photographer," she opened quite casually. "Then you must be also adept at retouching. Could you perhaps show me some of your work?"

"Why, yes, madam, if you like I could drop some examples of my work off tomorrow. If it is to your satisfaction, we can do business. Okay? Oh, and what is your address?"

"Thank you, Mr. Bijl, I would like that very much. Come to the little bookshop on the main street; do you know it?"

"Yes of course I do." Ben was now smiling. Occasionally people would bring their old tattered photos to him to repair. Retouching involved using a magnifying glass and charcoal ink with a very fine nib. The artist would completely fill in the ruined or spotted areas with tiny dots, one after the other, until the original scratch or spot was unable to be detected. It took painstaking skill and great patience.

That afternoon he entered the bookshop with the photos as promised. Surprisingly, the lady closed the doors of the bookshop as he entered, placing the sign "Be back in five minutes" on it and then drew the blinds.

Mrs. Miele, as she was known, took Ben to a large mahogany table. A brightly shining candelabrum hung above the table. Seating herself, she pulled it down close to the table's top, thus giving her extremely good light.

After carefully studying the retouched photos, she removed her spectacles and looked directly at Ben, saying, "Mr. Bijl, I wonder, do you know why I want your services?"

Ben sensed her intentions. "Why yes, Mrs. Miele, I think I do!" He had never seen this woman at any of the cell meetings, though he sensed she must be involved.

"We help with the Underground work of moving the Jews out of The Netherlands to Britain or any other safe-haven outside Europe, before the

Nazis find them. In the end, most Jews end up here in The Netherlands trying to make their escape. Ben, your rare artistic skill would be welcomed.

Your work will not involve you in anything but forging passports and taking photos for our clientele. You understand even this is dangerous, but it does not give so much direct exposure to the enemy."

"My contacts recommended you. They tell me you are a man who can be trusted. Were they correct in telling me that, Mr. Bijl? You see, if you have any—and I mean any reservations about helping— please leave with your photos immediately. The work I am involved in requires the utmost care and honesty, since we are dealing with people's lives. We cannot afford to have indecisive people working with us." She placed her spectacles on her nose, stared at him again, and then added, "Do you understand me?" Ben's piercing eyes looked directly into hers. "Yes, I do."

She looked at him with a wily twinkle in her old eyes. "But as I was saying, do you understand the requirements to be of use to us?"

"Yes, madam, obviously utmost secrecy and confidentiality would be needed on my part to be useful to you." Ben's brow furrowed; he lapsed into silence, but a moment later added, "You have no worries with me. I am both able and willing to cooperate. Now what do you want me to do?"

"Nothing for the moment. We will contact you. All orders will be delivered to me at this book shop via a courier at the time specified, and you must tell no-one. Not even your wife. However, I would like to see you this evening at seven-thirty sharp, to show you what we require. You will come to this shop but come to the back entrance, which I will show you now. You will tap once. Stop, and then after the count of two, you will tap one, two, three in succession. Then I will know it is you at the door. Clear?" He nodded. "Also, Ben, you must have an alibi, in case you are picked up and questioned. So, think of something else you could do, and arrange to have someone trustworthy cover for you, should the worst occur. Do not come unless your alibi is water tight."

As Ben took his leave from Mrs. Miele, she said softly, "And if ever you tell anyone of this conversation, I will deny it completely—it never took place! Understand?"

Ben nodded. "I certainly do, madam."

"Then I perceive you and I will get along very well, Mr. Bijl." She removed the sign on the front door, and as he looked back, it was business as usual.

He walked away from his encounter with Mrs. Miele with something he had not brought with him when he arrived—a reverberating shiver running from the tip of his head to his tailbone. This old woman was certainly deceptive. She was every bit a grandmother with nothing but eyes for her offspring. Her grandchildren's photo sat on the hat stand nearby. Indeed, she looked the epitome of innocuousness—shy, quiet, timid. She spoke so softly, yet her voice was as strong and unyielding as iron. Ben recalled the old saying: "An iron fist in a velvet glove." That was Mrs Miele.

Funny, and I thought the owners of this bookstore were NSBer supporters! Ben thought as he walked away. Things are not always as they appear to be.

Ben arrived home as Em was preparing dinner. He hedged around her in the kitchen for a full half-hour before it was ready.

"Is there anything I can do to help, Mama?" he asked, smiling at her surprised face. Ben was not really a domesticated male.

"Why, Ben, what's wrong? Are you just hungry, or is there something else lurking behind those eyes of yours?"

"Well, I'm going down to the Billiard Room for a game with the boys for an hour tonight." He knew she wouldn't like it.

Em was annoyed. She threw the vegetables onto the plates. "I wish you wouldn't go."

"Sorry, schatje. I've already given my word. But I will be careful." He looked at the alarm in Em's eyes and gave her a hug and kiss. "There, there. It will be okay, I promise." Em knew he was not a man to easily dissuade. She shook her head.

"Please be careful. You know if you get picked up after curfew - you're in big trouble."

Ben silently slipped out with Em's precious bicycle at a little after seven. It was really only about five minutes by bicycle to the main street in Zeist during the day, but he had to ride warily. There was a curfew every night. Under the German Occupation, no-one was permitted to leave his home after dark without a special permit. Of course, Ben didn't have one. In time he arrived, tapping as she had specifically instructed him to do, on the back door of the house behind the bookshop. It took some time for the lady to come to the door, but he was finally inside behind bolted doors and heavily blanket-clad windows.

Ben and Mrs. Miele examined passports. "This will be your draft, Ben. It must be an exact copy, except for the individual information. We have an appointment for you to do the photos, which will be in two days, at a specified location. We will ring you, or a courier will let you know, on another pretext of course, just a short time before the meeting." Mrs. Miele looked up at him, her small, aged eyes searching deep into Ben's. "Any questions? Do you understand?"

He nodded. "I understand."

"I cannot underscore how important it is that you do exactly what they ask of you and when they ask you to do it. Time is of the essence in this game. A few minutes can cost a life."

Ben nodded. "Now, about this draft." She folded it carefully into a narrow, flat parcel. "Take off your shoe and sock, Ben."

He immediately cooperated, getting her drift. "Slip this inside your sock, and when you get home, find a foolproof hiding place for it. Okay?"

"I have one in mind already, Mrs. Miele."

"Don't tell me where, Ben … don't tell anyone … just do it."

"Mrs. Miele, I am aware of the serious implications, and I give you my word, I will abide by all that you ask as far as humanly possible." She cautiously let him out.

"Good evening, madam."

The door closed. Fumbling around in the darkness, Ben looked for Em's bicycle, which he had hidden under a leafy bush. For one moment he thought, Where is the damn thing? Eventually his hand came to rest on the triangular seat. He breathed a sigh of relief.

Ben stared into the inky darkness—the moon was merely a sliver—focussing his eyes and ears, looking for prying eyes or straining ears. After a few minutes of observation, he moved forward, wheeling his wife's faithful bike until he reached the end of the lane, and then stealthily he rode the rest of the way home.

*

As Mrs. Miele had promised, two days later the phone rang. It was eight-thirty in the morning. Em was downstairs and answered it. "Good morning, Foto Bijl. How may I help you?"

A rather deep voice on the other end of the phone replied, "I wish to speak to Mr. Bijl, please."

"Just one moment, and I shall call him." She called her husband to the phone.

Ben listened carefully and jotted a cryptic address on the pad in front of him. He gathered up his coat and photographic bag, saying, "Em, I'll be going directly into Zeist, as I have two urgent photo sittings to take. Then I'm going for a game of billiards." He dusted her cheek with a gentle kiss.

"Remember, old Ben loves you!" Em frowned.

When the first completed passports were handed over, Ben breathed a sigh of relief. He hoped everything was perfect, and to him it appeared so. The next few days he was noticeably anxious.

Em sensed her husband had something afoot.

One of Mrs. Miele's acquaintances rang, asking for Ben. "Excellent photos! Marvellous work, Ben."

Ben placed the receiver on its cradle. Em noticed he was looking very satisfied as he raced back upstairs to his darkroom. His state of mind gave him away—he was whistling a happy tune—"In Holland staat een Huis…"

During the weeks and months that followed, Ben's photography and artistry helped many unknown persons escape the vicious clutches of the SS soldiers, a cluster of humans who seemed devoid of compassion. One afternoon, when Ben had not been forging very long, he delivered his package to an intermediary as previously designated. Ben had arranged to bring the package to the Billiard Room in Zeist. Ben suggested this location as it gave Ben a fairly safe alibi, if ever he or his family were questioned. He was careful to let Em know where he would be. It did not appear to her to be out of place as he was a regular billiard player.

Arriving at the Billiard Room early, Ben started playing a game to while away the few minutes he had to wait for Guido, his contact. Guido walked into the room. Ben noticed him out of the corner of his eye, even though he was looking at the pool table. "Hello, friend. Time for a game or two?"

"Not this time, my friend." Guido looked toward his jacket, and Ben got the message, although nothing was said directly. The two men understood the password they had been told to look for. They moved into the men's room to exchange the 'goods'. With a nod and wink they immediately returned to the pool table.

"Perhaps next time you'll have time for a game or two with me," Ben suggested.

Guido smiled. "Yes, I hope so, friend. Must be off today, I've got another appointment." He turned on his heel and quietly left via the back of the establishment.

Ben stood finishing a drink, contemplating. That guy's like a cat, he's so smooth and inoffensive. Just the man for the job.

The hallway clock struck four. Ben looked at his watch, thinking out loud, "It must be just about time for Bert and Jaap to arrive." He put down the glass and walked toward the front entrance in anticipation. Their weekly game of billiards had become ritualistic since Ben and Em moved into Veldheimlaan. They were neighbours who lived behind the Bijls' house. They had become good friends since they helped move Em's piano into the house on the day it was delivered. Ben and Bert often talked about migrating. Bert, the young son, was always talking about moving to New Zealand.

CHAPTER 10

Apprehended by the Nazis

Ben had just come through the front doorway and took one step on the short set of stairs to the street when a military vehicle pulled up directly in front of the place he was leaving.

A high-ranking SS officer approached him, clicking his heels as he saluted, barking the Nazi greeting, "Heil Hitler!" followed quickly by the frigid command, "Sir, your papers, please!" His shiny black, knee-high boots were reminiscent of a scarecrow hovering menacingly over a cucumber field.

Ben fumbled around in his pockets and produced the required documents. He handed them to the officer, unflinchingly looking into his hard eyes.

The officer examined them closely and then, raising an eyebrow, said, "So you are a photographer. We are very interested in people who are of your profession—and your work. What may I ask are you doing at the Billiard Room?"

"I come here regularly to play billiards, sir, and I was to meet my neighbours at four o'clock. As a matter of fact, I just came out to see if they were arriving."

"And you are going to tell me you were here to play a game or two with them? Yes?" The officer sneered, clearly disbelieving Ben's story.

"Yes, sir, that's exactly what I was going to do," Ben stated. "You can ask the drink waiter. He knows I come here regularly. Or the manager."

"Stop stalling, you. You will come with us now!"

"What for?" Ben dared to ask, continuing to look him straight in the eye.

"We'll see. Now move!" The officer nodded to the two soldiers accompanying him, and they pushed Ben into the waiting vehicle. It sped off to the Zeist Nazi Military Headquarters, in the town's old Veldheim Slot (castle), not far from where Ben lived.

Ben's mind raced, especially as the vehicle sped past Veldheimlaan. *I wonder if I will ever see my precious wife and children again. I can't think of any slips I've made. Please, God, let those passports do their job successfully. And thank you for letting me hand them over before this happened or I'd be a goner!* He kept staring out the window, trying to give the impression that he had nothing to hide.

Next thing he knew he had arrived and was being led into the Nazi headquarters emblazoned with long red flags and ominous black swastikas at every entrance. These flags billowing in the wind sent a feeling of dread into his heart at the "blackness of the SS" and the whole sickening scenario he now was entering. Ben's thoughts were abruptly interrupted by the sound of the clicking of soldiers' heels.

"Heil Hitler! Mr. Bijl, this is our commanding officer, Herr Schneider."

"Heil Hitler!" Schneider barked. "Papers, please," he enunciated with cynical eyes. "I am told you are a photographer, Mr. Bijl. Pray tell, what need for photography do people have in these troublesome times?"

Ben looked him in the eye without wavering. "Very little sir, very little, I can assure you. However, we do provide a service to your military personnel, and I still need to feed my family, so I get what I can."

"What were you doing in the Billiard Room this afternoon? Our sources tell us sometimes people meet there for clandestine activity."

"Well because I have little work these days and I love a game of billiards, I go there often to while away an hour or two. Today I had arranged to meet my friends for a game at four."

"I find it suspicious that a photographer should be where we consider possible clandestine activity could be taking place." He looked at one of his men. "Take this man to Officer Heilman. Get him to ascertain whether this man can actually play billiards, for starters."

The soldier responded instantly, "Ja, mein Herr, immediately. Heil Hitler!" To Ben he said, "You! Come with me!" He almost yanked Ben off his feet as he led the way.

Ben began to whistle, "In Holland staat een Huis…" as they walked the long corridor in search of Officer Heilman. The encounter with Officer Heilman would be revealing because if they thought he was lying, they would be sadly mistaken. He was a talented billiards player.

Finally, he was taken back to the commanding officer, who asked, "So, can Mr. Bijl play billiards?"

The soldier relayed Officer Heilman's findings and his opinion: "This man can indeed play Carom billiards, and he understands the methodology of the game exactly."

The commanding officer's eyes lifted off the report he was scribing, with much surprise. "Is that so?" Then after taking a deep breath, he said with annoyance, "Take him away. Hold him in the cells until we find out more about him and today's happenings. Oh, and find out if he has a reputation as a champion in this game."

He immediately continued writing his report. Ben's heart sank as the man spoke. But his determination continued to shield Ben's true feelings. His face remained calm, which did not go unnoticed by the commanding officer. Led by the guard, Ben turned to walk out of the office.

Ben didn't relish the thought of a prison cell, but he was tough, and if need be, face it he would. But he thought, as they marched him off to the dingy cells, At least they have no obvious proof that I am connected to the Underground, thank God. I am, however, in grave danger if they caught up with my intermediary. And if he squeals, I am undone—that is if he hasn't offloaded his package already. Only Em … Em … she'll be frantic if I am not home for dinner tonight. Thank goodness I prepared her: if anyone asks my whereabouts, she must say I am at the Billiard Room. At least if they question her, she will give the same answer as I have.

Ben spent a very uncomfortable night in the freezing stone-walled cell underneath the old castle. "Now I know how the Count of Monte Cristo felt!" A bitter laugh came from his mouth as he rubbed his aching back.

*

That evening Em had been distraught. Oh, dear God, please let Ben be all right. Where on earth is he? The SS must have picked him up! Why else would he not be home before curfew? Now Em, calm down—you must not worry. Think of the children. Mmm. What will I tell them when they ask where Papa is?

The next afternoon, a knock on the door brought terror into Em's heart. "What if it's the Gestapo?" Her heart pounded madly. She felt the colour rising in her neck and face, her normally low blood pressure rising acutely. Quickly she opened the door, and no, it wasn't the Gestapo, but it was a black-uniformed SS officer standing on her doorstep. Soldiers stood behind him, their rifles leaning on their shoulders at the ready.

She took a deep breath, trying to keep her voice calm and under control. "Good day, sir."

"Heil Hitler!" came the terse reply. "I am wondering if you know the whereabouts of a Mr. Ben Bijl?"

"He is my husband. Why? What's wrong with him?"

"Do you know where he is, madam?"

"No, I don't. He didn't come home last night!"

"Well then, perhaps you could enlighten me. Does your husband like to play billiards?"

"Oh yes, he is an excellent billiards player actually. He's won many tournaments. He often hangs out in the Billiard Room downtown since he loves to play and is always looking for someone to pit his ability against. Actually, he told me he was going there yesterday afternoon."

"Mmm. So how long is it since you've seen him? Did you say?"

"Yesterday," Em stated fearfully.

"I have orders to search your house for incriminating information, madam." He and several soldiers raced inside and searched for quite some time. They pounced on the negatives in the darkroom and confiscated them.

Em was terrified. Did they find anything incriminating? she wondered. "What are you looking for anyway?" She was thankful Mrs. de Rue had taken the children for a walk around the block.

"Never you mind, madam. Thank you for your cooperation." He clicked his heels with rhythmic precision and turned, saluting once again. "Heil Hitler!"

Closing the door, Em breathed heavily as her thoughts began to run riot and she tried to imagine her dear Ben's fate. She murmured,

"If he should be discovered to be helping the Underground!" Of course, Ben had not told her this, but she soon detected something was going on. "Why else would he need an alibi?" She wept silently but as the children came in the back door with her neighbour, chattering, she pulled herself together, scolding herself for talking to herself so much.

"Is that Papa home now, Mama? We saw soldiers leaving our house. Did they bring Papa home?" Gerda exclaimed.

"No, sweetheart. Just some soldiers asking for directions. That's all."

Mrs. de Rue looked kindly at Em and said, "Now don't worry yet, Em. He may soon be home."

"Oh, I hoped it might be Papa—where is he, Mama? I miss my Papa." She began to whimper. Charles too. Tears welled up in the children's eyes.

"Come here, my son," Em said, holding her arms out to reassure her little children. "Papa will be home soon, I'm sure."

As each day drifted into the next, Em began to resign herself. "Perhaps he has been taken from Zeist to a concentration camp— perhaps the Vught camp." She dared not think of anything worse. That was bad enough.

*

At the Nazi headquarters, Ben was interviewed and persistently accused of being involved in helping the Resistance. After many a trick question in order to catch him out if indeed he was a "resister" to the Nazi cause, he was told, "So you spoke the truth about your talents with billiards. But we believe your story about being at the Billiard Room is merely a cover-up for other activities. Subversive perhaps? Now tell us the truth, Mr. Bijl, and we will go easy on you. If we find you are lying, you will only live to regret it for a short time. Do you understand, Mr. Bijl?"

Ben stared back defiantly. "I already told you the truth and you don't believe me, Sir."

"Guards! Take this man to the interrogation room. Rough him up!" Ben was marched handcuffed into a room in the bowels of the large old castle.

"Inside, Schweinhund!" a guard yelled as they hit him on the back with their rifle butts.

Ben staggered and fell into the cavernous stone den. His eyes moved slowly around the room. Many instruments of torture—whips, metal rods, clamps, and batons—hung on the walls, closing in on him, sending his mind into a frenzy of horror, especially as he heard the lock turn behind him. Was he to be tortured with these?

Now, Ben, he thought anxiously. You're not going to let this frighten you—that's probably just what they want! They want to terrify you into admitting the truth. Ben's eyes sank to the floor. "God give me strength to remain calm and face whatever comes!"

Then after waiting for what seemed like eons in the blood curdling room, the door's rusty hinges squealed and scraped open. In walked two guards along with their commanding officer.

"Mr. Bijl, you have doggedly stuck to this story about being a great billiards player and how that was your only reason for being at the Billiard Room. We believe your story is camouflage for subversive activities. We hope your time in here to think about your future has helped your memory. Speak up, man—tell us the truth." The commanding officer looked slowly around the perimeter of the room, Ben's eyes following. The commander menacingly tapped his boot as he surveyed the room.

"This is the moment of truth … come now, tell us, Mr. Bijl, and we shall go easy on you."

"I have already told you I don't know how many times. That is the truth!" Ben stared back obstinately.

The commanding officer lit a cigarette and nodded to his guards. Immediately they rushed on Ben, punching him in the stomach and around the head. Ben fell to the ground, but he used his feet, knees and arms to a degree to protect himself. Finally, after being repeatedly belted, he fell to the ground unconscious.

Ben awoke to one of the guards shaking him, the sound of the commanding officer's voice ringing in his ears, "Mr. Bijl, come now. We do not wish to harm you further. It's truth time. Come on, speak up."

"What more do I have to do to convince you? I've already told you the truth." Ben's head was thumping with pain. Everywhere else he felt numb.

The commanding officer struck him across the neck one last time. "Take him back to his cell!" He snarled as he thundered out of the room.

Ben didn't recall much of the return trip to his cell. He fell in a heap on the filthy wooden bench—a bed. Then nothing until the grating of his food window woke him in the evening. He could hardly move.

Stiff and bruised, he struggled to get to the meagre rations set on the ledge for him.

A full week passed. No more beatings. The longer they keep me, Ben realized, the more chance I have of survival. It's obvious they have no real proof—merely strong (and of course correct) suspicions.

The Nazi headquarters failed to find anything concrete with which to charge Ben. Only Ben's strength of character and determination not to give in helped him survive the ordeal without cracking.

He was taken before Commander Schneider again. "Mr. Bijl, we are going to release you tomorrow. But be warned: if we find you anywhere in the vicinity of the Billiard Room, you will not escape so lightly. We are going to keep an eagle eye on your whereabouts from now on. Take him away!"

The next morning, fully two weeks after he had been apprehended, the prison cell door was unlocked after breakfast. The guard quickly hustled Ben. "Okay, Mr. Bijl, out you go. You're free to leave."

Ben hurried out of the Nazi headquarters unable to believe his good fortune. Momentarily all his aches and pains left him. Each guard he passed ignored him. Greatly relieved, he reached the imposing front entrance, and as his foot stepped off the last step, the old familiar tune came swirling from his throat, "In Holland staat een Huis…"

About twenty minutes later, Ben reached his home. A feeling of great emotion soared through him as he sneaked along the side of the house to the back door. A gentle knock, and he heard Em race to answer.

"What's for lunch, my schatje?" he asked, smiling from ear to ear as he quickly stepped inside and closed the door.

"Ben, Ben, it's you. Thank God it's you! Come in." She threw her arms around his neck and hugged him. She looked at her husband, and he was dishevelled and whiskery, which for Ben was unusual, since he normally had a very light beard.

"Oh, Ben," she said, "phew! You need a bath!"

Ben laughed and looked down at his clothing, and after sniffing, he said, "Yes, come to think of it, I smell like rotten fish."

Em was amused at her husband. "Haven't lost your sense of humour, Ben. Let me help you get these filthy clothes off. Let's get them out of here."

Ben joked again as he removed the grimy gear. "These clothes are so stiff, I believe they'll walk out to the laundry on their own."

Em was horrified! As Ben undressed, she saw welts, cuts, and bruises all over his back and neck. "What did they do to you, schatje? Look at your back. It's a mess."

"I imagine it would be, Em, but it's a lot better now than a week ago, believe me. They gave me a really bad beating, hoping I'd admit I was involved in underground activities. Anyway, thankfully I lived to tell the story. You know me, Em. I keep turning up like the proverbial bad penny."

"Thank God you're okay." Em took the revolting bundle to the laundry area, wondering how she would ever clean them.

When she returned to the kitchen, she said, "Here, put this clean dressing gown on before I call the children down."

Meanwhile Em went to the stairwell and called the children.

"I can't believe it's you, Ben. It's been two whole weeks. I thought you were in Vught—or even worse. So, what really happened?"

Before Ben could actually answer, the children came tumbling down the stairs.

"Papa! Papa! What took you so long in coming back home?" Gerda asked as she ran and jumped into his arms. "Naughty Papa!"

"Papa, I missed you," Charles added, hugging his father's legs as his sister hung in her papa's arms above him.

"Well?" Em asked in couched terms.

"The mouse got away from the cat—smart little muisje!"

"Where's the muisje, Papa?" Gerda's quick little ears intercepted the conversation. "We haven't got a cat. Whose mouse? Whose cat?"

"Never you mind, child, never you mind." Ben's eyes danced again as they so often did when he was triumphant, and his children laughed along with him.

"I'll be the cat then, Papa. Charles, you be the mouse, okay?" Gerda said ever so innocently.

"You've heard of the old tomcat? Well, this is the story of the old 'tom mouse' who got into a scrape!" Then he whispered to Em, "Ittleley igspey avhey igbey, arsey." ("I'll tell you later, honey.")

Em nodded and exercised much restraint, but inside she was deeply concerned about Ben's experiences. "Well, Ben Bijl, wherever you have been, you would have kept them entertained. The kettle is whistling.

Water's ready. Now come on up and have a bath."

"You don't have to ask me twice, Em."

Gerda and Charles playing during the
Occupation by Nazis during WWII.

Em couldn't wait to put her children to bed that night and drag the whole story from her freshly bathed and totally exhausted husband.

"Well, Ben? I'm waiting, and I want the whole story."

Ben took a few deep breaths and gradually revealed the whole frightening saga. Em cried as he retold what happened. "I don't mind admitting I thought I might never see you or the children again." He stopped and clung to her. "Yes, my schatje, I'm amazed to know I'm a freeman. But they warned me they'll keep a close eye on my activities. So from now on I will have to be extremely cautious. One more episode and I'll be shipped off to Vught all right."

"So that's how you came to have all these bruises and scrapes over your body. Ben, they could have killed you!"

"Has any one ever told you how beautiful you are, Em?" She looked up, surprised. Ben took her in his arms and kissed her passionately. "Come to bed, dearest. Now!"

"Don't change the subject, Ben. I've known for quite some time you've been working with the Underground."

"You are an astute woman. But not really, my sweet—I just take photos and forge papers. My work is only incidental."

"That is what you want me to believe, is it?"

"Yes, dearest—it's the truth."

"Maybe you should stop doing it."

"Don't be ridiculous. Can you see Ben Bijl backing down on such a serious thing? You know how much I hate injustice. And I wouldn't be any sort of man if I didn't fight for justice!"

"I know. I'm proud of you, but I'm scared for you too. Ben, Ben… you are the worry of my life! So, does that mean you are still going to frequent the Billiard Room?"

"Yes, I must, to show my innocence. They'll keep watching me —of that you can be sure. But I'll have to find some other obscure meeting places now."

"So, you're still going to do this—it's so dangerous!"

"I know, but I must. Would you have it any other way? What if it were our family in this terrible predicament?"

"Life is precious. But you must promise me, dearest, for our sakes, be careful."

He nodded, the slightest hint of a smile on his lips, but she saw he was not listening. He was busy undoing the buttons on her night gown.

CHAPTER 11

The Masquerade

Ben loved his beautiful Saralaya motorbike, his pride and joy. His fore-thought paid off. Where most of his friends and acquaintances complained bitterly that their motorbikes or cycles were confiscated, Ben smiled in agreement and sympathy. "How sad!" he would say. "The things we have to put up within this war!" Not even his relatives knew what he had done. "But my magnificent machine is resting in peace, safe as money in a banker's safe!" He had carefully smeared it completely with thick grease, wrapped it in canvas, and dug a huge hole in the corner of the yard, into which he had laid his prized possession, covering it with sandy loam. The sand dunes from which most of The Netherlands is reclaimed are not good grass producers, but for once that lifeless sand was an advantage! You could disturb it, and a few minutes later, no-one would know it had been interfered with, unlike other soils and grasses. It just looked like a child's play area.

Em marvelled at his ingenuity.

Curfews controlled all comings and goings. Roadblocks were set up at the entry of every town, and identification was mandatory. Often the Jews were caught whilst trying to escape from The Netherlands before the Nazis could capture them and send them off to concentration camps and death in the gas chambers. Those who dared stand against the "establishment" were brutally crushed by the greatly feared SS troops! Food grown for the

Dutch community was confiscated for the German army, and the locals had to make the best of a tragic situation.

Most people in The Netherlands lived in such closely confined dwellings that they did not have enough room in their backyard to grow food in order to survive. Most would be hard-pressed to play a game of hopscotch in their tiny backyards. So, within a short time the roads were strewn not only with military vehicles and soldiers but the ordinary citizens walking outside the towns and villages looking for enough food to keep their families alive.

The days wore on, and food from normal sources became even scarcer. At the beginning of the war, Em breastfed baby Charles for a long time. This helped prevent another pregnancy and sustained her young son better than anything else. Predictably, however, in January 1943, Em was pregnant again.

Ben decided it was time to dig up some of his treasured butter, soap, and cigarettes to barter for food under the cover of night. He placed a small stash in the cellar, which he would be able to move in small quantities more easily, and if anything were to be discovered, only what was in the cellar would be confiscated.

"Who will you sell to, Ben?" Em asked. "And more importantly, how are you going to do it without been nabbed by the Germans?"

"I'm going to gradually spirit them away on the black market in exchange for … not money," Ben said, thinking. "No, not money … but food to keep my family alive!" What could Ben do to enable him to sell his goods on the black market and also distribute his forged passports without being detected?

"Em, I've devised a plan I'm sure will work!"

Em rolled her eyes heavenward. "What next will this man come up with?"

Ben's confident reply was much more than even she who knew his ingenuity had bargained for!

"I'm going to borrow your midwife's uniform, bike, and medical bag and make my own identification papers, complete with passport photo. So there you have it—I'll be out of town on the pretext of attending a confinement. I can't see them—the roadblock officers— holding me up too much, can you?"

Em laughed. "You've got to be joking! Do you really think you can pull this off, Ben Bijl?" Inwardly she reasoned, Common sense would say it's doubtful!

"There's one sure way to find out. I'll go for a trial run."

"And where, pray tell, will be your first trip?"

"I think I'll go visit my family. We'll see how good my disguise is then."

"What? All the way to Amsterdam? You're mad, Ben! Why not try something less adventurous first up?"

"No, Em. If I can get to Amsterdam undetected, I can go anywhere. If I can deceive my own family, then I'll know my disguise is a success."

"So you are dead serious. Not joking?"

"The only time I was more serious about something, my dearest, was when I asked you to marry me." Ben's mischievous eyes danced, but suddenly he stopped and kissed her passionately. "I've told you before, Em, I'll do anything to protect and feed my family."

Em's eyes looked glassy. "And that's why I love you so much, Ben."

"Now don't you think it's a good idea? Agree?" Ben urged.

Em nodded hesitantly.

"Okay, Em, let's get started. First, one of your uniforms will need some alterations."

Together they set about disguising Ben. Ben's being short in stature, a smallish build, very fair, and not at all hairy now placed him in good stead. In Ben's earlier days his size had been the bane of his existence. He'd hated his height, and if being tough was how you proved your masculinity, Ben rose to the challenge—tough he was. The blonde wig he had purchased some months after the Occupation began from the local actor's guild while business was as usual, now had a use. Where most men would shrink from the extremes of ladies' underwear, he wore the bras, panties, and nylons! He wore the dark, long, brown nurse's uniform with white cuffs and collar along with a matching fabric belt around his waist, as well as the tell-tale brown veil with a white band around the face. The other essential item to the outfit was the large white apron worn over the great expanse of brown. He also wore Em's horn-rimmed glasses! He shaved his arms and legs as well as his face, so he, with the blonde wig, really looked female. Not a pretty woman but nonetheless a woman. Ben was a man before his time!

"Well, what do you think, Em?" Her husband stood before her dressed like her professional counterpart.

"Ben, it's a miracle. And I hate to admit I think you pass very well as a woman, that is." Em giggled at her manly husband. "But there is one thing horribly amiss. You might be dressed like a woman, but your mannerisms are totally male."

"Woman, I'm not Houdini, you know."

"This is very important. You have to study me for a couple of weeks before you attempt to go out. You not only have to be dressed like a woman to be successful here but have to act like and speak like a woman. This is the hard part! Otherwise you will blow your disguise." For once in his life Ben was speechless. Of course, she was right!

"Look in the mirror. It will be obvious if you watch yourself as you move and speak."

Ben followed Em, and as they conversed, he saw what Em meant. It was half a lifetime ago that Ben had attended acting school. That was only for a short while, being cut short by the Great War. But he did have a penchant for acting.

Em coached him in feminine mannerisms, how one walks, talks, and sits and gets onto a bicycle as well as many more details that would be necessary to deceive others into thinking he was a midwife.

After some time, Em ceded, "I think you've been a good student. I think you will succeed."

"There's one more thing we need to do—take a photo of me for my identity papers." Ben added excitedly.

Ben developed the film immediately. The rest of the evening he spent with the passport forging his name and particulars, then at long length, around midnight, he came to bed.

"Have you finished the papers?" Em yawned.

"Yes, they're done, but I'll have you check them in the morning to make sure they're perfect." He yawned, and in seconds she heard the familiar rhythm of his snoring.

*

Ben (Bernadina) masquerading in Em's midwife's uniform.

Em studied the passport carefully. "So who are you? Bernadina Kossen. Where did you come up with that name?"

"Kossen is my grandmother's maiden name. Why? Now if anyone calls me Ben instead of Bernadina, I'll truthfully be able to react to it without arousing suspicion."

"Well that's smart—good thinking. And yes, I think the papers are fine too, your eye for detail is acute, like Opa's. It's amazing!"

"Those are the words I want to hear. Now if I can deceive my family, I'm sure our plan will work. Today I'm off to ride down Veldheimlaan. Monday fortnight, I'm off to Amsterdam!"

"What if one of the guards at the boom gates discovers you're a fraud?"

"They won't," he replied confidently. "You worry too much. Have faith!" Ben kissed her good-bye at the door to the backyard and walked around to the front via the sidepath. As he rode sedately down Veldheimlaan, none of the neighbours seemed to give him any recognition. He looked exactly as they would expect of an older midwife.

Em encouraged him to ride up and down the streets for a week or two, and he continued to ride regularly during the next two weeks, venturing farther from home each trip. Now it was to Amsterdam! With a wicked smile he rode off down their street with the bulging medical bag strapped to the back of the bike. In it he had a small cache of goodies to barter. Some medical equipment lay on the top of the hidden goods, should the bags be searched.

"So far, so good," Ben said as he peddled farther through Zeist and on until the first roadblock, which was situated at the outskirts of town. He breathed deeply, trying to keep calm. So much depended on the outcome of this day.

As the bike drew close to the boom gate, a guard stepped forward, saluting and saying, "Heil Hitler. Halt!"

Ben/Bernadina got off his bike, smiling and looking the officer in the eye. He said, "Guten Morgan, mein Herr," in precise German.

"Papers, please." He took his job seriously—not a hint of a smile or friendliness.

"Ja, mein Herr," Ben said, handing him the passport to examine.

The officer looked them over quite deliberately, satisfying himself that this was indeed the person in the photo, "Where are you going Sister?"

"I'm going to Amsterdam." Ben's voice cracked a little, and he coughed. "To help my younger sister. She is almost due. I don't want to be late arriving, you know."

"Surely someone in Amsterdam could attend," the officer said, raising his eyebrows, slightly suspicious.

Naturally they could, Sir, but you understand it's my sister and she wants me to attend to her. You know sisters and all." Ben smiled sweetly. The officer looked a bit confused, but he seemed satisfied and handed back the papers. "Okay! Don't forget curfew. There will be no questions asked if you are out on the road after six pm. Be warned!"

Having satisfied himself all was well, Ben relaxed and even smiled ever so slightly. He thanked the officer. "Dankeschon, mein Herr!" Ben rode off.

He heard the soldiers making some snide remarks and then laughing at his expense. After all, "she" was no beauty! First smiling and then chuckling away, he thought, Well, Ben, you are to be congratulated! It worked like a charm. His deception had been successful indeed.

By the time he arrived at the boom gate on the outskirts of Amsterdam, it was later in the afternoon, being well more than seventy-five kilometres from home. He lost count of the number of times he had to show his papers in and out of each town along the way, but without exception, there was no suspicion. His plan had worked beautifully. But would he succeed in deceiving his family?

Along the route he passed people—walking, trudging with a few scraps in bags, some coming to Amsterdam, others leaving—all of them sad, gaunt, and tired looking. Their shoulders drooped in disconsolation; their gait slow and aimless, the eyes of many deep hollows of despair. Clothes were ragged and shoes worn out from wandering.

Most looked enviously at him on his bike, hating the Nazis even more for confiscating their own bicycles. A look of bitterness hovered on many faces, whilst others were still quite friendly, forever to be optimists, kindness shining in their eyes despite the deprivation of those dark days.

Now came the acid test. The highway into Amsterdam was known as the Hoofdweg. This was where his parents lived. In a short time he arrived at Number 88. It seemed like an eternity of knocking before Guda finally opened the door. Her fair complexion was like her father's and Ben's. She wore her wavy hair loosely in a bun on the nape of her neck, modestly elegant.

Smiling expectantly, Guda greeted him. "Good day. What can I do for you, Sister?"

"Good afternoon, miss, I would like to speak with—I assume— your father, Mr. Bijl, and Mrs. Bijl."

"Just step inside and wait one moment, Sister. I'll get my father directly." She ushered him into the front entry of Adrian's home.

Guda walked briskly through the comfortable living room where Leni sat on a chair beside the upright piano. She was conducting a music lesson with Hans, the neighbour's son. He was about twelve years old. Leni nodded at the lady entering perfunctorily, and added, "Pay attention now, Hans … one, two, three, one, two, three. Keep going … very good, Hans."

While Ben waited, the boy played a sweet but simple waltz. Ben's father walked down the hall toward the entry a few moments later. Adrian Bijl didn't seem to notice anything unusual.

"What can I do for you, Sister?" he asked in his usual friendly manner, hand outstretched in greeting.

Moving toward his hand to shake it, Ben smiled glowingly. "I was asked by a friend of mine, Ben Bijl, to make a house call on you and your wife while my work brings me to Amsterdam. I have a small parcel for Mrs. Bijl from her son." He opened his medicine bag and fumbled around for the parcel.

"Ben sent you, did he?" His father laughed. "Come through to the kitchen!"

He stepped quickly down the hall, Ben hot on his heels carrying the medicine bag along with the small parcel he had retrieved from it. There bundled up in front of a small wood fire sat his mother. In contrast to his father, Adrian, who was spritely and obviously well and had a zest for life evidenced by an almost constant twinkle in his eye, Catherina, Ben's mother, was an invalid. However, she didn't look frail. The old lady had long, dark-brown hair neatly plaited down her shoulder. These days Adrian was quite thin, but his proportions gave evidence that he had lived a comfortable life. He had brown hair now, but even approaching sixty he only had the beginnings of silver intermingled through it. Unlike Ben's hair, which had already begun receding and had a slight baldness developing on his crown, Adrian's was thick and wayward.

Ben followed his father. His mother had been helping Guda top and tail a small handful of carrots for the evening meal, which Guda had grown in their tiny garden plot outside the kitchen. There was little she could do these days, poor old lady. Ben smiled broadly at his mother as he walked in, holding in his hand the "parcel for Mrs. Bijl." "This lady is a friend of Ben and Em, Mama," Adrian said. "The nursing sister comes from Zeist and has a parcel for us—or should I say for you, Catherina!"

She looked up with great anticipation when she heard the word parcel, as gifts in such difficult times were rare. She looked intently at the face of the lady delivering the parcel. "Don't I know you?" she asked, her eyes squinting at the sister, quite puzzled. "You look like…" She laughed heartily. "Oh! It's Ben, Ben, Ben! I can't believe it! Papa, you didn't recognize your own son!"

Ben's family, Adrian and Catherina, and three sons (fair-haired Ben is on the far right).

Ben threw his arms around her. "Hello, Mama dear. How are you? Fancy, I couldn't pull the wool over your eyes, could I? What is it about mothers? They always seem to know these things! What gave me away, Mama?"

"Your eyes, son. Your eyes. I would know those eyes anywhere, in any setting. Ben Bijl, you always wanted to be an actor. I can remember you at school—you just loved clowning and acting it up. Then when the war came, work was so hard to get, especially in the theatre."

Ben bent down and hugged his frail mother once again. "You always said I'd be a good actor, Mama, but how could I make a living?"

"Well son, you must admit photography has been good to you.

And you do love it, don't you?" Ben beamed, but he wasn't going to admit to it. "Anyway, it is wonderful to see you. It's been a long time. Now tell me, what brings you here to Amsterdam in this get up?"

Before Ben could answer, everyone came running into the small kitchenette. His younger sister, Leni came rushing in, curious to know what had caused such a commotion in the kitchen.

"Ben, it's such a surprise to see you," Leni said as she hugged him and then looked up into his face. "Brother, what are you up to?"

Ben listened with great elation. He had obviously mastered the disguise well! "It's my disguise. I needed a safe disguise so I can go out and barter."

"What do you have to barter with?" his mother asked, stunned.

"Do you remember during the Great War how we were almost starving and how scarce everything was?" Catherina nodded.

"Well, I have never forgotten that dreadful agitation one feels when hunger eats away inside you. And so, as soon as I could see Germany building up armaments, even before the war broke out, I started buying up all the tobacco, soap, and butter I could afford. I buried it, and now that we haven't got enough to eat anymore, I'm going to use this to get food for my family." Ben looked around the room for their reaction.

"Ben, you seem to have thought of everything," Adrian said, shaking his head in disbelief.

"So, Papa, how is the photography business going? I would imagine it would be pretty good—perhaps even better—what with all these soldiers in the city."

"You hit the nail on the head, son. Never been better. Especially since we moved into the Amstelstraat shop. I am quite busy. If one could buy food and necessities with the money I'm making, we would be okay. But how does one get blood out of a stone?"

"If ever this war ends, and we survive it," Ben said, highlighting the evils of war, "I believe we should all consider emigrating to Canada or South Africa, or maybe even New Zealand or Australia. Every time there is conflict, it seems to rear its head in Europe, and here we are in The Netherlands in the very midst of it. What do you think?"

"Oh, Ben, you're right of course, but your mama and I are too old to consider such measures. Let's get washed up now for dinner."

*

The following morning Ben rode to the markets to exchange his soap and cigarettes for food, and vouchers to get food or necessities from the government.

"Cigarettes! Soap! Cigarettes! Soap!" Ben called, holding up a few at a time. Men and women flocked to him. The men were mainly after the cigarettes, and the women wanted the soap.

"I'll take all you have, madam!" one man yelled in his face, anxiously holding out his trembling hands.

"Not so fast, my friend. What will you give me in exchange for cigarettes?"

"How many will you give me for this loaf of bread?" The trembling hand held up a scruffy-looking loaf.

"Three cigarettes," Ben countered softly.

"What! Only three! Too dear!" He turned on his heel and began to walk away. He suddenly turned around, coming back and offered Ben the loaf.

"Are you really sure this is what you want?" Ben asked, feeling pangs of conscience.

"Give them to me!" The man grabbed at the insignificant little sticks between Ben's fingers. "Give them to me."

Ben took the loaf as the man scuttled away into the crowd. Ben shook his head sadly. As he turned to walk on, someone else tapped him on the shoulder. She was a pregnant woman with children in tow.

"Please let me have soap? What will you barter for? I have this bunch of turnips and some watercress."

"One piece of soap, madam." Ben smiled at her as he held out the soap.

"It's too much!" she mumbled, looking longingly at the soap.

"Take it or leave it, madam."

"This is the first soap I have seen for months. Yes, I'll take it. But how will I feed my children? God only knows!"

They exchanged goods. Within an hour Ben's supply was depleted. As he rode out of the Amsterdam markets, he was extremely pleased with his bartering efforts and the success of his mission. Then as he headed down the Hoofdweg, a well-dressed man called out from behind him.

"Excuse me, Sister. I saw you exchanging goods in the marketplace. Have you any more cigarettes?"

Ben stopped and waited until the man was abreast of him. "Sorry, Sir, I have no more."

"What? You haven't got any more?"

Ben recognised the man was a doctor. His medical bag gave him away. "Sorry, Sir!"

The doctor rode off, obviously frustrated, and just a few feet up the road he stopped abruptly and dived onto the ancient cobblestone pavement, picking up the butt of a used cigarette, frantically trying to light it.

Ben kept riding but under his breath he muttered, "Disgusting! How could grown men, especially an educated man like this doctor, be so hooked on such a filthy habit?"

The return to Zeist was uneventful and the checks at the boom gates were much easier, seeing some of the guards remembered the little old sister riding through a few days earlier.

However, although he was successful, there always remained a healthy amount of wariness within him. Ben wore a look of complete satisfaction though when he rode his bicycle into Veldheimlaan 20 after the long ride home. Understandably, Em was over the moon when she looked out her front window and saw Ben cycling through the front gate. She raced out the back door, reaching her husband before he could even get off the bicycle.

"It's you, schatje! I'm so happy to see your trip went well." Em threw her arms around the "little old lady" still sitting on the bike seat, almost ready to hop off. "Thank goodness you're home safely. I was really getting worried. So how did it go?"

"It's good to be home, Oudje," he said, bending forward and hugging her and kissing her.

"Don't do that here," Em whispered. "Someone might see us!"

"You worry too much, Em!" He teased her for her concern. The backyard was very secluded, with a high brick wall separating them from their nearest neighbour, but caution was in order. Especially since the owner of the other half of their duplex, Mr. Dijkstra was a control freak. He couldn't be nice even if it meant something in his pocket. His poor sisters were terrified of him, and Ben's family often heard them quarrelling. The women often were heard screaming out in fear or perhaps in pain as he struck them. Ben's blood boiled at the very thought of a man striking a woman. So perhaps, he was not to be trusted.

"Haven't you heard 'the walls have ears'?" Em chided, holding her finger to her lips in caution.

"Perhaps you're right. Let's go inside." After Em closed the back door, he added, "I'm really amazed just how smoothly it went. I never missed a beat or aroused suspicion at any of the checkpoints. Can you believe it?"

"What about the family? Did any of them recognize you?" "Yes, but only one. Who do you think recognized me?"

"Your mother," Em said unhesitatingly. "It would have to be your mother."

"It strikes me, Oudje, you are always right. What is it, women's intuition? I don't know, but women have it in greater measure than we men folk, that's for certain!"

Ben went out and unloaded the bag and brought the bicycle inside the house. There was no way they could risk leaving that life-saving device outside for someone to steal—either Nazi or fellow countryman! "Now, Em, how about a hot cup of—well—something? And my kids, where are they?"

"First though, quickly go into the cellar and change, before the children see you. I'll get some clothes for you and then call the children." Em smiled as she went upstairs.

A joyful reunion ensued.

CHAPTER 12

The Game of Cat and Mouse Continues

Mid-1943 saw a downturn in Hitler's great conquests throughout Europe, and his greed in trying to take on Russia turned out to be a disaster. He had not learned from Napoleon Bonaparte's earlier disaster when trying to overthrow the Russians! The tide of history could have been very different if Hitler's greed for power had not been so great. The chilling result of this blunder manifested itself in a great shortage of manpower for the war effort, which he desperately wanted to continue in the west and the south in order to maintain his hold on those countries already conquered. All countries annexed by Germany were now called upon to supply manpower to augment the dwindling number of soldiers he had at his disposal. Even in small towns like Zeist, the military police began taking eligible men off the streets to transport them to Germany to work in the munitions factories or other essential services. Initially the government proclaimed that all men between eighteen and forty-five appear ready to leave, knapsack in tow, on specified mornings in the cities. Ben knew it would only be a matter of time before they would look for more "volunteers," as they put it, from the smaller townships.

It was necessary to keep Ben out of the public eye from then on, as he was obviously under suspicion and had thus far evaded being caught by the surprise raids that were regularly held on the townspeople in order to catch some unawares.

Every day Em lived in fear that another attempt might catch her husband and leave her, with two children and another on the way, without anyone to fend for them.

Meanwhile, one morning there was a strange phone call. In order to protect him, she had denied having a husband at home. This meant she had the added responsibility of answering the door and the telephone in case someone was out to trick her husband out of hiding! The Nazis were fully aware of the Dutch women's ploy, so they constantly tried to catch them in a moment of weakness or forgetfulness.

On this particular morning, when the phone rang, a man's voice asked for Ben Bijl. Em froze. Finally, she stammered, "My, my husband left me quite some time ago, but if it's in relation to photography perhaps I can still help you, as I am also a photographer."

"Mrs. Bijl," the voice continued, "if you have a bird out of its cage please lock it up as there is a cat in your area today."

"Thank you, Sir." An all-too-familiar feeling of dread filled Em's heart. She ran upstairs to Ben, who was working in the darkroom developing film and processing photos.

"Ben, there's going to be another raid in our area today! You must hurry now. Leave this. I'll finish it. Just go and hide! Oh, and make sure there aren't any incriminating negatives or photos laying around in here."

"How do you know, Em?"

"That phone call was from someone asking for you, and I said you'd left me and weren't here."

"Mmm. Did he say anything else?" Ben asked, swinging around to face Em, very suspicious of the information he had just relayed to him.

"He just said, after I told him you weren't here, that if I had a bird out of its cage, go and lock it up as the cat will be in our area today."

"Yes, and?"

"That was all, he just hung up."

Ben initially looked relieved, but then he smiled, and his expression changed. "It would have to be today, wouldn't it?" He was irritated. "I promised these would be ready in the morning—early! Quickly then, please go downstairs and prepare some food and water for me."

"Who was that man?" Em was still worried about who actually had made the phone call.

"The Underground prints a weekly paper called Trouw for those who are involved in their work, to prepare them for trouble and keep them abreast of the Nazis' plans and new laws. An educated guess tells me one of them realized it was in our area and of course they are anxious to protect me, as I am invaluable to them in providing the legal paperwork to get people out. I know for a fact one of our cell members works in the Zeist police headquarters and feigns being on the Nazis' side in order to act as an informer. It was probably him. Now don't worry. Go get everything organized."

Ben grabbed some reading material, his glasses, a deck of cards for a game of solitaire, and some candles and his flashlight with which to see in his hiding place. After some minutes, he came downstairs to find Gerda and Charles. They were playing on the seat in the bay window. Charles was watching his pet white mice through the window, which Em had taken outside because of their unpleasant odour. He had a book in his hand, but the mice appeared far more inviting. Gerda was playing with her toy tea set.

"Bye for now, my schatjes. Be good for Mama while I'm away, won't you?" He hugged them and went to his desk and took a sheet from the notepad.

"Where are you going, Papa?" Gerda asked.

"Oh, Papa has to get something upstairs and then he'll be going out for a while, schatje," Ben reassured her very casually.

"Can't I come with you, Papa?"

"No, schatje," he said, tussling her golden curls, "Oh, I just remembered—how could Papa forget?—today is your first day at school! Excited?"

"Well…sort of." Gerda hesitated, something unusual for her. "Do I have to go, Papa?"

"Now just one moment, sweetheart. We have to get a photo for your first day at school. Come on." Ben guided his unsure offspring to the front door, picking up his camera on the way. "Come on, pet! A great big smile for Papa!" Ben picked up his daughter and hugged her in an enormous bear hug. "Papa's little girl is growing up! Love you, sweetie! Now remember to be good. Yes?" Gerda nodded, for once at a loss for words.

"You, my dear, have to finish getting ready for school or you will be late." He tweaked her little chin, his eyes dancing and playful as usual "Quickly now; go inside, Gerda." They walked back inside hand in hand.

"Do I really have to go to school today?" She sighed again.

"Yes, dearest. You turn six in several months. You know from this day onward you go to school everyday except on the weekend or holidays. Right?"

"Yes, Papa, I know."

Em called her from the kitchen. "Hurry now, Gerda. We will have to go in five minutes. Are you ready? Cleaned your teeth? Lunch in your bag? Quickly now! You will be able to spend all day with your friend Marielle!"

That comment worked like magic. At her mother's bidding, Gerda rushed past Ben on the stairs.

Gerda's first day at school mid 1943.

Ben shook his head at the instant change in attitude. But then as he walked past the bedroom to the darkroom, he peeked in and heard Gerda say at the washstand in her bedroom, "Just why do kids have to clean their teeth all the time anyway? What a chore." Gerda frowned at herself as she shook a tiny pinch of salt into her palm and began the arduous and revolting task. "Yuk!" She added as she spat out the residue. "Yuk!"

Ben chuckled. "Kids—one minute you have 'em, next minute they're against you. Strikes me they're like the weather!"

Charles, meanwhile, was settling back into his ABC Book of Animals. "I wonder if there is a picture of my white mice in this animal book?" He carefully turned the pages, studying each animal, but no mice! A look of disappointment spread across the little fellow's face, but it immediately changed when he came upon a picture of Hendrika the cow and her calf. "Ah well! I like cows too."

Em had finished washing up breakfast dishes and heard Charles' last comment about the cows as she walked into the front room, where he sat.

"Mama, when I grow up, guess what I'd like to be?"

"What would you like to be, son?"

"I think I would like to be a farmer like Opa Flach. I do wish we could have some animals, like he has. Lots of them, Mama."

"Well, it takes a lot of food to feed animals, and we haven't got enough these days to feed even ourselves, have we?"

Charles was close to four year sold now. He looked intently out the window, as if weighing carefully the words his mother had spoken, and then said, "Well one day, when I grow up, I'll find lots of food for us and then we will be able to have some animals like Opa. Okay?"

She smiled at Charles as she headed upstairs to find Ben and check that everything was in order. Her third pregnancy was now in the third trimester, and she was feeling the strain. The treads always creaked on the way up to the attic, so as she rose above the stairwell and looked into the room crowning the house, Ben wheeled around on his knees. He was kneeling in front of the timber wall on the opposite side of the room. But as she entered, he quickly turned around and jumped up furtively.

"Oh! Thank goodness it's you, Em. I knew it would be, but I suddenly felt uneasy—what if it wasn't?"

She closed the door, and he immediately kneeled down again in front of the wall. Picking up a fine knife, he eased it into a section of the wood boards and in seconds had the boards in his hands. After removing half a dozen pieces of the timber cladding, which ran vertically around the wall, he lit a candle and placed it into the low narrow chamber on the other side of the wall. Up there, in the Dutch gable of his home, in the triangular space between the roof and the attic wall, Ben had prepared his hiding place many months before. And in recent months, he had used it often. It was quite remarkable, because he had carefully placed nails on the inside of the boards, which he had just removed, and when he settled himself inside, he could lift each of the boards back onto the wall, and no-one could tell they had ever been removed. After this, Em would place Hessian bags with fruit or turnips (but these days they were almost unprocurable) or some other available foodstuff in front of the hidden opening to divert attention from the wall. It looked just like any other attic—a storeroom-cum-spare-bedroom if needed. So far, his ingenious little hiding place had foiled the enemy. But would it continue to protect him?

Inside the small triangular area just over a metre wide he had placed an old mattress, pillows, blankets, flashlight, matches, reading materials, candles, something non perishable to eat, water and a bucket. Even hidden amongst his things was a revolver, which he kept for the worst-case scenario. Even Em was unaware that Ben had a gun, and it was doubtful Ben would have used it unless his family's lives were in danger. Here he also kept most of his clothes and information he still had to do with forging passports.

The day turned out to be a long one. At long last there was the knock on the door around three-fifteen in the afternoon. No real concern though. Ben had hidden himself some hours before, and all Em had to do was remain calm. It wasn't easy; her heart was always pounding as she opened the door—this time to two youthful-looking officers who promptly greeted her with the customary "Heil Hitler!" and saluted, clicking their heels in unison.

"Papers, please!"

Em handed over her papers, which identified her with a photo and names of her children.

"Where is your husband?"

"I have already told your officers. My husband left me not long ago. I am alone."

"I see; we shall look around all the same, madam. You are aware of the penalty for hiding volunteers for the Third Reich?" Em rolled her eyes at the word "volunteers."

After conducting their search and once again warning her of the consequences of hiding anyone, they left. With the closing of the door, she breathed a sigh of relief. Yet again Ben and others had been protected by being given an early warning.

Once she had satisfied herself that the soldiers and their wagons had completely left Veldheimlaan, Em went up the attic stairs, whistling their prearranged "all-clear" password, a birdcall. Instantly like a spring-loaded Jack-in-the-box, Ben appeared. Boards flew in all directions as he came out of hiding. Ben came out smiling with satisfaction that once again they had eluded the enemy.

"Foiled 'em again!" he cried as he sprang forward. He stopped dead in his tracks—cramping in his legs meant he needed to have a long hard stretch. "Wow! It gets a bit confined in there. Glad to be out!"

"I'll bet you are." Em grabbed him, kissing him tenderly. "But sorry, schatje, I have to go immediately to pick up Gerda. It's almost four already, and I'll be late." With a long, drawn-out sigh, she added, "Can you look after Charles? I'll be as quick as I can. Bye."

Before he knew it, she was gone. That faithful bike was indeed a Godsend. Ben cleaned up around him and walked down the squeaky stairs to check on his third son.

CHAPTER 13

Survival the Paramount Issue

There were regular raids on houses at random, not only to find the ones who had refused to answer the "call up" but also to make sure nobody used electricity.

The Veldheim Slot was now taken over by the Nazis as their headquarters in Zeist. The day the electricians came and took away the power fuses from the meter box in the front foyer of their house was one of the most frustrating days of Em's life.

"Ben, what am I going to do now? Life without power is going to be unbearable."

"Don't fret yet; old Ben has an idea that just might work." Em's eyes immediately registered extreme interest. "How?"

"Wait a minute and you'll see, my dear," he said confidently. He rustled around in the basement for a time, and shortly thereafter came to Em with strips of well-worn silver foil—the cigarette wrappers from yesteryear, with which he was busily bartering. He had also found some old ceramic materials.

A few days later Ben and an electrician, probably working with the Underground, cut a piece of wood out of the floorboards in the foyer where the power supply came into the house. The electrician peeled back the shielded cable and tapped into the power supply.

"You see, Em," Ben explained, "he is now going to reconnect the power using this temporary fuse board that he has made out of silver foil and the ceramic material I found." He connected this to the cable and bypassed the meter box so no electricity would register as being used.

"Let's test it first, Ben," the electrician suggested, "before we cover everything up. Got a lamp?"

"Yes, I'll get one immediately," Em offered enthusiastically. Shortly she returned, and after making sure all the windows in the adjoining room were securely covered with blankets, they switched the power supply on. Instantly there was light!

"I told you it would work, Ben my friend," the electrician said, patting him on the back.

"I will never cease to be amazed, Ben. It's amazing! We actually have electricity again. Thank you so much for your help, sir." She added excitedly.

"No, madam, we thank you for your help." His was a look of earnestness. "Now remember, you must be very careful. If the authorities find out, there will be big trouble—the least of which will be a fine, but it could be much worse."

"We have to be extremely cautious or else we could be caught. So, no half-measures Em. Thankfully because of the curfew, no-one can be outside at night after six, and all windows have to be blacked out completely with blankets anyway."

The purpose of blankets is to make it difficult for enemy planes to drop bombs on towns, which are clearly defined by light of any kind. At least covering the windows did not cause any suspicion since that was what the Occupation Government wanted them to do anyway.

"These sheets of black paper I have in the darkroom will have to be attached to the windows as well as the blankets now, Em. We cannot afford to let even a whisper of light be seen from the street or it may be my death warrant."

This having been done, it was possible to have light on inside the house. To be safe, Ben limited its use to the kitchen light. The first evening they tried it out, and Ben went outside and did an inspection of the whole house to make sure that even the smallest sliver of light was not seen.

"The first rule will have to be this: always keep a cold bulb close by, to switch over before answering the door should we be caught unawares.

Especially seeing it will be in the kitchen at night where I forge the passports. If the Germans come into houses on this street, they will feel the light bulbs because they know the power is still going down our street to the Slot. So, we have to be one step ahead of them all the way!"

*

During the weeks that followed, Ben helped their neighbour Mrs. de Rue rig up the illegal power supply in her kitchen as they had done in theirs. Her daughter Willy had a bakery shop in Zeist until her marriage, and then her husband's work took them to live in Germany. From the end of November until late February, the sky was seldom anything but dark, grey clouds and freezing winds from the Arctic. There was little sun for weeks on end and dismal rains day after day. Even during the day, lights would normally be used to be able to see adequately, and it was on one such day that a Nazi raid occurred.

Mrs. de Rue had been busy in her living room trying to do some sewing, remaking a long, full-skirted dress into a "new" skirt when the soldiers made the inspection. She was caught unawares by the Nazis. The threatening knock on her door made her freeze. Her brain scarcely registered what she must do as paralysing fear swept across her. She only had time to turn the light off, but the tell-tale materials, such as thread and scissors, were still on the table when she opened her door.

"Heil Hitler!" came the greeting. "Papers, please!"

Mrs. de Rue fumbled around and eventually produced the papers. This did not go unnoticed by the officers. Why was she so nervous? They knew only too well that all houses in Veldheimlaan were on the direct line to the Nazi headquarters.

With suspicions aroused, they insisted, "We will conduct a search of your house, madam."

As soon as the men walked into her living room, their suspicions were confirmed. They immediately discerned what she had been doing, as it would be almost impossible to see inside on such a day, especially with the drapes drawn. There was no evidence of candles on the table, which could have been an alternate light source. Seeing this, the younger officer reached out and felt the globe above the table. Yes, it was very hot!

"You have been using the electricity without permission! You know, don't you, what the penalty for using electricity is?" He then drew a revolver to her head. "Schnell!" ("Quickly!") "Tell me, old woman. Why did you disobey the Government's decree?"

She burst into tears as he threatened her. Shaking, she asked, "Do you see that photo on my mantelpiece?"

The sergeant nodded, stepping closer to examine the portrait on her mantle in the dimly lit room. "Luftwaffe!" ("Air Force!") His voice sounded incredulous.

"Who do you think that is?" She began to sob, pointing to a portrait of a young man in a German Luftwaffe uniform. "That is my daughter's husband. She and my grandchildren live in Germany, and he is at this very moment fighting for your cause. What would they say if they knew you intend to kill me, their grandmother, because I, an old woman, am using a little electricity?"

Instantly the officer dropped the revolver from her forehead, and looking at her, said, "Mrs. de Rue, we will let you off this time, but don't you ever use the power again or next time we will not be so lenient! Verstehen? The fine will be twenty-five gulden, which you must pay at the police station tomorrow without fail." He wrote out a fine and handed it to her, and with that irritating click of the heels, they stormed out, hailing Hitler.

As soon as they moved further down Veldheimlaan, Mrs. de Rue ran across to her neighbours' and knocked frantically. "Em! Let me in!"

Em opened the door, and the woman fainted in her arms. "I'll bet she was caught using the power!" Em's conclusion was predictable.

After Mrs. de Rue revived, she related her experience. A warm chicory coffee helped immensely, and soon they were laughing about her luck.

"Well, Mrs. de Rue, you must remember, always keep a cold globe at the ready near the globe you are using. If there is a knock on the door, you must exchange it before you answer the door, and always keep the doors locked so you will not be caught unawares as happened today!" Ben ended his lecture with a reassuring pat on her shoulder.

"It would also be a good idea to keep a small stick of candle, if you have any candles left, on the table as well. Even if you can't light it in a hurry, you could say you were in the bathroom and had been sewing earlier," Em added kindly.

"Thank goodness Henje's husband is in the Luftwaffe!" Ben said.

"Yes, yes, until today, I was sad to have to say that to anyone, but perhaps it saved my life today!" Mrs. de Rue smiled, colour returning to her face.

"I believe so." Ben sighed.

Shortly after, Mrs. de Rue's daughter wrote with the news that the Nazis had rounded up anyone from Allied countries, including those who had joined the German military forces, and executed them as traitors. Her young Dutch husband was amongst them. The many injustices of war!

For everyone it had become a full-time job just providing food for their children as the years dragged on. The last two years there was virtually no help from the Occupying Government feeding their subjects, so it was "eke out a little using your wits!"

Consequently, for Ben to get the forged passports into the right hands, he used his nurse's disguise. He was well known by the German soldiers at the road checks, so well that they soon waved him on without even checking his papers. This worked to his advantage in transferring the lifesaving passports for Jews and others to his various contacts in the area. Whilst he was out of town, he would take some of his "treasures" and barter with them for food, no matter its description or how unappetising it was. Cigarettes and soap, his main tools for trading, were sought after like gold, just as Ben had observed during the Great War.

As the bombing of Germany and east of The Netherlands under German control became a nightly exercise by the Allies, life became a nightmare. The Netherlands being in the direct flight path of the Allied Spitfire Mk1s meant that the Dutch people were like "the filling" in a sandwich. The district of Utrecht where they lived was smack-bang in the middle of the pathway.

In preparation for that possibility, Ben had brought buckets of sand into every room, which could be used to extinguish fire, should that occur. As soon as the air raid sirens sounded, people were instructed to go to the nearest bunkers in their town or hide in the cellars of their homes if they had one. Sometimes there would be no time to run downstairs, so the family had an escape plan, which was for the children to get out of bed and stand in the nearest doorway so the parents could reach them quickly.

Eventually, Ben moved their children's mattress into his and Em's room. The children were put to bed at night fully dressed for protection, should they need to make a quick getaway. Bombs landed on some of their neighbours' homes. Night after night an eerie droning of planes slipped across the velvet sky, punctuated with brilliant but terrifying flashes of destruction. As the Americans became more involved in the air attacks on Germany, the planes began a different tack, and started flying across in broad daylight.

One morning Em set off to take Gerda to school, and Charles straggled along beside her. As they advanced down Veldheimlaan, a fairly long street, the results of the frighteningly close air attacks the previous night became evident. Not that their area, the District of Utrecht was actually under attack, but often as the Allies flew over on their way to bomb German industries, dams, and power plants, the German ground artillery would find their targeted plane, and the plane of course would drop from the sky in flames, whilst the occupants endeavoured to parachute to safety on the ground. Often planes would land on buildings and houses, wreaking much havoc and injury on the people inside.

Occasionally, actual bombs landed on residential districts, although usually they were not meant for them—but the result was horrific. Bits and pieces of wreckage were strewn across the streets; some buildings fell from impact. Fire had consumed parts of them. Great craters where bombs exploded could be seen in some streets.

On one particular morning, as they approached one of the areas hit, hanging there in one of the trees lining the sidewalk along the street was a parachute hugging a large chestnut tree. Charles and Gerda ran forward to examine the sight.

"Looook! Looook!" Gerda shrieked, pointing up into the shaded underbelly of the tree. "It's a dead man, Mama! Yes, I think he's dead." Caught up high in the tree hung an Allied pilot, his light khaki uniform, as well as the markings of his parachute, distinctly identified him. Charles joined his sister, looking up inquisitively, but instead of frank interest, he was terrified and immediately began to wail, running back to his mother's side. It was a terrible sight for anyone, let alone young children.

Em quickly took them across the street and moved on, but Gerda kept talking about the macabre scene, asking lots of questions.

"What happened, Mama?"

"I don't know, schatje."

"But what do you think happened? Do you think that was the plane we heard going down, that crashed last night?"

"You know it would have been. You've stood behind the curtain at the attic window with Papa, and he has pointed into the sky at flaming planes falling from the sky."

"Yes, yes," she answered impatiently.

"Well, that is what happens when the plane hits the ground. It causes great damage, and often the poor pilots have a bad landing in the parachute and are killed."

"Like that man we just saw hanging in the tree?"

"Yes, Gerda. Now let's talk about something nice, shall we?"

"I don't like these things, Mama," Charles said sadly, wiping his teary eyes. "Why do they happen?"

Em thought it all went over his little head, but she saw from his comment, he understood more than she had thought. "Well, sometimes people hate one another, or one country wants what another country has and so they begin to fight over it, much like you and Gerda sometimes fight over the ball or trikes."

"But I wouldn't want to hurt my sister, Mama!" he added in shock.

"No, of course you wouldn't, but when it's a big problem, people sometimes resort to terrible things, like this."

"How sad," Gerda said. She had been all ears and was now crying with Charles.

He looked at his big sister, and after a big sigh, said, "Gerda, I love you. I wouldn't do that to you."

She hugged him for a moment and then quickly turned away, looking for something more interesting to do. Em laughed despite herself.

The Christian School was now in view. The Christian Brothers and the Christian Sisters School's were on opposite sides of the avenue. A huge playing and assembly area separated the two wings of the separate schools. Parents and children converged on this central location, as school was about to commence. The respective schools were on either side of this magnificent avenue of trees, leading from the town centre to the beautiful Slot Zeist with its moats and gardens.

"Well, Gerda, have a lovely day, and make sure you behave yourself." Em kissed her strong-willed little girl on the forehead.

"Oh Mama, there's Marielle. I must catch up with her! Bye now." With a perfunctory kiss, Gerda ran forward, calling, "Marielle! Marielle!"

"Bye, Gerda! Bye!" Charles' voice faded away.

Em shook her head, smiling at the focus and independence her young daughter displayed. "I guess she's like her father. And Em, what would you expect?"

"What did you say, Mama?" Charles asked as he heard his mother mumbling.

"I was just thinking about your determined sister, that's all."

"What's determined mean, Mama?"

"Ohh, that's hard to explain….It means she has a strong will to do what she wants to do. Understand?"

"Sort of—she makes me do things I don't want to do. Yes?"

"Well"—Em stifled a laugh, "that's fairly close to the mark, Charles!"

CHAPTER 14

A Death and a Birth

The summer had been very pleasant, perhaps unseasonably hot that year. A blessing considering little else was good news, with the war in its fifth year still raging around them. After school, Ben, Em and the children passed the time sitting in the sun in front of the double-glass doors facing into their backyard. Here on the grass they had a little table and chairs and would often eat—or try to pretend they were having an evening meal or lunch. Sometimes it was just a cup of "tea" enjoying those pleasant summer days and long twilights.

It was half past four. Em and Gerda had just returned home after picking Gerda up from school. Em's pregnancy was fast coming to an end.

Ben examined his wife's face, understandably worried. "Em, you look so tired." She was under a lot of pressure and getting near to her next confinement. "How about you sit here on the lounge with your feet up for a while, and I'll get something for us to drink and eat."

He kissed Gerda, taking her by the hand. "Come with Papa into the kitchen. I want you to tell me all about your day at school."

"My new teacher's name is Mrs. Groen. She is so very nice. And she likes my drawings too!"

"Really?" Her father's eyes twinkled.

"Yes, Papa. Mrs. Groen said my dog and cat were the best in the whole class!"

"And how did you come to draw a dog and a cat? Could you draw whatever you liked?"

"Oh no! Mrs. Groen asked us to draw a picture of what we saw coming to school today."

"And did you see the neighbour's cat and dog this morning?" Ben's brows danced up and down with amusement.

"Well, not exactly." Gerda drew a deep breath. "But we walked the way Mama takes us when we go for walks, so I have seen Mrs. Engel's cat and Mrs. van der Molen's dog fighting many times." Her little cheeks were turning rosy red. "That was all right wasn't it, Papa?" She studied his face, looking for approval, her head cocked to one side. Ben chuckled and chucked her under her chin. "Oh, my pet, it wasn't the exact truth, but I think Mrs. Groen would allow that in this instance as she really wanted to see what you could draw, not actually what you saw on the way to school. Understand?"

"Thank you, Papa, I'm so glad! I didn't mean to tell a lie."

Ben bent down and kissed her rosebud lips. "Off you go now. I must make Mama's tea. Right?"

She skipped off happily to find her brother.

It's amazing, Ben mused, how children can block awful memories out of their mind. She did not think to write about the dead airman they had seen in the tree that Em told me about earlier today.

Ben returned to his resting wife. "Here you are, my dear. Drink this excuse for tea. I'll get the meal tonight. You just rest up a bit, okay."

"Thanks, Ben. I've just been wondering how we're going to feed another mouth." Her eyes searched his, fighting to hold back tears. "I'm so worried." The strong emotions of pregnancy were really manifesting themselves, as usually she did not cry easily.

"Now don't worry; we have managed so far. Worry doesn't change things, and it makes you sick. Please leave it in God's hands. You, at least have faith, unlike your doubting husband, don't you?" He patted her kindly on the shoulder. "Now stop worrying. We'll talk about a few ideas I have when the kids are asleep tonight. All right?"

She sighed and silently sipped her "tea" – at least it was hot and vaguely soothing.

The children finally in bed, they had time to talk while the tranquillity of the summer twilight faded oh-so-slowly into night. It was quite late when they sat down at the open double-glass doors off their living room. They looked into the backyard, and further beyond that at the darkening night sky. The gnawing pain of hunger, like a relentless toothache, was wearing them down, especially for Em being with child. Ben's bartering tools had helped wonderfully. Until his stash began to dwindle, things were not too bad, but by May 1943, his little cache had virtually been depleted, and people had far less to barter with, except their precious family heirlooms and jewellery that could not be consumed.

"Is it really true that many families are so hungry that they are reduced to digging up dahlia corms and the like—actually eating them to help stave off the hunger?" Em was wondering about others worse off than they were.

Ben studied his distraught wife. He hoped they would not be reduced to such things. Dahlia corms are relatives of potatoes but of course are not as palatable.

"Console yourself, Em, with the fact that corms and bulbs are pretty good fare compared to rats, birds, cats, and dogs!"

"Oh, Ben, stop it! I'll vomit everywhere If you keep talking about such things." Next second, she stumbled to get out of the armchair, racing hurridly up the hall, holding her mouth.

Ben sat musing over their conversation. Animals of every kind appear on many tables disguised as something far more appetising. Hunger prevents most people from asking exactly what it is, I guess. He surveyed the heavens before him. It's so peaceful tonight, one would never know there is so much pain in the world. His face twisted in torment. When will this war ever end? Please, God, let it be soon!

His thoughts were cut short as the sound of Em throwing up reached his ears. He jumped to his feet and ran to her aid. He steered her toward the stairwell, and her bed, turning back the covers. Tomorrow was another day. Ben prayed for his distraught wife. Something that he not done for many years.

July and summer were almost spent. Em had about six to eight weeks to go before the baby was due, though she was not very big.

"Coffee's ready. Come, Ben, come children!" There was a rattling and scuttling of tiny feet, and soon the family gathered at the table. The chattering suddenly stopped as they each examined what was laid up on it. "Enjoy." Em smiled half-heartedly as she handed Ben a cup of chicory coffee and the children a glass of water.

"I'm not really thirsty, Mama," Gerda said as she pushed away the tiny porcelain glass Em had half-filled with the precious fluid.

"Drink just a little, schatje," Ben urged.

Gerda wrinkled her nose. "But I don't like water. Can't we have some milk?"

"You know we haven't got any milk," Em said. "Then, don't keep asking, understand?"

Gerda rolled her eyes heavenward and walked away, shaking her head, mimicking her mother, "We haven't got any …" She bared her teeth in utter frustration, not really understanding with whom to be cranky.

Meanwhile, Ben sipped the "coffee" Em had encouraged him to enjoy. He looked carefully at his wife's wearied yet lovely face.

"Thank you, schatje. How are you feeling today?" Ben leaned toward her and patted her rounded belly as he drank from the cup. "Sit down and relax in this beautiful sun for a few minutes, Em. You look so tired." She sank into the seat beside her husband, "Yes, I'm really tired—sick and tired, I guess …"

"Don't let it worry you too much, Em. This war can't go on forever."

"It just feels like it is, that's all." She gave him a wry smile.

"Hey, look at Charles playing in his car." Ben quickly tried to distract Em onto a more positive subject. Ben had set up chairs with rugs over them and made what looked like a car for the little ones to play in. "He plays for hours on end in that thing. Going here and going there in his little make-believe world far away from reality. Thank goodness children can get away from it all with their wonderful imaginations!"

Unexpectedly, disturbing their pleasant little interlude, the doorknocker began its monotonous thud, thud. Since the war, Em felt it was like a drum sounding a death knell. It instantly set her on edge. "Oh, who's here this time?" Em asked, rubbing her eyes from the glare. She looked imploringly at Ben.

"It's all right, Em, I'll answer it," he said kindly, but before he could say anymore, Em forced her bulky frame up from her relaxed position and said forcefully, "Don't you dare, Ben Bijl. Quickly, get upstairs and in the attic, just in case. I'll answer it!" She took her time getting to the door in order to give Ben a chance to disappear.

After several repeated knocks, she heard footsteps, as if the person knocking was walking away again, thinking no-one was home. Em peeked out from the front office window. She saw a man walking down the path. Relief! It was their friendly postman.

With haste she opened the door and called him back. "Mr. de Jong! Don't go! I'm home. Have you mail for me today?"

"Yes, Mrs. Bijl, it is a letter for you. Here you are."

"Thank you, sir." Em took the letter from his hand and turned it over. It was from her mother. She smiled and looked relieved. "Thank you."

"My pleasure, Mrs. Bijl, good day." The postman turned on his heel and walked down the path. Before he closed the gate, he was humming.

Em turned the letter back to the front and rushed inside, closing the door. "Thank goodness this will be good news." She turned it over observing that it was not edged in black, the customary envelope to announce a death in the family. Now in a much more light-hearted frame of mind, Em quickened her step and walked as briskly as she could up the two flights of steps to the attic.

"Ben, Ben!" Em called excitedly. "It's okay, you can come out, it was only the postman with a letter from Mama and Papa!"

Boards started flying off the wall the instant he heard her voice. "That's good! What's new?"

"Let's go downstairs and read it in the sun, dear." Arm in arm they negotiated the two flights of steps to the ground floor, Em savouring the pleasant sensation of news from someone you love.

She excitedly ripped open the letter and began reading.

> "Bleke Hei"
> Meerleseweg Chaam
> July 14, 1943
>
> "Dear Em and Ben,
>
> It is with much sadness I write to you today. As you know, Papa has had many stomach upsets over the years, and although

we have never known exactly what was wrong, we have grown accustomed to his bouts of illness.

Last week, Papa took ill again, but this time he began vomiting fresh blood. I called for Dr. Blumsheim to come and see him. He said that Papa probably had a bleeding ulcer. Anyway, despite all his efforts, he was not able to stop the bleeding. Em, your dear father passed away this morning. We found out later that he had a brain haemorrhage.

I'm devastated. He was only sixty-six years old. I felt we would have many more years together, and I cannot believe it's true. I will have to face the future alone."

The awful truth hit right to Em's heart. "Oh no, no, no!" Em whispered as she sank to her knees in shock and disbelief. "I can't believe it, Ben! My father—Papa—gone! No! It can't be!"

Ben cradled his wife in his arms, trying to calm her, gently rocking her. "Em, schatje, I am so sorry," he whispered.

But his wife was not registering the words, just the disbelief of shock and that initial numbness of grief. "Ben, would you please read the rest of the letter? I, I can't ..." Em whispered as sobs again erupted from her heaving chest.

Ben took the letter from Em's shaking hands, squeezed them tightly, nodding sadly and quickly skimming the page to find where she had left off.

"In my mind I know he has gone, but in my heart, I keep thinking it's an awful dream and I'll soon wake up to reality, and the whole awful nightmare will have vanished.

We are holding off the funeral until Saturday, though I know you may not be able to get down to Chaam to attend, your being so far advanced in your pregnancy. However, if you can, dear daughter, please try. Perhaps Ben could come to represent the family. Whatever happens, Em and Ben, I know one of you will be here if it's humanly possible, but if not, please pray for me and your sisters. God has taken my dear Johan, your dear papa, to a better place.

The funeral will be at the old Dutch Reform Church in Chaam at 1:00 pm this Saturday.

May our Lord comfort you and the rest of our dear family, who are still grieving for our precious Gerrit, whom we lost so long ago. May He help us in all our tribulation as He has promised to do. With great sorrow and love,

Your Mama."

"Oh, Ben. No! It can't be! He's far too young to die!" Em's hands were gesturing her continuing disbelief. "No, no, it can't be true!"

"Why are you sad, Mama?" Charles climbed out of his car and patted his distraught mother on her leg. "What's wrong?"

"Mama is sad because her dear papa has just died."

"Like the man in the parachute, Papa?" His eyes were little grey marbles.

"Yes, son, like that."

"Ohh! Mama's sad. Sorry, Mama!"

Em cuddled her little boy on one arm and Ben on the other. She continued to weep. Ben rocked her all the while until finally, exhausted, she stopped and said, "I'm very tired, Ben. I must go to bed."

"Come on then Em, I'll take you upstairs right away. Don't worry now, I'll look after Charles. I'll make you a warm drink. Just close your eyes and rest." He immediately guided her up the stairs, helping her into bed, and then hurriedly ducked downstairs.

She slept the rest of the day. Ben realized rest was probably the body's way of helping her cope with the stress. Their kind neighbour Mrs de Rue offered to go and fetch Gerda from school.

He prayed she would not go into premature labour. "Actually, she seemed to take it pretty well," Ben told Mrs. de Rue. "But the stark reality hasn't hit home yet."

He roused her in the early evening, for a little food, which he had prepared for them. The children didn't want to eat the "gooey" pearl barley he had boiled. Ben was beside himself after two hours of trying to get Charles to swallow a few mouthfuls of the awful, insipid stuff. Ben was not the most patient soul, but he tried playing games with his son to encourage him to open his mouth.

"Look, Charles, here comes an airplane! Whoosh!" Ben glided the spoon full of mush through the air and dive-bombed into Charles' giggling little mouth.

Immediately his son spat it out, crying, "I hate this stuff, Papa! Please, please don't make me eat it. It's yuk!"

Determined not to be outdone, Ben carefully tried to retrieve the precious morsels scattered across the table and start again. "Here comes the airplane. Open up!"

On the odd occasion his son didn't spit it straight back out, he would sit there just stirring the sticky tasteless mess around his mouth with his tongue until Ben felt like retching himself. Over and over and over and over!

Ben was furious and finally threw the spoon down in utter frustration. "Son, you must eat or you will die!"

That held no fear for the child, who just cried even more seeing his papa so angry with him.

Gerda learnt soon enough that even if it tasted bad, she could go away and play or draw and read as soon as she had forced down the revolting excuse for food they were given. It was either eat it or go without! This was not a case of choices, and even if the food was disgusting, the empty, nauseated feeling was worse.

When Ben finally went up to Em with some food and a weak tea, it was very late. "See if you can eat a little of this." He looked at it. "God knows it isn't much, Em, but you and baby both need something to sustain you."

"Thanks, Ben," she said sadly, her eyes red from crying. He sat on the bed whilst she ate a little and contemplated. What would be the best and safest way to get to Em's father's funeral?

"Sweetheart," he said a little while later. "Let me go in my nurse's get up. I will be able to bring a little food home and be there to comfort your mama and sisters. It's too dangerous for you to ride a bike at the moment—and it's at least seventy-five kilometres! Even the train would be too long and uncertain, if we could get a ticket in time."

He had expected Em to put up a fight, but she was surprisingly reasonable. "Mmm. I would dearly love to go, but I have an obligation to this little one." She gently patted her bulging belly and once again wept. "I am also a midwife—and I know what advice I would give someone else. Don't go! It's too close to the delivery, and too far away, and our child has the right to arrive safely. I have no control over my father's future now, but I do have some control over our baby's."

"Em, you are such a sensible woman. Have I ever told you how lucky I was to have married you?"

"Yes, schatje, and I too. I am so glad you did. What would I do without you, Ben?"

"Dearest…" He tried to swallow back the lump rising in his throat. Since words weren't coming freely, he pulled her to himself. They sat there until the sun sank and finally Ben said, "Em, dearest, we must make preparations for me to go as it is Thursday tomorrow. Tomorrow I will go to the Police Station and get the required permits for Sister Bernadina to attend her - shall we say, uncle's funeral in Chaam?"

"Yes, Ben," Em said, "I know Mama understands." She dabbed at her swollen eyes as she spoke.

Her husband kissed her cheek, caressing her hair. "Em you are agreeable for me to attend on your behalf, aren't you?" Em slowly nodded, her head drooping.

"I'll take your bike and ride there since I'm going alone. I think this is the safest way for me to get there."

Em said nothing in response, merely nodding her assent.

Ben continued, "I will ask Mrs. de Rue to keep an eye on you and the children until I return. And you know she will, dear lady. She's like an Oma to our kids. If you need a doctor before I return, she will ring one for you. How does this sound to you?"

*

Johan Flach was laid to rest on the Saturday. Another dark cloud hung over his family's head. What would the morrow bring? Anna prayed for her husband and for Em's baby, that the infant would arrive safely. Despite her sorrow, she smiled at the thought of a new grandchild. Anna and Em's younger sisters gathered at the front door as Ben mounted his bicycle. He balanced on it carefully since it was laden with foodstuffs from his mother-in-law's farm.

Jannie and Johanna were giggling at Ben's disguise.

"Ben, if you could only see yourself!" Jannie said, dissolving into laughter once again.

"Now, Ben, do have a safe return to Em and the children. And thank you so much for coming so far, for Johan's sake. You don't know what this means to me." Anna dabbed her eyes as she spoke to the man she had once shunned.

"Mama Flach, it was nothing. I only wish I could have done more for you and stayed on for a week or so to help you sort out all the legalities. But as you know, Em is only five or so weeks off confinement, and I am afraid to leave her for too long, especially if she goes into labour early."

"Don't give it another thought. You must consider Em and the little ones first. Besides, Jannie's boyfriend, Gerrit, is here, and he too has been so good to me." Anna turned to Gerrit as she spoke, smiling gratefully into his honest eyes.

"Ben, don't worry. I'm working in Chaam supervising the renovating of some old buildings. I work for the National Trust. I will be in Breda for the next six months. Hence you see, I'll have plenty of time to assist Mrs. Flach where necessary. It won't be a problem since I board here with the Flach's." Gerrit looked lovingly into Jannie's pretty face. "Believe me," he smiled, "The pleasure is all mine."

Ben winked at him. "I'm sure it'll be pure pleasure, Gerrit. Thank you." Then he held out his hand and shook Gerrit's enthusiastically. Ben hugged the girls, and with a final wave, he pedaled down the lane towards the Meerleseweg.

Gerrit ran alongside him, grinning from ear to ear. "And for goodness sake, Ben, take care and don't forget who you are!" Both men chuckled wickedly.

*

Em's sisters watched at the front door as the men went down the lane. They guessed why they were laughing so much. That was humorous enough, but as Ben almost toppled off the bike making the turn into Meerleseweg, all of them burst into peals of laughter.

"Just look at that fellow, Mama. Em's husband certainly is an original! Have you ever seen anything like it—Sister Bernadina?" Jannie said.

She and Johanna began cackling all over again.

Anna quickly regained her composure. "Now, girls, calm down. You'll make yourselves sick. All right girls. We have much work to do. Come now!"

In those few moments, "Sister Bernadina" rode out of sight as the tall trees on either side of the Meerleseweg hid him from their view.

Meanwhile Gerrit Kleinhout was returning from the lane. "What on earth is wrong with you girls?" he asked. "It sounded like a hen fight from down there."

"I said, 'If Ben could only see himself!'" Jannie said, meeting Johanna's eyes again—and off they went again. This time Gerrit joined in, and even Anna, who had walked into the kitchen, couldn't help herself.

"He's something else, that Ben. Guts of steel," Gerrit said admiringly, looking in the direction of Chaam.

"How do you think you would look dressed up in that midwife's garb?" Jannie teased him.

"That, my dear, I dare not contemplate," the tall, angular man replied. "Not as good as Ben, I'm afraid."

*

The journey home was long. Ben rode steadily for the rest of the day and arrived home before curfew, tired but satisfied. He passed through all the roadblocks with ease. The soldiers always waved him on with the biggest grins on their faces. Ben had great satisfaction in hearing the raucous laughter at Bernadina's expense each time he cycled a few feet down the road from the boom gates.

The foodstuffs arriving with him on the back of Em's trusty bike from the Flach farm were gratefully received and hungrily devoured by Ben's starving family. Eggs, a little bacon, a variety of fresh vegetables, some oats, and a little milk and butter—wonderful fare in wartime, although sadly, the pleasure of such a variety in foods ended all too quickly, despite Em's best efforts to spread it out.

"We are so lucky to have your bicycle, Em. These bags full of 'medical stuff' are such a great way to hide the food I bring back and forth."

"Yes, honey, it truly has been a Godsend," she replied wearily.

On August 26, Em's confinement commenced. Her labour started about four in the afternoon. By ten she had delivered.

"What is it? A little girl?" Her face suddenly lit up, her eyes searching excitedly for evidence of the baby's sex, as the doctor pulled the infant from between her legs. For one moment there was panic in Em's eyes as she instantly understood—it was another boy!

"A boy." She fell back on the pillows, tears streaming down her cheeks. "Another boy."

"Yes, Em, another beautiful boy for both of us to love. Here, schatje. Look at your second son. And what would you like to call him?"

"I am still happy with Louis Anselmus, after your Papa," she replied.

Ben could hear the apprehension in Em's voice. "Then it's settled. Louis Anselmus it is." Ben held the newborn out to her.

As soon as Em reached out to take him from his father, her tears abated. It was magic! Her disappointment was only momentary; it was not having a son that she feared, it was Haemophilia. Wiping the tears away and gently nestling the infant to her breast, Em smiled at the tiny life given to their care, lovingly kissing the downy little head.

"He's beautiful, Ben. Naming him after your father is nice—he's such a lovely man."

Em had a reasonably good delivery, considering the fact she'd been malnourished throughout her pregnancy, and the very recent trauma of losing her father. Their little one was very thin and his chest quite sunken, and four years of war had taken its toll on his mother's physical stamina.

Ben studied the newborn as he looked for his mother's nipple, "He looks remarkably well considering, Em."

"Yes, I think we are very lucky; he looks strong. See, Ben? He's healthy—see how he's latched on already? That's a good sign."

Ben leaned over his wife, kissed her and his newborn, and said, "Happy, Em?"

She stared pensively across the room. "My father would have been proud of our sons, Ben."

"Yes, I'm sure he would have. And speaking of forebears, I see a lot of Grandfather Niestadt in this little face."

"Perhaps you're right." Em lifted the sleeping infant closer to her face to examine his more carefully. "Perhaps he is—the shape of his face and forehead—yes, I think you may be right."

"So how about I call the children now?" Ben turned away from the bed and made for the door. Mrs. de Rue was faithfully minding them downstairs.

"Yes, they'll be so excited. I'm surprised they aren't asleep though."

"Wild horses wouldn't keep Gerda from seeing this baby before she went to sleep! She told me we just had to call her immediately after the baby came."

"Sounds like my daughter—doesn't want to miss anything." Em rearranged the baby's shawl as Ben hurried out.

At the entrance to the living room, he called excitedly, "Come quickly, we have a wonderful surprise for you. It's another baby brother!" Moments later, Gerda came racing up the stairs and threw open the bedroom door. She peered around the room, scanning it carefully. The new arrival in his mother's arms was not the object of her attention. She raced past her beckoning mother in the bed to the open window and gazed out into the gathering night.

"Ohh! I've missed him!" She stamped her foot and reeled around to her mother and the tiny brother nestling in her arms.

Ben and Em looked at each other, wondering what she was talking about.

"What on earth are you looking for, Gerda? Your little baby brother is over here. Come and see him, schatje." Ben pointed toward Em and their infant again. "See here, Gerda. Here he is!"

"I know he is, Papa," the little girl said icily. "I'm looking for the angel who brought him to us—Mama, you said angels bring little babies, and I've missed him. He must have been quick because the baby has just arrived here, but he's gone already!" Tears welled up in Gerda's eyes. She added, sniffing, "And I so much wanted to see the angel. Why didn't you call me sooner, Papa?"

"Better luck next time, schatje." Ben tried to keep a poker face, but his eyes were dancing. So that was what Gerda was about. Her parents tried to stifle their laughter.

After quickly regaining her composure, Em called Gerda to her side, saying lovingly, "Don't worry, sweetie. The most important thing is that 'he' called and left us our baby boy. Come on now, come over here to Mama and give our baby a welcome kiss."

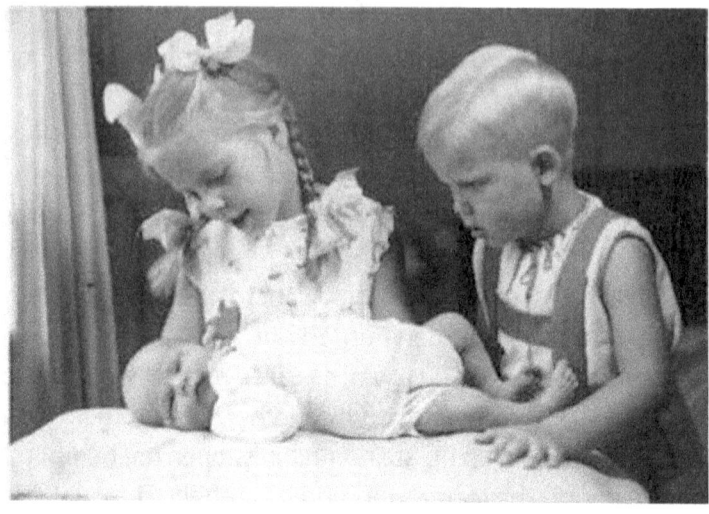

Louis' welcome photo into the world for friends and family.

Gerda moved across the room toward her Mama, still frowning fiercely, and when she finally took a look at the infant in his mother's arms, she said rather matter-of-factly, "He's awful red-lookin', Mama." Then she crinkled up her little nose quizzically and said with finality, "Sort of wrinkly looking, isn't he? Can I hold him, Mama?"

Charles, who had been asleep, had awoken to the commotion. He came running across the large bedroom to see the new arrival. "Mama! Papa! Where is it? Ohh!" His eyes shined with wonder as he examined the baby at his mother's breast. Charles stroked the baby's head. "Isn't he cute?" Then he planted a kiss on the soft, downy head and launched into chatter with Mrs. de Rue.

True to his tradition, Ben took a photo the next day of his three children. This time they were posted out sparingly, and the photo was not accompanied by a printed introduction but written by hand. It was just the same a lovely welcome into the world for baby Louis Anselmus. Em's family were particularly happy to hear that her child had arrived safely and was relatively healthy. During the following year, they rallied around, deriving comfort from Louis, their gorgeous baby . One door closes, another opens.

Another reason for joy was Jannie and Gerrit's engagement announcement.

"Ben, this letter from Jannie has details about their engagement. She says they are to be married next May in Chaam. Gerrit is going to be based with the National Trust in Breda. That's great news. I can hardly wait."

"Yes, you know that's how he came to meet Jannie—through his work. He has been working in Chaam for some months. Such a nice, genuine person," Ben said. "You really have some lovely sisters, Em. But I haven't met Cien's husband yet—what's his name?"

"Cornelis van Tiggelen. They only have one son, also named Cor. He must be about nine or ten by now."

"They didn't come to our wedding, did they?"

Em shook her head. "No Cor didn't, Cien came alone, but Cor and Cien are dark horses. They seem to have cut themselves off from the family a bit, I feel. However, it may be just finances or plain distance."

"Well, they weren't able to get to the funeral either."

"Cien and Cor live in Putten. It is a long way to Chaam."

"That's what your mother said too. Its about one hundred and thirty kilometres, she said. Ah well, perhaps at Jannie and Gerrit's wedding."

Breda, not far from Chaam, was where Annie, another sister of Em, and her husband, Gerrit de Graaff lived since their marriage in 1941. They had one little girl, Ada, born in January 1942, about a year before Louis arrived. Then came along Anka in 1944. Ben and Gerrit (he had two brothers-in-law called this) got on famously. They agreed to get together after the war. She and Ben discussed her family at some length and concluded that Em's only brother (also called Gerrit), who had died so long ago, was a lot like her eldest son Charles to look at.

She was painfully aware of the seriousness of Haemophilia and constantly worried about Charles and of course the possibility that Louis too may have the condition. They would have to make the right choices to protect their children, particularly if they had Haemophilia.

CHAPTER 15

Manpower Called up in Zeist

Those last few months of 1943 were precarious indeed, and Ben and Em had to summon all their strength and mental ability each day to eke out enough to survive. On September 8, Ben came downstairs smiling and whistling.

"What makes you so happy, Ben?" Em asked. "What news from the crystal set today?"

"The Italians have finally switched camps. They've surrendered to the Allies and now support them in the war on Germany, which means that the Americans should be able to move in a lot quicker! It means unless I am terribly mistaken, peace won't be long in coming. The tide is certainly turning against Hitler."

"Oh, Ben! I'm so glad! Let's hope so. Everyday now I wonder where our next meal will come from."

"So do I, my pet. If something doesn't give very soon, there won't be a man left in Europe."

"Don't say that, Ben. You frighten me!" Em shuddered at his comment. "Life seems so cheap these days."

"Yes, I agree. Sad as it is, it is a fact."

"I was just thinking about our seventh wedding anniversary not long past. Thank goodness there are some bright spots in our lives Ben. We're still happily married and have three delightful children."

"Yes, my sweet and with God's help we'll keep bread in our mouths despite all this for many years to come."

"I certainly hope so Ben."

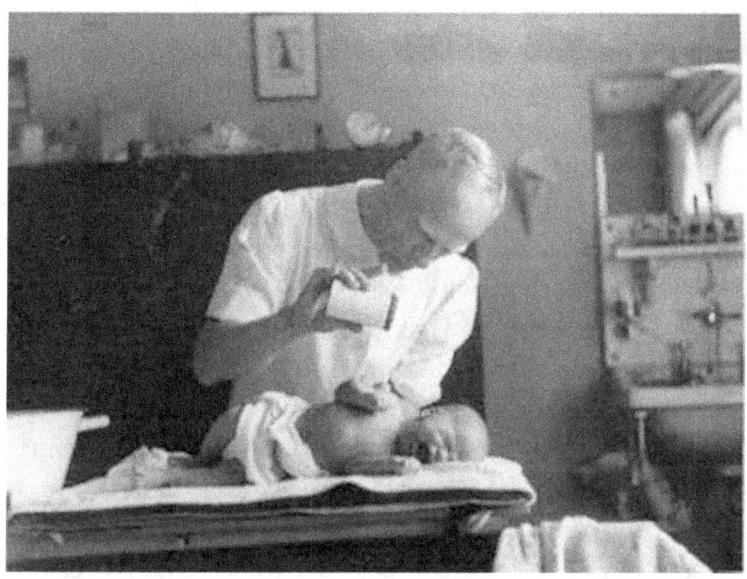

Louis born in August 1943, Ben the midwife. Louis has Haemophila too.

Then one cold November morning, Ben and Em woke to the crackling noise of loudspeakers. They progressively got louder as the sound neared the Bijl home. Ben jumped up with a start. His work for the Underground meant working undercover of night and often late into the night, so as you might expect, Ben did not get up particularly early.

"Lord, what's that racket?" he mumbled as he rubbed his eyes, trying to discern the time. "It's obviously morning and it's a loudspeaker with a message for us."

Gerda also heard the commotion and immediately focused on the loud, heavily accented voice rumbling over the loudspeaker. "What are they saying, Papa? Get ready by eleven o'clock this morning? What's he talking about?"

"I'm not sure, schatje. But that's what I thought he said too."

Understandably, with all the noise, the whole family was awake by then. Gerda raced down the hallway to the windows in the stairwell, with Charles close on her heels.

"Now, children, stay at the stairwell window and don't go downstairs or open the front door, do you hear?" Ben warned.

"Yes, Papa." Gerda sounded annoyed and mumbled under her breath, "We can't do anything around here. Come on, Charles."

"You'd best go downstairs and listen at the front window, Ben," Em said as she hurriedly got out of bed. "We really need to hear it clearly!" "Em, I've heard it clearly already!" He paused, looking for her eyes. "The men of Zeist have been called up to go to the factories and work for them. The Nazis have finally reached us in Zeist. I knew it must eventually affect us here too. I've heard they have already rounded up close to half a million of our countrymen from larger communities."

"You said it was coming. Each day I have been praying the war will end and it wouldn't get to this. I'm frightened for you, Ben. If they find you, now they will kill you for hiding, you know."

"Don't worry. We know what to do and I am prepared. So are you. You know what to say. All we have to do is keep calm. Remember. Keeping calm will save your husband's life. So far our hiding place has been our Saviour."

She nodded as she clung to him. "But that is easier said than done."

"Yes." He drew in a deep breath, trying to retain his composure for her sake. "Now enough of this. We need to get going and carry out the plan. Can you organize something for me to eat?"

Em rushed out of the room whilst Ben contemplated for a few seconds, and then he too dashed into action. It was seven-thirty. They had plenty of time to prepare—or did they? Maybe that was a ruse to catch men unawares.

*

"O Lord, please let my Ben come through safely today." Em kept praying, but she continued to be distracted. *Now what do I need? Ohh! That's right—some barley, a jug of water, and some matches. I think Ben's got most of the other things he needs already. I must take up some extra blankets for him too. It will be extra cold up there lying still in the dark for God only knows how long.*

That done, Em hurried up to the attic. He was almost ready to go into the wall.

He said, "I'll just rush down and say good-bye to the children for a few minutes. You know - just in case something goes wrong today." Em's eyes registered alarm.

"Now don't worry. I'm sure everything will be okay," he whispered.

She nodded and hurried out of the room, brushing tears from her eyes. A few minutes later she called the children to the dining room for breakfast.

Her husband appeared. "And how are you, Gerda?" He patted her on the head, as he often did. "You haven't got Mama to comb your hair yet. Hurry up and finish your barley. You'll be late for school if you dawdle! Oh, on second thought, perhaps we could let you have the day off today. How's that, sweetie?"

"Really, Papa? Oh, goodie!" Gerda got up to share the good news with her mother, who had now returned to the kitchen.

Ben said, "Hang on, young lady. You must eat all your breakfast first. Now come back and sit down at the table and eat. You too, Charles! That's my good children."

Gerda reluctantly returned to the table with its unsavoury fare sitting there like sticky flour paste waiting to be consumed.

Charles cried and kept regurgitating what he had already tried to swallow. Ben looked at Em, who finally sat down to eat with the children. A look of frustration written all over his face.

"This morning is no different from any other, as you can see, Ben. How he survives is beyond me. He doesn't eat enough to keep a mosquito alive! I think its time for you to go to work. Yes?"

Ben nodded. He kissed his family, hugging them, and disappeared upstairs, saying, "Papa will grab some photos and then I'll be off to town. Bye now." They responded cheerfully, "Bye, Papa."

"Come on, Gerda. Upstairs—get dressed and clean your teeth while Mama feeds Loeki" (Louis' nickname).

"It's all right, Mama. Papa says I don't have to go to school today. So, can I play?"

"Yes of course, dear, but you still need your hair combed. I'll be upstairs feeding Louis if you or Charles want me. Oh, and don't forget, if anyone knocks on the door, neither of you are to unlock and open it. Got it? You come and get Mama."

It was a little after half-past ten. Ben had been cocooned in his hole for a couple of hours already. By then Em had finished nursing the baby. She settled him back in his cot.

She then called from halfway down the stairwell, "Gerda! Come into Mama's room. I'll plait your hair now."

"Coming!"

Gerda skipped into the room, and Em said, "Listen very carefully to me, schatje. This morning the soldiers are looking for Papa. So you must not say anything to them about him. I am going to tell them he's left us. If they ask you where's your father, what will you say?"

"I'll say Papa's not here anymore." She nodded. "I know! I know! He's hiding in the attic really!"

Em looked stunned. "How did you know that, Gerda?"

"Last time the soldiers came, Papa said he was going down the street, but he went upstairs."

"And?"

"Well, I followed him, and he went up into the attic. Then the soldiers came inside looking, but he never came downstairs, so I thought he must have been hiding in the attic."

Em couldn't believe her ears. Her six-year-old daughter knew everything! Thank goodness she had enough understanding to know it must be kept a secret.

"All right! Now remember, Gerda, this is very important. They might take Papa away and we may never see him again if you say he's here. Understand?"

"Yes I really understand, Mama. Really I do."

"Good girl. When they come stay with me and don't say a word, even if the soldiers ask you a question. Just act dumb. Right?" Em picked up the hairbrush and ribbons and commenced plaiting her hair.

A sudden rapping on the front door jerked Em back into fearful reality. "They're early," Em mumbled.

"There's knocking. They must be here, Mama," and Em dropped the half-twisted plait. "You'd better go and answer it."

Em resolutely walked downstairs and answered the door.

"Heil Hitler! Madam, we are here to pick up your husband. He is required by the Third Reich to volunteer. You've heard the loudspeakers this morning.

He should be on the street with his knapsack and ready to leave now. Where is he?"

"My husband left me some months ago. He is not here." Em returned their cold stare.

The officer smirked. "Somehow I believe we've heard this story before." He gave a sideways glance at his companion. "Haven't we, Kurt?"

"Ja, mein Herr, ja!"

"We regret, madam, we must make a thorough search. You understand why, I presume. Many people are not telling us the truth. We will find out for ourselves."

"No doubt you will," Em said icily. She stepped aside as they marched in. Lord please protect him, a voice said within her palpitating heart.

For fully fifteen minutes they ransacked Ben and Em's house, searching thoroughly for the man of the house to no avail. Em and Gerda returned to the main bedroom when the men returned from inspecting the attic.

"Madam, we are leaving now, but be warned once again. If we raid this house and find your husband here, he will be shot on sight for refusing to cooperate with us. And you—you may be sent to Vught for aiding and abetting."

Em kept her eyes averted on the pretence of plaiting Gerda's hair. She did not want them to see the look of exultation in her eyes—again they had failed to suss Ben out!

The soldiers marched down the hall and into the stairwell when Gerda suddenly cried, "Mama!" They didn't find him! They didn't find him!" Em almost had a heart attack. Instinctively Em clamped her hand over Gerda's mouth.

"Shhh! Shhh!" That was all Em could whisper at Gerda's emotional reaction. Did they hear? Their search was unsuccessful, and now, God forbid, has my child innocently given him away?

She hurried down the hall trying to muffle the girl's loud and profuse sobs! She gazed out the first-floor stairwell window. She could see the soldiers. Em wondered, did they hear Gerda's excited cry?

She heard the young soldier saying, "Did the child say they didn't find him? Perhaps we should check again." He turned back. Em's heart froze. Were they coming back to take a closer look?

The sergeant, being a more mature man, smiled at the youth's conscientious question, much to Em's surprise. Perhaps, he had a family too at home, but he just brushed the lad's comment aside and said. "I don't think so, Kurt. They're just glad we've gone. Let's move on." Em reconsidered her first impressions of the Sergeant. Perhaps at heart, he was glad they did not find Ben. It would not do to give the impression he was ignoring his orders, especially with a young soldier who had been systematically taught the rightness of the Hitler Regime, was with him. She sensed his humanity, despite the terrible stresses of war and loyalty thrown upon soldiers at such times.

At this point Em's legs felt like they were collapsing under her. She sat on the stairs for a moment to recover. Then she walked down to the open front door and looked outside onto the streetscape.

A military truck, with a dingy-looking canvas cover over an iron frame on its back, stood idling menacingly in the middle of the cordoned-off street, and a number of very hunched over men in great coats sat in the truck, while others of the neighbours were getting into it with their sparse belongings. Various other military personnel stood around with rifles in readiness. Wives and children stood around crying and embracing their loved ones. Although Em registered this was happening, her mind was arguing—this isn't true!

She backed away from the open door and shut it resolutely, as if trying to forever wipe away the vision she had just seen. Tears darted down her cheeks.

The truck and its entourage moved a little farther down the street, and all the while Gerda perched on the front window seat, prattling on like a news reporter.

"Mr. van der Molen is coming out now, Mama. He has a bag and a blanket. Ohh, and look—there is Mrs. van der Molen! She's crying! Why is she crying so, Mama? Now the soldiers are making him get into the truck with the other people ... but I don't know exactly who they are. It's pretty dark inside there. Ollie and Hans are hanging on to his hands. Ohh! They too are crying. Why are they crying so much? Isn't he going to come home soon?" Silence.

Then Em forced herself to answer. "Gerda, remember what I told you earlier about Papa?"

"Yes."

"Well, their fathers have been taken away to work for the German army. They don't want to go either but are more afraid of the Nazis than Papa is. That's why they allowed the soldiers to take them away."

"So that's why their children are so sad and crying. So would I be if they took my Papa!" There was silence while she digested what her mother had explained and then added, "But they will come home one day, won't they?"

"I certainly hope so, schatje. We hope so." Gerda's eyes filled with tears. Silence reigned but not for long. Em stared into space, trying to blot out the scene Gerda had so graphically described. She was asking herself, What more can we do to preserve our family? Will we succeed in avoiding the enemy?

She was startled back to reality when she heard the front door open again. Then she saw the flash of Gerda's red ribbons flying though the front door. "I'm going out to the gate, Mama, because I can't see what's happening anymore."

Em leapt up, Charles sliding down her fullskirt onto the floor. She ran to the door, calling, "Gerda! Gerda! Don't you leave our yard! Do you hear me, child? Stay in our frontyard, both of you," as Charles and his teddy bear followed suit. When she had satisfied herself that they would obey, she turned back into the house, making for the kitchen. It was time for a cup of "tea."

During the afternoon, with the children's help, she was able to keep an eye on the events developing on the street. When she was convinced that they had left, and only after all the windows and doors were locked and covered with blankets did she dare to give Ben the "all clear" signal. Em quietly approached Ben's hiding place and whistled the family's secret code, the bird whistle. In the tiny area about 1.2 metres wide and approximately 1.2 metres high at its highest point, Ben had sat or lain down most of the day. After a long hard stretch Ben proceeded to come out.

Planks flew off the wall. Ben stumbled out. He grabbed Em in an enormous bear hug, lifting her off her feet. "You were great, schatje. Great! I promised you I would never leave you or my children and I won't." Then he looked into Em's eyes and saw she was in a state of shock. The day had taken its toll. Suddenly the tears began to fall.

After comforting her, Ben suggested, "Let's find something to drink and tell me exactly what happened today, every tiny detail. I strained my ears until it hurt, but I could only catch what they actually said when they came to the attic."

"Wow, I wish I could have been there with you to see all this, schatje," Ben said almost wistfully. "But I guess I should be thankful that I'm still here and not on my way to Germany. You say Mr. van der Molen and Mr. de Fries were amongst those they rounded up? I wonder will we ever see them again?" Ben shook his head sadly, giving a silent answer to his own rhetorical question.

History revealed that of the half-million men taken to Germany from The Netherlands, only a handful returned from the forced-labour camps.

Ben's actual hiding place looking from inside the attic

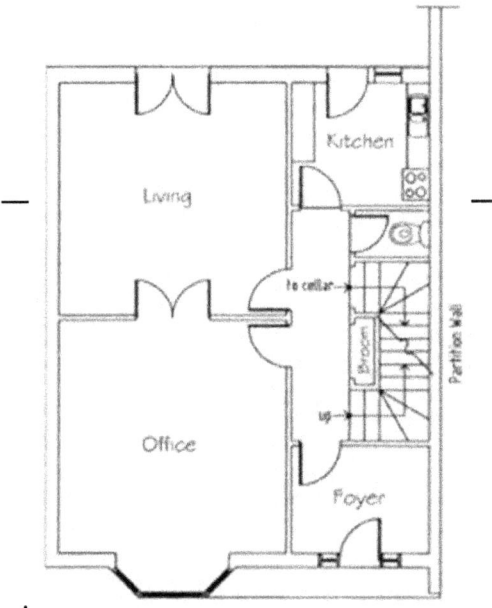

First Floor

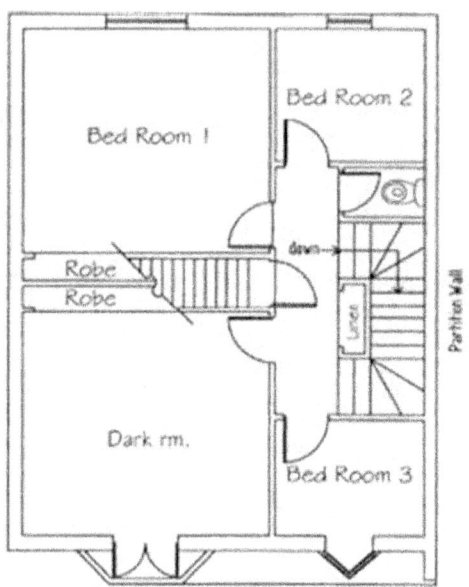

Second Floor

Plan of Veldheimlaan 20

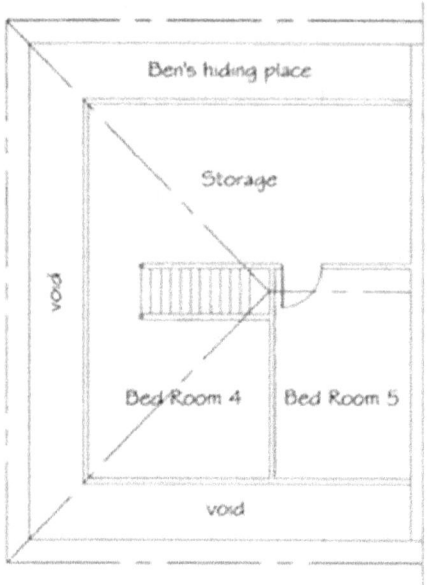

Attic

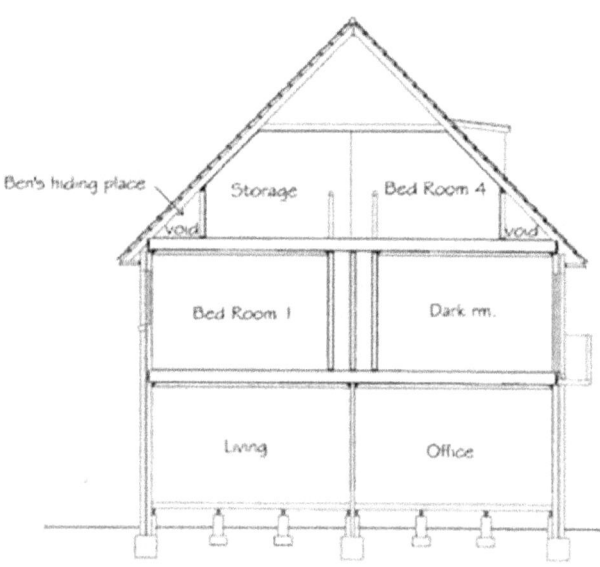

Section

Plan and Section of Veldheimlaan 20

CHAPTER 16

A People Betrayed

Christmas and St. Nicholas Day had passed with people everywhere praying it would see the end of the dreadful carnage that war had brought not only to Europe but to much of the world.

A knock on the door came. Ben had prearranged to be "out of circulation" until things quieted down, not even circulating as the midwife due to the extreme danger he was now in. Em, still masquerading as the deserted wife, moved to answer it. After making sure Ben was "safe," she finally approached the front door.

By this time, there had been several loud knocks. When she opened the door, a friendly face reeled back and swivelled around on his heel. He had just begun to walk away. It was the local postman, but he didn't call very much these days.

"Good day, madam. I thought no-one was home," the young postman said, smiling broadly at her.

"I'm sorry, Mr. de Jong, I was busy with the baby. You have mail for me?"

"Yes, madam. Here." He handed her a bulky white envelope. Jumping out of the bottom right-hand corner was:

AAA Bijl Photographer Hoofdweg 88, Amsterdam
"Thank you, sir. Good day!"

Em looked at the addressee more closely, wondering if she had imagined it. Her eyes were not the best without her spectacles. Trembling now, she prayed, "Please don't let it be what I think it is … bad news?" Very little mail circulated these days, and when it did, it was usually not good news.

Hurriedly she signalled Ben with their all-clear bird whistle. While he was coming, she found her glasses and bid him come into the kitchen for the coffee time, after which she anxiously opened the letter, which was indeed from Ben's parents and yes it was addressed to Mr. and Mrs. GBH Bijl.

Ben leaned over her shoulder, also anxious to hear what news the letter contained. Em read aloud,

> "Our dear Ben and Em,
>
> It is with unbelievable sadness that we write to you. Your Uncle Kees has been arrested by the Nazi SS troopers and taken to the Vught Concentration Camp. Auntie Greet is now staying with us until we have further news of his fate.
>
> You would not have been aware of it, for obvious reasons, but Uncle Kees and Auntie Greet had been hiding their long time Jewish friends, Mr. and Mrs. Joiakim, with them in their house, here in Amsterdam. Apparently, they have secretly hidden them for the last eighteen months.
>
> Two weeks ago, Kees and Greet went to visit your cousin Willie and Jannie, his wife, and the grandchildren. It appears that while they were away, someone discovered they had been hiding people and alerted the Gestapo.
>
> Greet feels it may have been their neighbours who alerted the Nazis.
>
> The following day, Monday the fifteenth, quite early in the morning they arrived and found the Joiakims' hiding place and took them away. And afterward, when Uncle Kees returned home they arrested him and carted him off to Vucht, even though he is a very old man. Auntie Greet says he stood calmly as they placed him under arrest. Greet said she ran to him, but they would not even let her say good-bye.

But I am proud to have such a man, my brother, and Greet, his wife, in our family. Anyway, Ben, we do hope this letter finds you, Em, and the children, especially our youngest grandchild, Louis, coping with the food shortages. The food lines are almost endless these days, and we can stand all day sometimes and receive nothing or just a cup or two of watery turnip soup or sometimes we think its perhaps boiled tulip bulbs.

Mama, Auntie Greet, Guda, and Leni join with me in sending you all our love and best wishes. Kisses and hugs for our precious Gerda, Charles, and Louis. May God be with all of you.

All our love

Papa and Mama."

Ben ran his hands through his receding hair. Em wept silently. After what seemed like minutes, he suddenly voiced his feelings. "Those poor Jewish people—and poor Uncle Kees!"

"Did you know them at all?" Em enquired.

"Not very well, although at parties when I was growing up, I recall meeting them. They seemed to be nice people. The only thing that can save them now is if the war ends very, very soon."

Ben sat contemplatively for a few minutes, and then he burst out in anger and righteous indignation. "If I could just get my hands on those NSBers! Ahh!" His nostrils flared as they always did when he was upset, and his eyes darkened and finally in utter frustration he pounded on the wooden table. Brooding.

Em patted him on the shoulders. "But Ben, just remember, two wrongs never make a right!"

"No, no, I know, Em, you're right, but at this moment if I could get my hands on one of them, well, I don't trust myself to do what's right. Why? Why does God let these things happen?"

CHAPTER 17

A Joyful Wedding

The new year was ushered in without rejoicing. In the middle of January, Ben came downstairs. "You're looking worried," Em said. "What news today?"

"According to the BBC, the tide is certainly turning against Hitler. But the big question is, how much longer can we survive on just fresh air?"

"Oh, Ben, we have to. Every day now I wonder where our next meal will come from."

"Mmm." Ben suddenly lapsed into quiet solitude, saying nothing. "This life is making a man old before his time." Ben ran his fingers through his thinning hair and down his face, the hallstand mirror unkindly revealing the fine lines beginning to surface.

Presently the brass doorknob began to thud, heralding another visit. Em jumped up, anxious as usual. "Who is it this time?" The unpleasant feeling of turning and knotting in her stomach resurfaced in the ever present grip of fear.

She met Ben at the hallstand and quickly whispered, "I'm going to answer the door. Quickly now, upstairs in case it's trouble. I'll try and delay them if it's another search."

Ben quickly aroused himself from his brooding and quietly slipped past the front door and sallied forth up the stairs, silent as a shadow. When she was convinced he was out of sight, Em looked discreetly behind the curtain to see who stood knocking.

No need for fear, it was the friendly postman again. Em quickly opened the door. His wide smile greeted her as she swung the door open wide.

"Mrs. Bijl, mail for you." He handed her a pale pink envelope. "I trust I bring you and your family good news."

"Good day, Mr. de Jong, and many thanks." Em's face broke out into a smile as she turned the soft envelope over in her hands. "Yes, it's from Mama. I'd say it's Jannie and Gerrit's wedding invitation." Excitedly she pulled the envelope apart and pulled out the folded sheet, opening it. Yes, it was Jannie's invitation!

"Yes sir, it's good news, my younger sister's wedding invitation!" Em responded cheerfully. "Thank you for being the bearer of good tidings." Em closed the door and raced up the stairs, calling, "Ben, Ben! It's okay, just mail. And it's good news, Jannie and Gerrit's wedding invitation.

The fifteenth of May in Chaam. And guess what? Jannie and Gerrit are asking if Gerda could be a flower girl and Charles the pageboy!"

"But what are they going to wear, Em?" Ben asked, rolling his eyes. "At this moment, we are paupers."

"Oh, don't worry, Ben, I'll make something for them out of something else. You'll see. Haven't you heard necessity is the mother of invention? Oh! Jannie said in this little attached note that Gerrit was able to borrow a beautiful old carriage for the wedding couple and the children to ride into the town hall for the civil ceremony, and then to the church and finally back to the farm for the afternoon tea. Isn't that special? Do you think we will all be able to get there, Ben? Really?" Then she added, "Please dear God, let us make it. Let something good and joyful happen in our lives."

"You're so right. How nice to receive good news for a change! It's going to be a real challenge getting all of us to this affair schatje," Ben said as he handed the invitation back to his delighted wife, "but I know how much this means to you and your family, so we'll just have to find a way."

*

After devouring the Telegraaf one morning, Ben sighed. "I don't know, if this war doesn't end soon, Em, we are all of us going to starve."

Em looked at him with pursed lips and sad eyes. What could she say? It was all true.

"I'm blowed if I know how we are going to have some food to take with us, let alone get to Chaam in this situation." Ben scratched his head, and then got up, hands on hips, staring out the kitchen window.

Em watched him from the table where she was trying to make an outfit for Charles to wear to the wedding. "Oh, Ben, you worry so." Em shook her head in disapproval. "Food is the least of our concerns at Mama's farm. It may be plain, but she will have something far better than we can find."

She observed him. He looked like a volcano, a little smoke coming from the top, with no-one knowing when or if he would explode that day or the next month. But, she thought, what can I do to change things? This is bigger than all of us! It's one day at a time.

Ben continued to relate what news the Allies had shared in the secret broadcasts, which he avidly listened to via his crystal set each morning. "You know how earlier in the war the Brits utilized the cover of night to relentlessly bomb German targets? Now since the American Air Force's entry into the war, they use another tactic, which is called 'pin point bombing.'"

"What's that?" Em asked raising her eyes in question at her husband, who had turned around and was now facing her as he spoke.

"This differs from the British approach in that the Americans fly at higher altitudes and drop their bombs during the day, on important targets. The obviously clearer vision allows them greater success in hitting their targets. Remember in February they bombed German aircraft industries with overwhelming success? This was followed up with putting all their raw materials out of supply. That's why they're bombing all the dams in Germany. This puts all their electricity plants out of operation, and of course they have always tried to target fuel supplies."

"Do you think at last the Allies are ascending? It looks like it to me." Em looked hopefully at her husband for his reply.

"Yes, and let's pray that it won't be too long. Am I hungry!" Em laughed at Ben's humour.

"I'm not being funny really. Em, I'm dead serious!" He opened the cupboard and shut it again. "Old habits die hard. Things are pretty bad when you go to the cupboard and it's empty! It's not natural. You must be able to hear my stomach rumbling from over there."

"I can't actually, but I can hear mine," Em replied. She was just putting the finishing touches on a small pair of trousers. "Well, how do you think Charles will look in this little jacket and pants?" She held up a little black vest and pants she had made from a suit from Ben's wardrobe.

"He'll look great, Em. You amaze me! What you can't do with a piece of material, some scissors, and thread."

"Do you recognize it? I cut up one of your old suits."

"That's fine. I guess old Ben will have to go in his underpants now, won't he?" Ben's eyes were dancing once again, which they rarely did these days. "I have got my wedding suit left, haven't I?" he asked, teasing.

Em was laughing now too. "Yes, my love, we haven't quite got to that stage yet."

The second week of May 1944 arrived with much excitement in the Bijl household. Ben had acquired the travel passes from the police station and they were ready. The family walked all the way to the Zeist Railway Station with Ben disguised as Sister Bernadina, carrying a mountain of baggage and pushing the baby Louis in the commodious pram with Charles at his side. Em followed him, supervising Gerda and a mass of other luggage. People would have thought Ben was her mother or perhaps a maid, or at least that was what they were depending on.

They arrived none too soon at the station. The station master announced, "The next train will be leaving Zeist for Utrecht Station in two minutes." From Utrecht, which was a major junction in the province, they would change trains and travel south to Breda. They were able to scrape up enough for the train fares. Money in itself was available, but cold cash could not put food or other necessities on the table at such a time as this.

As the family settled in on the train, the children, full of excitement, asked lots of questions. "What's that?" and "Why is that man walking across the railway track? Isn't that dangerous?" and so on as they kept looking out the windows and pointing at all sorts of new places and things. Their short lives hampered by the war, had not seen much outside their local town. Adding to the mêlée was the final whistle call from the station master. At last, a screech of steel as the wheels darted forward and the carriages lurched obediently after them—they were off! "I can't hear myself think anymore," Ben said jovially.

The sleeping baby Louis suddenly stirred from the din around him.

"Wouldn't you know it! Now Louis' awake too!" Em sighed, resigned to a long as well as restless but nonetheless exciting trip.

Gerrit Kleinhout, the groom, was waiting for them at the Breda Railway Station to assist with the luggage and the children. He seemed modelled after the style of Fred Astaire—refined, lean, and angular, not terribly handsome yet very appealing. His face was an open book; honesty and kindness shone from his eyes better than any written testimony to his character could.

"It's great to finally meet you, Em," he said with genuine warmth, kissing her on both cheeks in typical European fashion. "Welcome!"

Em was trying to disentangle herself from luggage and children. She smiled, bending forward, offering her hand and cheek to kiss him.

"And Ben, how are you? Surviving well?" Gerrit whispered.

"Good to see you, Gerrit. Yes, as well as we can be in such difficult times." Ben offered his hand to his future brother-in-law, pleased to note Gerrit had already seen him in his midwife's uniform. "Anyway, Gerrit, you and Jannie getting together is one piece of news that really thrilled us. We couldn't be more delighted! Could we, Em?"

"Yes, Gerrit, we are so happy for you both."

Gerrit said, "It's great all of you could make it. Jannie is so excited! I'm glad you both approve of me too." Gerrit gave a cheeky wink and threw his head back, letting out a mischievous laugh. "Now let me assist with all this luggage. The horse and buggy are out front. Come on!"

He hesitated, turning to them. "Beware—there are guards at all the entrances of the station, checking papers of course." Gerrit quickly relieved Em of her luggage and carried it out to the waiting vehicle.

The entourage approached the soldiers at the main door of the station. One by one they examined the family's papers. Gerrit went through first, since they recognized him as having arrived a little earlier. A perfunctory glance at his papers and he was urged out on to the street ahead. Next came Em. She held out her papers, which also identified the children as hers. The soldiers seemed satisfied and waved them on. Gerda and Charles chattered away on the way out to the buggy, asking a myriad of questions, and Gerrit delighted in answering them.

Then came Bernadina pushing Louis in the carriage.

"You are a long way from home, Sister," the soldier said. "Do you have a baby to deliver here?"

"Oh, no, not this time, sir. I am accompanying Mrs. Bijl since her husband left her some months ago. You can't imagine how difficult it is for a woman on her own."

The guard handed the papers back to Bernadina, looking rather dubious. Then he sighed, perhaps nearing the end of his shift, but he said, "Ah well, off you go."

The almost eleven kilometre drive home to Chaam was slow but exhilarating to Em as she reminisced about her childhood days. Anna, her mother, rushed to welcome her family and greet them at the kitchen door, which generally served as the front entrance into the house. She was especially interested in meeting baby Louis, who was about eight months old. It was a busy afternoon completing the last minute preparations for the wedding.

On the eve of the wedding, the Flach family gathered at the Chaam farm. Quite a few relatives were there, and Anna's house was bursting at the seams with family members. No-one would have thought it was the middle of a war that weekend. They were happy to be together and know they were still surviving despite the ordeals the Occupation had cast upon them. Reminiscing on happier days was good for the spirit. However, for Anna Geertruida, the sadness of losing Johan, her husband, still hung over her head, it being only about a year since. Even sadder for Anna was the memory of their only son, whose absence was accentuated by the arrival of all her living daughters except Francien, for Jannie and Gerrit's wedding.

Anna shed tears in the kitchen whilst the others laughed in the lounge. For Jannie's sake, she put on a brave face when she returned to the living room.

Although the Saturday turned out to be a rather cold, grey, late spring day, the family's excitement was not dampened. Gerrit had driven into town with Gerrit de Graaff in the morning to pick up the magnificent black carriage and horses to carry his bride, Jannie, as well as her party.

"Auntie Jannie, you look so beautiful today," Gerda said, head cocked to one side as she studied her aunt's lovely satin gown, borrowed from one of her sisters. Her delicate golden curls surrounding the soft beauty of her eyes, cheeks, and ruby lips. Jannie blushed with pleasure.

"And you and Charles, Gerda also look great."

Jannie had coached Gerda and Charles on how to act for the wedding ceremony, and soon the beautiful old coach arrived and took them to the town hall, and then on to the church. Storm clouds had gathered by the time the bridal party returned from the marriage ceremony to the farm in the carriage. All were eager for the wedding reception. It was really an afternoon tea.

The family then gathered for the family photos, which Ben delighted in taking. As the happy couple and the children alighted from the carriage, the extended family formed a guard of honour for them to walk under along the narrow lane that led to the farmhouse.

"Proud of your children, Mr. Bijl?" Em whispered to her husband as he was taking photos, rushing from here to there with obvious ease, immensely enjoying his work.

Ben's eyes twinkled. "They look like little angels. It's a pity I know better." He then laughed roguishly at the look of surprise in his wife's eyes.

Jannie and Gerrit's wedding in Chaam, May 1944

"They look beautiful!" she retorted. "And so does my little Loeki"—don't you, my sweet?" Louis wore a beautiful cape and hood, which Em had made for him.

Ben turned abruptly from the bridal party and said, "Smile for Papa, Loeki! Smile! We must have a photo of you and Mama too." Ben dressed in his male attire at Chaam, since it is a tiny village and far away from the bulk of the population, so it was not kept under surveillance to the degree of large cities. But he, along with any men without permits, had to keep an eagle eye out for Nazis.

The family then moved on to the farmhouse for the wedding reception. Food was scarce, but they all scrounged around in their own areas and tried to bring a little something, which when combined with other small items could be made into something special for the reception. It was a delightful day for all. About five in the evening, the family rose to wave the newlyweds farewell as they took the carriage for one more ride to the railway station and a short trip for their honeymoon.

Em embraced her sister. "All the best, Jannie. You have a wonderful man there. I'm sure you will be so happy together, and I am particularly happy that you are going to live in Breda because we will be able to see both Annie and you. I have missed being close to any of my sisters since we moved to Zeist, but your living in Breda with Annie will be great!" They hugged one another, lingering over the parting.

Eager to get going Gerrit said, with a proud and adoring smile, "Well, Mrs. Kleinhout, are you ready to leave?"

Jannie blushed slightly and smiled lovingly into her husband's eyes. "Yes, my schatje. I'm ready."

He took her arm and led the way to the sleek carriage amidst the resounding voices of loved ones shouting farewell.

*

Anna took Ben, Em, and the children the following Tuesday back to the Breda Railway Station.

"Good-bye, my dear girl," Anna said, hugging Em. "Please take care. And thank you, Ben, for coming with your family for Jannie's wedding. It was lovely despite all the problems we have had to contend with, wasn't it?"

"Yes, Mama, it was a lovely family gathering. Thank you." Ben kissed his gentle mother-in-law and added thoughtfully, "As soon as the war is over, you must come and stay with us, Mama. Yes?"

"Yes, Ben, I would love to," Anna said, smiling approvingly.

As they were boarding the train, she whispered to Em, "Watch out for Bernadina, Ma. She might steal your husband!"

Em laughed, surprised to see such humour coming from her mother. "In truth, Mama, you're spot on. Bernadina has already had a couple of proposals from older men—some honourable and others not so honourable. Curse her fatal charm."

"Really? Is it true, Ben?" Anna asked incredulously. "Tell me she's having me on!"

Ben sidled up to her and whispered, "Look at me, Mama. They just can't resist me!"

"Oh, you are incorrigible, Ben!" Then seriously, Anna said to Em, "I can see now you were right about Ben—he is one of those characters one reads about but never believes is real. I've never met a man like him." She stopped and looked at Ben again. "You said he was a good man, and I see now you were right!"

Ben was beaming, but tears sprang into Em's eyes. "Thank you, Mama."

The train travelled along the top of wide dykes, as most trains in The Netherlands do, as it hurried north toward its destination. At some of the railway stations, there was evidence of recent skirmishes, but thankfully this section of the country was not badly affected by bombings, being mainly farming polders. It was the industrial areas that were targeted, because naturally the German army had tried to preserve most of these farm areas for their own use.

When the train had travelled about halfway between Breda and Utrecht, the sound of airplanes whirring in the distance caused great alarm to all the passengers, since trains were often the targets of passing enemy planes.

Ben squirmed in his seat, trying to look out the window to see where the planes were coming from. "My God, Em, let's hope they don't start firing on us schatje," he whispered.

She immediately stiffened, although she made no reply, not wanting to frighten the children. Even so, Em's eyes spoke volumes—fear.

"I can hear planes, Mama. Can you hear them? They are very close!" Gerda was up and straining past her father, trying to catch some of the action. "Where are they?"

Almost immediately the train came to a shuddering, screeching halt as the steel wheels dragged on the tracks amid a flotilla of sparks. In the next second, loudspeakers crackled forth instructions: "Please remain calm and listen carefully! We repeat, please remain calm and listen carefully! All passengers are asked to evacuate the train immediately. Please move down the grassy slopes of the dyke as quickly as possible in order to hide amongst the trees at the bottom of the dykes! Hurry now! We repeat, please evacuate this train immediately!"

Children who had been sleeping awoke and began to scream. Adults white with fear tried to calm them. People scattered in all directions down the grassy slopes.

Meanwhile, the planes, which were identified as German Luftwaffe, swooped low, sending anti-aircraft fire crackling above the frightened passengers' heads. However, on that occasion, although it shook everyone up, especially those with little children, no-one was actually injured.

After some time of anxious waiting, the train's guard announced: "It is now safe to return to the train. Would everyone please return to the train as quickly as possible? Thank you. Please hurry, as we are now off our time schedule and will be arriving later in Utrecht than originally planned. Thank you everyone for your cooperation."

"Why did those planes shoot at us, Papa?"

Ben grabbed her hand and whispered, "Don't call me Papa, my sweet. We don't want anyone to recognise me." He looked keenly into her eyes and added, "Understand?"

Suddenly serious, she nodded and said, "Yes, sorry, I forgot." Just as quickly, she continued with her inquisitive prattle. "So why did they shoot at us?"

"I don't know, sweetheart. Now just be quiet and hurry back with us up the hill. There's a good girl." He grabbed her hand as he urged her on whilst carrying Charles in his other arm. Em struggled up the steep embankment with Louis in her arms.

"Well, I'm thankful nothing untoward happened today," Ben commented discreetly to Em as they settled back into the carriage.

"It all seems so senseless. Firing on civilian trains and people who are obviously not military personnel. Why do they do this?" Em was fuming. Her head was beginning to ache.

"Who knows? Will we ever know the mind of such fiends? Perhaps it was just a scare tactic, once they really saw the train was a passenger train full of civilians."

The rest of the journey was peaceful, and within an hour they were changing trains in Utrecht for Zeist. The guards at the station satisfied themselves that all was in order with the family's papers and allowed them to pass through onto the street. Half an hour later, the Bijl family arrived, very thankfully, at Veldheimlaan 20.

"It's good to be home," Em sighed as they walked inside. "I'm tired. It was a lovely few days, wasn't it? I'm so happy Jannie and Gerrit are moving to Breda. It's very close to Princenhage, such a beautiful part of The Netherlands."

"Yes, I did have some vague recollection that it was in the Breda district." Ben smiled at her. "You really loved that place, didn't you?"

"Yes. But I'm not sorry I left it. I found you! I even think I'm a little jealous. Jannie and Annie will be able to do so much together. I wish it was nearer to us."

"A man has enough trouble getting his wife to do the housework now, let alone when she's gadding about with her sisters!" Their eyes met. She saw him trying to keep a poker face, but his dancing eyes betrayed him every time.

Em laughed. "And wouldn't I enjoy it!"

CHAPTER 18

Trouble Comes in Threes

"Finding food," Ben complained, "is like looking for a needle in a haystack these days!" He shook his head. What more can we do?"

Em stared out the kitchen window, washing the breakfast dishes. Her silence was deafening.

"Anyway, dear. I'm upstairs for an hour or so. A man's got work to do." Ben patted his wife affectionately as he turned on his heel and walked quickly through the gallery kitchen into the hall, leading to the front door and the upstairs stairwell.

Some months had passed since the memorable wedding. Em was engrossed in thoughts of the wonderful days spent with her loved ones in an effort to eliminate the pressing problems of their daily lives.

The telephone rang in Ben's office. She jumped awkwardly, almost dropping the plate she was wiping. She hurried down the narrow passage to the office. "Good morning! Em Bijl speaking. May I help you?"

Gerrit's voice drifted down the line from his office. "Hello, Em. It's Gerrit. How are you all?" As it is today, landline phones were operational even if electricity was not available to the home. Gerrit rang from his office phone.

Em was surprised because usually it was Jannie who rang. She very much enjoyed the close association they had been sharing. "Gerrit! It's great to hear from you! How are you both?" For a few moments there was silence.

"Well, Em, that's why I'm ringing—my beautiful Jannie took ill last week. The doctor says she has polio." Em understood how serious polio was.

"Gerrit, that's dreadful. How is she? Recovering a little?" She hesitated and then added positively, "Jannie's young and strong. I'm sure she'll come through it all right, Ger."

"I keep praying you're right, Em, but …" His voice fell away. "Yes, Gerrit?" She waited with bated breath.

"Well … to add my concern—she's pregnant."

Em gasped hard. A feeling of dread enveloped her as the seriousness of the situation registered in her brain. "Gerrit, no! So how is she?"

"That's why I'm ringing. The doctor has been here, and he has done everything he can to help, but to date she is not responding. It's almost a week now since she contracted this terrible polio."

"What are you trying to tell me? She'll be all right, won't she?"

"We hope so, but as you well know, there is no cure for polio. We just wait and see if Jannie is strong enough to fight through it. I'm so worried. She's getting weaker each day, and I can't do a thing about it!" Em listened to her brother-in-law in horror as she realized he was crying.

"What can I do? Is there anything we can do to help you or dear Jannie?"

"No, Em. The doctor feels we can only wait. Annie, your sister, is with her. All we can do is pray that she'll pull through—the fight is with her. My poor schatje."

The next morning the phone rang early. Em pounced on it, a feeling of foreboding rushing upon her. She immediately recognised Gerrit's voice.

"Oh Gerrit! How is she?" Her voice was hoarse. She strained into the receiver for news of Jannie and her child.

"She's gone, Em! My precious little bride is gone."

"Oh no! No! No! When Gerrit? When?" Em cried.

"In the early hours of this morning. She slipped away, both her and our baby! How will I ever be able to go on without her? I loved her so much, Em. Tell me it's all a terrible nightmare and that I'll wake up one day and find her alive and well. Oh, Em, how will I live without her?" His heartbreaking sobs sent stabbing pains through Em's heart.

"Gerrit, I am so very, very sorry! Does my mother know?"

"Not yet, Em, but Annie and Gerrit are going to visit her today on my behalf. I feel so much for your dear mother. She hasn't gotten over your father's death yet. It will be heartache upon heartache for the dear woman. Perhaps you could write to her as well. I will of course go to her too, when I am able."

"Of course, Gerrit, I will." Tears rolled down Em's flushed cheeks as she listened to the heartbroken young man on the other end of the phone.

"Em, I must go now as I have others to ring and a funeral to arrange. I'll be in touch," he managed to say, "Bye now."

"Bye, Gerrit. I'm so very sorry." As the phone line died, Em sat in the reception chair. The eerie feeling of numbness took over her shocked senses once again.

When Ben walked into the room, she ran into his arms. "She's gone, Ben. Jannie's dead! How is it possible?"

"I'll make a cup of "tea" Em. Come and sit down." Having drunk the tea in silence suddenly Ben pounded the table with his fists. Shaking his head in disbelief, he cried, "Why does God let the good ones die? Life is so unjust!"

"It's not God's fault. But why, I don't know either," Em said sadly. Bitterness was not in her makeup. Acceptance was.

Some members of the Flach family were able to attend Jannie's funeral. Anna, Em's mother, was absolutely devastated yet again. Only time could ease but never erase—a pain she already knew only too well would never leave her until she herself took her last breath.

*

The Allies were making good progress; having knocked out the supply of German airplanes, they were now in a likely position to retake France. The British, Canadian, and American forces were able to successfully land in France in June, on what was later known as D-Day, about a month after the wedding. And at the time Jannie died, they were moving north. Soon Paris was captured (in August), and the Germans began their retreat. The Dutch people languished, weak but eager to help the Allies succeed.

The October 1, 1944, issue of the Telegraaf contained startling news. Ben read the Telegraaf ritualistically each morning, keeping abreast of the ever-changing tide of the war as much as possible, and listened to the BBC reports. He rushed out to Em with two very important news items.

She was trying with great difficulty to wash nappies in cold water with no soap. Rivulets of blood ran down her fingers as she scrubbed them, trying to get them at least a little clean. The constant rubbing tore her skin, and the daily ritual was her worst nightmare.

"Listen to this, Em. 'In the countryside around Putten and Nijkerk, yesterday there was another skirmish between the Nazis and the Resistance. It appears that a German soldier was killed and another badly injured in the conflict, and the Resistance members and the persons they were trying to help escape got away. It says the people in the district are afraid of reprisal."

"Putten? That's where Cien and Cornelis live. But it would be a long shot if they were in the line of fire," Em said with interest.

"Time will tell, Em, time will tell." Ben shook his head doubtfully.

"The Nazis are not likely to take that lying down. Anyway, we'll see."

"Mmm," Em replied, deep in thought. "That oldest sister of mine is a closed book, Ben. I guess we'll have to wait and see if she contacts us. I hope she would if Cornelis was involved."

"By the way, on a brighter note: as you know, the Polish army was fighting to break through the German lines around Breda. Annie and the two Gerrits must be greatly relieved. It won't be long now, and then it'll be our turn."

"Wonderful news, Ben! I'm so glad something good has happened in that regard." She looked sad, her mind obviously in another place.

The following week's edition of the paper bore the blazing headline "658 Men Taken to Work Camps." Ben quickly read through the article. Nine men were shot as a reprisal. He was horrified.

"Em, here it is! What did I tell you? 658 men and boys between eighteen and fifty have been rounded up from the Putten District and sent to the work camps in Germany as a reprisal for the death of the two Nazi soldiers killed last week. Not only that—"

"Oh, dear God, no! I wonder if—" Em's eyes registered renewed panic.

Ben stopped momentarily and shook his head, doubtful that Em's brother-in-law was safe. He continued. "It says German soldiers and the local police came to Putten because it was the closer of the two nearby towns from where the incident took place—it was out in the country between those towns, apparently.

They ordered all the men and boys to the church and the women and children to the school, saying they would burn down the whole village. At least a hundred houses went up in flames, but the church and school remained. Poor devils! As if things aren't hard enough already in this rotten war."

"So, they let everyone go after destroying their whole life's work in a few minutes!" Em sounded bitter, something she usually was incapable of. "Please let Cien's house be one that didn't go up in the flames!"

"I wish that was all! But no."

Em threw her hands to her head, covering her ears. "No! I don't want to hear it. I knew that was too good to be true." But after a moment she asked, "What happened?"

"The women and children were driven out of the town, but the men were taken to the railway station and herded onto freight cars like cattle. It says about 120 escaped from the train during the trip to Germany, but most of them were shot trying to run for cover."

"Knowing my family's luck, something will happen to Cornelis, poor thing."

"I'll tell you now, Em, it will be well nigh a miracle if any of those 650-odd return home after the war. Their lives aren't worth living."

"I hope Cien's Cor isn't amongst them. I guess she'll let us know. What do you think?" Putten is a country area like Chaam, and many people on farms did not have telephones. Therefore, mail would be the only way to make contact in those areas.

"Yes, I'm sure she will. Now don't worry! I'm sure he'll be all right."

"On the other hand, Cien is such a dark horse. She never keeps in touch with the family, like the rest of us. Perhaps it includes her husband. But she didn't contact us about Jannie's wedding recently— oh, I think its just Cien—she's a loner! Keeps to herself, you know. Funny though."

A week or so after the newspaper report on the Putten disaster, Em and Ben did receive a letter from Cien. Em's blood ran cold.

"Please Ben, will you read this letter? I'm afraid to. She never keeps in touch. I fear the worst." Em sank into the lounge chair waiting for Ben.

He quickly opened the letter, and Em watched the expression on his face.

"Its bad news isn't it? I can tell by the look on your face! Lord, what happened to him?"

Ben kept reading and finally looked up. "In fact, you were right, Em. Cor was amongst the 658 rounded up and taken away."

"Oh, so he's been taken to Germany then. It's not so bad as it could be. Poor Cien."

"I don't know about that, Em." Ben's eyes rushed over the words in front of him. "It's like I said, he'll probably never be seen again. His life is worth absolutely nothing to them." Ben read the letter further:

> "My poor Cor was one of the unfortunates! Little Cor and I are still finding it hard to believe. One day you are minding your own business, and the next day your heart is torn in two!"

Ben stopped reading, observing Em's distress.

Finally, she urged, "Go on, please!"

Ben continued with the unhappy details whilst Em wept. Then she said, "Cien and I have never been close, but my heart goes out to her—poor thing—left now with her only child to rear alone. Thank goodness she is a good tailoress. At least she will be able to make a living. But ..." Em started weeping as she tried to explain about her sister. "But, Ben, what if this was you, and it was me who had been left like that?"

"Now don't worry about such things until you have to!"

Ignoring what Ben said, Em continued. "They say all sad or painful things come in threes. They were right. First it was Papa. And then it was Jannie—and now Cien's husband. I'm numb, Ben! God forbid, what next could happen?"

"Don't jump to conclusions, sweetheart. If he stayed on the train, he just might return after the war—that is if the end is not too long in coming."

Ben walked sadly toward the stairwell, vehemently shaking his head. "If he returns," he muttered out of earshot, "I'll eat my hat!"

CHAPTER 19

Hungry and Pregnant Again

Em's family had derived joy from Jannie and Gerrit's wedding. Obviously, it was quickly eroded with the terrible news of Jannie and her baby's death, as well as Cornelis' departure to God only knew where in Germany. As the months wore on, there was one thing that helped them cope from day to day. It was the continuing progress the Allies were making from the south.

In the meantime, men especially could not venture outdoors because if they were even seen, they were just picked up by the SS soldiers and taken to wherever the enemy felt help was needed–no exceptions. The German army was desperate for manpower. Now travel between towns was extremely hard and dangerous. Besides this, they lived daily with the fear of falling bombs landing on them, either in their houses whilst they slept or even as they walked down the country lanes in search of food. Especially in the south of The Netherlands, between Rotterdam and Arnhem, it was dangerous. Zeist lay almost on the route of the daily line of travel of bombers from Britain to Germany.

Many nights Ben stood with Gerda and Charles up in the attic, and they would look out the window and see myriads of planes going over. "What are those lights moving backward and forward across the sky, Papa?" Gerda asked incredulously.

"They are search lights, Gerda," Ben explained. "They light up the sky, and if the army on the ground sees an enemy plane in the lit-up area, they will fire rockets at them." No sooner had Ben finished speaking than the sound of anti-aircraft guns reverberated through the night, and as the bombs hit their targets, a fantastic array of fireworks plummeted from the plane.

"Wow, Papa! Just look at that! It's so beautiful, all those wonderful colours and lights. I'm going to try and draw that tomorrow." Gerda gasped excitedly.

"Yes, it looks fantastic, but it is war, and many good men die in those planes as they fall to the ground, schatje. That means it isn't really nice after all, is it?"

"I guess not, Papa." Gerda contemplated the immensity of what her father had just said. He could almost hear the cogs going over in her young mind. She was going to be seven on her next birthday; she was really beginning to understand. "Like the man in the tree we saw." He nodded.

After tucking his children into bed that night, Ben tapped Em on the shoulder as she was finally dozing off after another lot of planes had crossed over. "Em! Em, I think tomorrow I should build an escape route in the basement. Some of those planes and bombs have been landing too close for comfort. If one should fall on our house, the basement is the only place we might be protected, but if the house fell in on it, we would not be able to escape through the stairs because of the debris."

Em's ears registered what he was saying, but tiredness swirled around in her head like water gurgling down a drain. He sounded so distant; she thought she was dreaming.

At breakfast the next morning, Ben broached the subject again. "As I was trying to tell you last night, I'm going to make an escape hatch down in the basement today."

"What are you talking about?" Em looked at him vaguely.

"I guessed as much when you didn't answer me last night. I decided to let you sleep, you poor dear. All these sleep interruptions certainly make you weary, don't they?"

"You're so right!" Em yawned. "What do you propose to do?"

"I'm going to build a ramp up to the cellar windows and replace the windows at the top of the ramp with a hopper-type window that we can hopefully wind open and crawl through to the backyard if needed." There were fairly narrow windows just above ground level in the cellar.

"Wonderful idea! But we can't afford to buy timber. Where will you get some to build it?"

"Never you mind, Em. I'll find something. If I can't buy any, I may have to borrow some from an already bombed house. But I must get some today and get into that job immediately before something terrible happens."

A couple of hours passed. Ben struggled up the driveway, pulling some planks on the end of the bicycle. Ben incognito as the "old midwife" pulling planks on the back of his bicycle was quite amusing! The ordinary people at that time didn't take much notice of men or women doing things out of character, since life was so abnormal anyway. The only thing they could do was acknowledge the humour in it and laugh.

"If you could only see yourself, Bernadina! How about a cuppa?"

"Why thank you, Em. I hope it will help you, dear, since that rotten husband of yours took off. We poor women have to do men's work, don't we?"

Em nodded, trying to look sad and angry but bursting inside with amusement at his antics.

Bernadina carefully stacked the wood at the back door and went off again. In a short time, "she" returned with more, also depositing them. By mid-afternoon, she had enough timber to build the ramp.

"You'd better come in for something to eat, dear," Em said as Bernadina finished unloading. "You must be starving!"

"I am, Em. I am! What's for lunch?"

"Come into my restaurant and let me tempt you with the menu," Em added as she walked inside. "You can have barley or barley or barley…"

"How exciting!" Ben said under his breath as he washed his hands in the kitchen sink at the back door. "I can't wait!"

"Oh, and there's another letter from your parents."

Ben ripped open the envelope anxiously, before he would eat. He was worried about his sons and the rest of the relatives in Amsterdam. In the big cities, conditions were even worse than in the outlying areas. There was so little food in Amsterdam that food kitchens were set up to help prevent starvation.

In part, the letter read:

"Miep, her parents, and your boys are fine.

Thankfully, although Miep's family has a Jewish background and a wealth of money, they meet the requirement of being more than four generations in The Netherlands, and thus their bloodline will not come against them. So your boys are safe, Ben. Also, they are still relatively better off than we are because of their high connections, and I wonder perhaps if it is not with the opposers to the House of Orange. Although having said that, I am not really sure if that is the true situation. Hopefully I misjudge them in that, but whatever the reason, so far, they are all right.

The majority of people these days are like us—living from hand to mouth. Now if it weren't for the soup kitchens, we would literally be starving to death. To conserve on energy, often one person from a family will spend the whole day standing in a food line, hoping for a meagre ration to be doled out to them. We are hopeful too that those in line will not be told to go home because the day's supply of watery soup or straw bread has already run out! I believe its more saw dust than straw!

If the volunteer for the family strikes it lucky, he will still come home with precious little to share with the other members of his household. Try sharing one small loaf of this 'bread' with six or more family members. Consider too that that one small loaf—for the whole family—is all they will have to eat for the whole twenty-four-hour period or often longer if food runs out! Nothing is left—no coal, no coke (a form of roasted coal), no wood, and no electricity is available for warming, and little can be purchased by way of warm blankets or clothing. Trees are becoming as scarce as hens' teeth.

Generally, the rest of the family as of this winter are only able to survive by going to bed all day and trying to sleep while one member haunts the line. They try to spread out consuming one slice of bread through out the whole day in order to stave off the hunger pangs, letting it dissolve in their mouth. In the very last few months, city dwellers have become so weak that they can hardly get out of bed to go and stand in a food line. Little children often stand, many bare-foot and under-dressed, waiting to get a handout. It's heart-breaking to see!"

Granted, Ben and Em's situation was not as bad as Ben's family in Amsterdam, where it was even more dangerous to be seen in public if you were a man—even older men.

Ben said, "The local paper says it appears the Government will turn a blind eye to anyone cutting down trees on the sidewalks. Well, it goes without saying why people are doing that, doesn't it? How else are the poor things going to keep from freezing to death this winter? You can't blame them, can you?"

"No, you can't. But where, I ask, will it all end?" Em was mending some of the children's clothes. "Are you going to run the risk of being caught to get some wood for us? I don't think you should—at least not while we can still use the electricity."

"Tell you the truth, Em, I feel like running the risk to help us, yes, but then I think of all the other poor souls who can't do it for themselves—you know, like the old lady I've been giving food and a little wood to already. She has no family, no-one to look after her. Shouldn't I help her too? Maybe I will."

Em stopped sewing and surveyed her handiwork. She had woven such neat little basket-weave stitches in and out to fill in the holes. "I know what you say is true, but we can't help them all."

During the next week or so, Ben slipped out at extreme risk, with the intention of cutting down trees and giving some of the wood to the elderly neighbours around them. Em was in a panic when he did not return too early. Eventually though, Ben knocked on the backdoor just as curfew was commencing.

"Thank goodness you're home! I was getting worried, Ben."

"Yes, Oudje. Remember me? I'm a hard man to catch." He seemed quite jovial as he removed his hat and great-coat. He risked being "himself" to do it and that was extremely foolhardy in his wife's mind. "I hope that doesn't mean you were almost caught," Em ventured.

"No, not this time, schatje, although some one taking my photo while I was in the act of felling the tree didn't impress me too well. I just hope they were anti-Nazis, or I'm going to be in for it."

(Interestingly, in 2004, a documentary by the BBC called The World at War featured an episode on the Occupation of The Netherlands. There was movie footage of people cutting down trees for firewood. And right at the front, cutting up the tree after it fell into the street, was Ben Bijl.) A grimace spread across Ben's face, as if the thought was possible. Quickly though, he tried to allay Em's fears. "Is there anything to eat? I'm freezing and starving!"

"Sit here and try to warm up while I get some hot broth for you.

There's not much in it, but it is hot and will warm you up a little."

Ben nodded enthusiastically, rubbing his hands together, trying to restore the circulation.

"Meantime, here is a mug of hot water to sip." Em patted him on the shoulder as she handed him the mug. "My, Ben, you are half-frozen."

"So, give a thought to the elderly and babies who haven't got electricity as we have. Things are tough in the Bijl household, but others are far worse, believe me."

Em nodded, feeling somewhat guilty. "I'm glad you care about others, but it doesn't prevent me from worrying about what could happen to you, you know. I thank God every day we still have my bicycle."

"And I agree, but as it stands, even that is at risk now. Food is getting harder and harder to find, and it takes longer and longer trips away from the towns to get any. The Germans take every, last bit they can get their hands on from the southern polders for their soldiers."

"And of course, the other thing is that people are getting weaker by the day from malnutrition, so they can't walk far for food if it can be found either. Realistically it must soon end, Ben, or we'll die."

"We won't give in yet. The end is in sight! Be positive!" Ben sat warming himself, anxious for nourishment. "Now is that broth hot yet?"

She handed a bowl of steaming watery soup to him. She saw the look on his face, and said, "You said to think positively. Now eat up!

Imagine it's creamy mussel soup."

He gave a contemptuous laugh. "Touché, Em!"

*

Around the time the news from Putten filtered through in 1944, Ben hurried into the bedroom, highly excited to share some good news with Em.

"Em! They've done it! The Americans and Canadians have taken back Belgium and are now flooding north. They're passing into The Netherlands right now! Do you hear?"

Em sighed with relief. "That means it really will be over soon, thank goodness—thank you, God!"

"Prince Bernhard has asked all those loyal to the House of Orange to unite with a rail strike, in order to further cripple Hitler's efforts to keep the war ongoing."

"That's a pretty brave thing to do, Ben. What if the Germans just line the strikers up and shoot them?"

"I guess that's a risk we'll have to take. There's not a doubt in the world that they will retaliate harshly. But as Prince Bernhard says, we must stand unitedly against the tyranny even at the risk of our lives. The Trouw encourages us to strike in order to bring the war to an earlier finish. It says the railway workers are determined to carry it through. There'll be skin and hair flying when they do, I'll wager!"

On October 29 news arrived. The Polish Division of the Allies had freed the town of Breda and districts to the south of Zeist. Em and Ben rejoiced that her mother and some of her sisters and their families had seen the end of the Nazi Occupation.

It was about this time Em suspected she was pregnant for the second time during the Nazi Occupation.

Her husband said, looking up from the Trouw, "I wouldn't worry yet, dear, with all the stress we're under, you're probably just a little out of kilter."

"Well, I am feeling queasy. But I'll give it another week or two before I really begin to worry."

Ben smiled broadly. "That's a good girl. You know old Ben loves you, don't you?"

Em's face radiated with warmth yet concern. "Yes, my dear Ben, thank you. I know—it is exactly that—because you love me!" She laughed at and yet feared what his love had done for her. Ben, however, did not appear fazed.

But call it what you will, Em's intuition was correct. A couple more weeks revealed she was pregnant again.

Ben said, "Well, dearest, don't worry, God will provide for one more. Or at least we can see the end just has to be in sight now, surely! That rail strike really set the cat amongst the pigeons, as the saying goes. The British and Americans are fighting right now at Arnhem, trying to take back the bridge. It is vital to the Germans that they control that bridge. If the Brits get it, Germany is on its way out. You were right a few days ago when you said you thought you heard cannon fire. The paper says it can be heard in this district at times. The war is soon going to end, so take heart."

"Let's pray that this infant will be born in a time of peace, for all our sakes." Em stood up as she spoke, a sudden desire to vomit sending her racing for the toilet. "I'm tired of fighting just to keep us alive. Please, dear Lord, let it end soon." She came out of the toilet with tears running down her cheeks, her nausea somewhat relieved, and began to retrace her steps to the empty kitchen.

"Ben, I am anxious to try to get more food. You know how vital nutrition is, especially now I'm pregnant again. I've been thinking about the situation, and what I can do? Do you remember at Jannie's wedding? Mama spoke of her brother, Uncle Adrian. She said he had written and offered to help Mama and her family with food if we could get to him."

"When you consider how far away your mother is, you could safely say he won't be able to help her. It's far away even for us!" Ben replied, a cynical look on his face.

"Well, he may be surprised because I intend to ride to Zwolle and accept his generous offer, Ben."

"Now that's the silliest thing I have ever heard you say, Em Bijl." Ben raised a single eyebrow. It was a really intimidating look indeed. It seemed to almost question his wife's sanity for even thinking about it. However, when the Telegraaf headlines jumped off the frontpage a few days later: "Bread Basket Flooded as Reprisal," Ben was livid—that meant thousands of people in the cities would literally starve that winter. Em stood at the sink looking into the backyard. A single tear rolled down her cheek. With her fourth pregnancy commencing, Em was truly feeling ill. Being deprived of proper nutrients in the first trimester had resulted in extreme morning sickness. She and Ben were thinner than they had ever been. Ben and Em, being only in the thirty to forty age bracket, were probably in their prime, whereas babies and children, and the elderly suffered much more.

"Please, God, give us food before we all starve to death." Em wiped the tear away and kept washing the dishes. "No food, very little heating, and freezing weather—how much more can we put up with? Ben! That does it! I'm going to ride to Uncle Adrian in Zwolle. And don't argue. I've made up my mind."

"Em, your uncle lives more than ninety-five kilometres north-east of Zeist—in Zwolle. Surely you don't really intend riding all that way!" Ben walked out of the narrow kitchen, throwing up his arms in sheer frustration.

"Yes, Ben! I do! And I am! There are few trains running north to Zwolle as you know –and we must save our children. I have no other choice!"

"Em!" Anything could happen to you riding all that way at any time. He stopped mid-stream and walked back to her.

"For God's sake, we are in the middle of a war! Everything about it is dangerous. Don't even think about it. If anyone goes, it'll be me, do you hear?"

Their eyes met. His eyes were piercing; her usually serene expression was gone. Em's eyes flashed. Suddenly they were almost black instead of the sapphire-blue he loved so much. This was a face Ben had never seen, driven by desperation.

"Ben, I know it's a long way, but I am still early in the pregnancy and I still have my bike." Em studied his face with cool determination. "We have no other choice! And," she said, gently caressing his rigid shoulders, "if you are caught, that's it! Your children will never see their father again. With me, at least I am not being hunted. I'm not wanted. They have no reason to do me harm. Perhaps being pregnant will be an advantage."

Ben stared at his wife, admiring her for her courage. He knew when he married Em she was quietly determined. Once again with her back against the wall, she showed she had pluck. He stared out the window, contemplating.

One hundred kilometres in The Netherlands is like asking someone in Australia to ride from Sydney to Newcastle! Even to this day, a trip of forty kilometres by car is considered a long way to the Dutch mind.

Uncle Adrian was still relatively well off since they were wealthy and some of their estates were farms. The one they lived on was a rich farm and was well north, away from the conflict in the south. There was plenty of German artillery close by the route to Zwolle, it being at the top of "the corridor," which ran from Belgium in the south to the mid-northeast of The Netherlands. This was the only safe supply route the Germans had left, so it was a target on all sides and was heavily protected by the Nazis to prevent the enemy from succeeding. Many Allied troops lost their lives at Arnhem, close to the district of Utrecht where Ben and Em lived.

In fact, the British and American air forces set out in broad daylight just a few months before in September, and many had lost their lives in the efforts to take the Arnhem Bridge. Their aim was to completely choke the enemy supply line in the corridor. Most of the city of Arnhem lay in ruins, but the Germans still held the vital bridge. One could hear the sound of artillery fire night after night, it was that close. The Germans paid close attention to the activities of the Dutch in these areas in the event they were helping Allied troops escape. Roadblocks were set up everywhere.

Em realized Ben was mulling over what obstacles she would have to face in order to get to Zwolle successfully. They studied the map.

She interrupted Ben's thoughts. "You know how desperate it is for us to find food for the children. All we have eaten for months now is a little boiled barley."

"Then I'll take the bike and go to your Uncle Adrian, Em," Ben again urged.

"No, it's far too dangerous for you now. I'd rather see us hungry than fatherless. If they discover your disguise now, that will be it! I'll go, I'm only four months or so along, and now I'm in the second trimester, I'm not so sick as I have been. And being pregnant may mean the difference between keeping the bicycle and having it confiscated. You know they grab every single bike they possibly can from us. Also, remember too, Ben—you're needed here. Many lives may yet depend on your expertise. You should stay."

"Ah, but I don't want you to go, Em; it's far too dangerous. What if anything should happen to you?"

"Ben, you must—you must let me do it this time, we must get food. The children are so thin now—they need some different and more nutritious food. Uncle Adrian will give me some butter and eggs at least. Ben, I know it's a long way to ride but going via the canals on a barge isn't very safe either. I think this is the safest way for me, as I am legally able to have the bike—at least for the moment anyway." Ben reluctantly agreed.

CHAPTER 20

The Ride to Zwolle

Two days later Em set off. Cycling north, she passed the signs to Amersfoort on the west of the highway, and then around four in the afternoon on the outskirts of Harderwijk, she stopped off at a smallish home set back off the road amongst a cluster of beautiful chestnut trees. Dismounting, she walked to the door and knocked, hopeful the people would be kindly.

"Good afternoon. My name is Em Bijl, and I am travelling to Zwolle, but I need a place to sleep overnight. Would you allow me to sleep in your barn? I would really appreciate your help." Em looked tired and wistful but the honesty in her face shone through.

The lady at the door smiled approvingly, "Do come in, Mrs. Bijl. I am sure we can find somewhere here for you to stay." She nodded to come inside her house.

"Oh, thank you so much, madam. You don't know how much I appreciate this!"

The farmer and his wife put her up for the night and gave her a hearty breakfast—two slices of dry rye bread! It tasted like heaven after nothing but barley. "How can I ever thank you Mrs. and Mr. Blumen?"

"Just have a safe trip and safe return, Em. If we ever need help, I'm sure you too would offer assistance."

"Yes, sir, I certainly would. If you are ever in Zeist, this is my address." She handed them Ben's business card. "Once again, thank you so much!"

Her journey took her northeast. She rode past the sign to Nunspeet and Oldebroek on the left-hand side of the highway, known as the Zuider Zeestraatweg. Excitement began to rise in Em's heart as she pedalled into the OverIJssel region, where the city of Zwolle lay. Much of the countryside was covered in rivers or lakes, both natural and man-made like the IJsselmeer. The ride there was fragmented with some overnight stays and short rests in little villages, where the people were friendly and kindly for the most part. Some said if her search for food proved unsuccessful, they would perhaps be able to find a little food to share with her on the return trip.

She arrived in the outskirts of Zwolle, a very large city of almost one hundred thousand people. Four rivers surround Zwolle, which was built on a hill. Actually, the town was just 4 metres above sea-level. (It was really what most people would say was a hillock) When the rivers flooded, which was often, the city remained safe. Zwolle had a major fish and cattle market, only smaller than the markets in Rotterdam, as well as a lot of other industries. It was a rich town.

At the general store she got off her bicycle and enquired within. "I am looking for my Uncle Adrian van der Waal. Could you please direct me to his farm?"

"Adrian van der Waal! Ha! Everyone knows the van der Waals!" the man at the counter replied, almost with contempt.

Em wondered what he was inferring, but she didn't have to wait long.

He continued, "The van der Waals own half this district. And you ask me, do I know them? You must be a stranger in these parts madam, to ask such a question."

"Yes, sir, I am." Em tried to remain polite both in spirit and tone of voice. "Would you be able to give me directions to Adrian van der Waal's residence? I am really tired, and I want to get there before curfew."

"You go straight down the main street here and follow it out of town, then about four kilometres from the town sign on your right, you'll see the enormous gateway and their name plastered across the gate in gold letters. Can't miss it, madam!"

"Many thanks, Sir." Em walked out of the store smarting at his lack of neighbourliness, but then experience suddenly made her put her immediate feelings aside. Her grandmother Opoe was Uncle Adrian's mother, she also thought, and she was a haughty old lady. Perhaps Adrian was like that too.

She remounted her bicycle and shortly the notorious gateway loomed ahead. Obviously, this is Uncle Adrian's farm. Everything from the fences to the buildings indicated he was a man of considerable wealth. A few minutes later she was riding around the huge circular drive. The garden was mostly greenery at that moment, coming into winter, but she imagined it would be a kaleidoscope of colour in the spring. The bright yellow crocuses were just about finished, one of the few bulbs that flower before winter.

Em stepped off the bike and walked up the commanding stone steps to the ornate, oak front door. She rang the doorbell and waited. Em wondered, I haven't heard from them, although they should have received my letter by now. It was three days since she had left home. Her boots and coat were covered in slush and mud, her legs were sore, her face red and raw from the prevailing northerly winds off the IJsselmeer. Although she had had a good night's sleep the night before, the half-starved state she was in and her pregnancy were depleting her strength.

Having reached her goal, she was rapidly tiring.

The door opened. "May I help you, madam?" A housemaid asked.

"Yes, I am here from Zeist—I am Uncle Adrian's niece, Em Bijl. I think they are expecting me," she said softly.

"Oh, you must come in then, madam. I will get the mistress. One moment, please." She ushered Em inside the lovely entry and walked down the spacious hall to find Auntie Corrie, Uncle Adrian's wife. Presently she returned and beckoned Em to follow her into the house. In the beautifully appointed living room sat her aunt. She rose as Em entered the room.

"Hello and welcome, Em! We have been expecting you. Thank God you have arrived safely. Come and sit down, dear."

The maid took away Em's overcoat and boots, and her aunt gasped. "You look exhausted, girl! You're so very thin! You've scratches everywhere, and your poor face. Let's see what we can do for you."

"Thank you, Auntie Corrie. It's good to see you." Em pursed her lips, along with a little shrug of her shoulders, as she often did when she didn't know how to reply and said nothing. She thought, What can I say? I am exhausted. She sank gratefully into the luxurious sofa.

In a short time, her uncle came into the room, smiling warmly. "Well, if it isn't Em. How are you? I think I timed that well—I was just returning from business." He warmly embraced her.

Their house was delightful; larger by far than most of the homes she had encountered along the way. The farmland looked well cared for and gave evidence of being well provided for, even in this time of great deprivation.

Having money certainly helps at times such as these. Em thought wryly.

"I'm very tired, Uncle, but I'm glad to be here and thank you for your offer of help. My family will always owe you a debt of gratitude."

"That is the least we can do, for you are family, my dear. Now, my dear, a cup of coffee and something to fill that emptiness." Auntie Corrie added kindly, "How long since you've eaten?"

"I had a little for breakfast today. A kindly old couple in the Harderwijk district put me up one night and shared their food with me. It's been quite awhile since we've had bread at home. What I mean is real bread! The foodlines are so long, and when you finally get there, all they offer is 'fake bread,' as Ben calls it."

"Fake bread? What is it really?" Auntie Corrie asked, raising her eyebrows in astonishment.

"Well, it's supposed to be a mixed-grain loaf, but it tastes like it is about 70 percent saw dust and straw. In fact it makes me ill, but a lot of people eat it and say, 'It's better than nothing!' At one of the places where I stayed overnight along the way, the old farmer's wife gave me two slices of rye bread. Even without butter it was good after what we've been trying to eat lately."

"Have this coffee, Em, and here are some slices of light ryebread— with butter!" And Em breathed in the aroma of freshly brewed coffee— real coffee!

"Thank you." She took a tiny sip and closed her eyes, "It tastes even better than I remember!" After two slices of bread though, Em felt rather ill.

"Too much too soon, perhaps?" her aunt suggested. "How about a nice warm bath and a good sleep. You'll feel like new."

"Yes, Auntie, I believe I have had too much already, and yes, a bath would be wonderful!"

After Em's rest, the family shared the evening meal. More like a feast, Em thought as she watched the table being laid. Her cousins Adrie and Wim, being the youngest in the family, were still living at home and joined the family for the meal. They were young men but still single and assisting their father in his farming business.

Over the meal, the family caught up on the events since long before the war, and Em spoke in an animated way about her three little children and how much happiness they had brought her and Ben. She proudly offered the photos of their children, which she and Ben had so much enjoyed taking.

Bijl Family at the end of 1943, not long after Johan's death.

"This is Gerda, our eldest. She turned seven in November, and yes, she has a mind of her own! Gerda is the apple of her father's eye!"

"A beautiful child indeed, Em!" Uncle Adrian said.

Auntie Corrie concurred. Looking at the photos again, she added, "These are professional photos. Do you know a photographer, Em?"

"Yes, Ben, my husband, is a professional photographer, Auntie," Em said proudly. "Here are some more of my younger children, our sons Charles and Louis.

"This is Charles; he turned five just a few days after St. Nicholas' Day. And this is Louis; he is just starting to walk now. He is about sixteen months old."

Her aunt looked carefully at Louis' photo. "Oh, but he does not look well. Is he ill? Or is it just hunger I see?"

"You are very perceptive, Auntie Corrie." Em sighed. "He is not well, and although you didn't notice it in Charles, neither is he."

"Whatever is wrong, Em?"

"I'm afraid both of my sons have the same problems that my brother Gerrit had. We know Charles definitely does and I'm quite suspicious about Louis, but not entirely sure yet."

"Oh, nooo!" Uncle Adrian added. "Surely not! Are you sure, Em?" He turned to his wife. "That's also what Opoe believes my two brothers who died had. Did you know that? I'm talking about the bleeding problem of course."

"Yes, we recently found out that my brother, Gerrit, had what is now known as Haemophilia."

"Haemophilia? But tell us what causes the terrible bruising in this condition, my dear?" Auntie Corrie asked.

"Dr. Meyer, our Paediatrician in Utrecht, explained that Haemophilia is a genetic blood disorder. Do you remember how Gerrit had what we would describe as arthritis in his legs and elbows, which caused him great pain even if there was no bleeding?"

They lived with chronic joint bleeds resulting in swelling and severe bruising. Uncle Adrian remembered his two brothers living in almost constant pain. They inherited it from their mother's family, the van der Giessens.

The rest of the evening was spent reminiscing with her cousins about their childhood visit to Em's father's farm at Chaam, which to the cousins, only little back then, seemed like an eternity away. Distance was the most common reason for not visiting relatives.

"How about a cup of hot chocolate before we retire tonight, Em?" Auntie Corrie asked, changing the subject.

"Chocolate! Are you sure I'm not dreaming?" Em answered. "That would be delightful Aunt! It's impossible to get in Zeist. The trouble is, Zeist is not far from the German and Belgian borders, and all the military machinery coming and going comes and goes right past our back door. You must be thankful that you live north of the actual war zone. You seem to have access to more food here. Only the Nazis and their supporters can get chocolate at home. Anyway, yes, I'd love a cup of hot chocolate—only just a little chocolate, please, or I'll be ill. Thank you."

"Yes," Uncle Adrian clarified, "we are lucky in that respect, but it is still very difficult for us because the corridor runs near us into Germany, and we get all the traffic going south to the front quite nearby. When I travel to another town, it takes so long because of all the road checks along the way. It's really frustrating, especially if it's near curfew."

That night and the next were some of the best night's sleep Em had had in years. For some reason, there was perfect peace and quiet all night long, unlike at home.

"Although," Auntie Corrie explained, "it is not always this peaceful, Em."

Em replied, "At home we put the children to bed fully dressed in case we have to rush them down to the cellar, if there are any planes dropping bombs overhead. And it happens often. Ben and I can be up and down all night. So, it's good to just sleep."

"That really is a grave concern for you and your family," Auntie Corrie said sadly. "Let's pray it will all end soon."

On the second morning after her arrival in Zwolle, Em woke to the sun shining. This is unusual in The Netherlands. She took it as a good omen for her return trip, so she was anxious to leave early.

The family gathered in front of the house to say good-bye to Em but not before her bags were packed to the brim with carefully wrapped eggs, butter, rye bread loaves, various vegetables and fruits, and a few special treats. Em placed the last of the smaller gifts into her overcoat pockets. She juggled another bag, holding onto the handle bars of the bike. At last she was ready to leave.

"It was wonderful to have you, Em. I'd feel a lot happier about you returning home by train with this load. But – you did make it up here. I guess you'll make it back. Godspeed. If you need help, please come to us again. If not before the war ends, then when peace has been restored. There are rumours that the Nazis must soon concede defeat," Uncle Adrian said encouragingly. "Let's pray for it each and every day," Auntie Corrie said softly. "God bless, and safe return, Em."

"Thank you all so much for your love and help. My family appreciates your kindness more than you can know. Please come and visit us after the war is over. I must go now. I love you all." Em waved gingerly as she negotiated the large circular garden. The bike was really top heavy. Once down the slope leading to the main road, she picked up speed and the ride became fairly smooth.

As Em rode down the path and turned left into the lane, she looked back, her spirits high, her heart beating with excitement. She thought, Now for home. She peddled strongly for the first few miles.

Her ride was uneventful until she neared the IJssel Bridge, which crosses the IJssel River as it flows from Germany through to the IJsselmeer. In the distance, Em heard the whirring of plane engines, and soon realized they were Allied planes heading directly for the bridge. There was the sound of heavy gunfire starting up from the ground, and Nazis were running to their positions and preparing to counterattack. The soldiers signalled Em to stop and violently waved her away. Their usual roadblock was left unattended as their attention was wholly bent on protecting the bridge.

Em stopped momentarily. I have to get across the bridge before the plane - if they drop a bomb on it and the bridge goes down, it will be impossible to get home. She jumped back on the bicycle, ducked her head, and took off at high speed. The soldiers ignored her, intent on the more pressing issue at hand. She rode as if Hitler himself were chasing after her. She did not look back.

She could hear bullets whistling past her on every side, as the planes descended low and began dropping their loads. Loud explosions cracked through the air; impact from the bombs, sending shooting geysers of water into the air and great rippling waves across the river's surface.

Just as she neared the far side of the bridge, there was a sudden deafening explosion. The bridge had been hit, but not enough to completely destroy it. The shaking of the bridge threw her off balance and she fell off the bike and landed on her right knee, skidding along the road's surface until the bike and its load came down on top of her—food items hurtling past and landing all around her!

She staggered to the road's edge and fell writhing with pain into the bulrushes at the bridge's edge. Em's heart was pounding. She lay silently in the long, spindly grass.

Until after what seemed like hours, there was silence. Soldiers came out from their positions of attack, and an officer began shouting commands. They were still too busy to stop her, asking for her papers. After trying to retrieve her food items—many of the eggs had shattered, and the slimy yellow dripping mess covered everything she retrieved.

Ohh! Yuk! The eggs of course! Em squirmed at the feeling of the slime oozing between her fingers. Thankfully the rest of the food stuffs appear to be intact. I'll just keep moving further away from the bridge ... She sneaked away quietly to the cover of some friendly trees and began to tremble uncontrollably. The awful reality of how close to death she had been struck home. Her trembling hands embraced her belly protectively. Her knees gave way. She sank into the soft grass.

She looked down at the road. "What's this? Blood! Oh, my knee!" Her knee was completely skinned, and bits of gravel were firmly embedded in her flesh. Only at this point did she realize how badly she had injured herself.

"What am I going to do now? I guess there's nothing for it but to try and get up and ride again." She mounted with difficulty and started peddling very carefully toward home. She had to stop. Out of her medical bag she brought some bandages, which she tied firmly around the injured knee to give it a little more support.

Finally, as the precious minutes ticked by, she stood up with difficulty. "I'll set off on foot and walk the bike along. Perhaps that will be less painful than riding." The pain was less intense, but of course she moved much more slowly. All day Em struggled along. Stopping and resting, stopping and resting but—the knee just got sorer and more painful and swollen.

"I just can't go on any further." Em sobbed. Looking down, she lamented "I've got a football for a knee, just like Gerrit used to get. Poor boy!" After a rest, she would bolster up her strength and with great determination, set out once again on foot, pushing along her heavy load. The lovely day, blighted by pain, was drawing to an end, and Em thought ruefully I've only travelled about ten kilometres all day.

As curfew time drew closer, Em reasoned, I have to find shelter for the night. There's a signpost coming up. There was a small village about a kilometre to the left of the highway. "Nunspeet," Em said as she approached the sign. "I'll take this turn. Hopefully I will find someone here to put me up for the night."

She turned left and walked the last few hundred metres in great pain, hoping someone would take pity on her and give her shelter. The ancient-looking police station in Nunspeet was well lit. Em resignedly hobbled up to the door and knocked.

"Come in," a kindly voice called from within. She entered. Engrossed over some reading matter at a table sat the police sergeant of the town. He looked up with a smile as Em entered the office.

"Sir, I had a bad fall today riding out of Zwolle, and I won't be able to reach my destination before curfew. I was wondering, is there anyone here with whom I might stay overnight—even a trustworthy person's barn would be all right."

The sergeant was an older man, and he immediately took pity on her, "The local minister of the Protestant Church. I am sure he would assist and provide you with a bed for the night, madam."

"That would be wonderful. Where does he live, sir?"

He stood up and walked with Em to the street. Then, pointing to his left, he said helpfully, "Just keep walking down the main street here. The church is on the next corner to your right. The minister lives next door to the church."

"Thank you." Em walked slowly to her cycle and looked in the direction he had pointed. There, not far ahead was the little church.

"Good evening, sir, and thanks," she said as the policeman walked inside the office. Seeing the end of her journey now in sight sent a sudden rush of tiredness through her, and her body, wracked with pain, began to feel faint. Em slumped against a fence and gradually slid down the fence onto the moist grass. For quite a while she lay there until consciousness returned.

"Please, dear God, please help me make it to the minister's house." Em struggled to get her body to respond to the urgings of her mind. Summoning all her meagre strength, she pulled herself up with the aid of the fence and inched her way along to the gate of the minister's house. Finally, she reached the front door and knocked shakily.

The door opened and an elderly man greeted Em with, "Good evening, madam. What can I do for you?"

"Please, Pastor, I need a bed for the night. The police sergeant said you would be willing to help me. I have injured my knee today and I am unable to ride my bike. Please help me! I am on my way home to Zeist from Zwolle."

"Oh, such a long, long way, madam? Yes, yes, my dear. Come in. My wife and I would be happy to put you up for the night. I will help you take your bicycle around the back and out of sight. Would you like to leave it in my shed tonight? I'll lock it up safely for you. My, you are very lucky to have a bicycle at all."

"Thank you, Pastor …"

"The name is Pastor van den Bosch, my girl. This is Ada, my wife." He put out his hand to shake Em's.

"It is very kind of you to give me a bed tonight."

"My dear, you are limping," Ada said. "Tell me, what have you done to yourself?" Em opened her coat, and the football-shaped knee was exposed. "Ohh! It's your knee, I see. Perhaps we can bathe your leg for you. Do you think that will help?"

She was middle-aged, tall, and buxom, rather rotund and most interested in Em's condition. The minister was also tall, greying, and sparse on top, but his eyes were alert, in an exaggerated sort of way, made more so by means of the horn-rimmed glasses he wore on the end of his narrow nose. Suffice it to say, although very helpful, they wanted to know exactly what Em had been up to since she left Zeist and why she had come so far from home alone.

"Whatever happened to your knee?" Mrs. van den Bosch asked again.

"Well, I thought the Nazis were going to take away my bike today at a roadblock when I crossed the IJssel Bridge across the River IJssel. They finally let me go, but I was frightened, so I went as fast as I could to get away from them, in case they came after me and changed their minds. It was then that I hit a deep pothole, skidded along, and fell off the bike, landing on my knee." Em carefully held her emotions in check and carefully edited the complete story of her day's ordeal.

"Oh, well, you know the saying 'More haste, less speed' is true," Pastor van den Bosch said. "Anyway, have a warm drink and something to eat. We haven't much, but you are welcome to share it with us. The bed in our spare room is warm and dry." Em went to bed very early, but her sleep was restless, and although they kindly gave her some herbal painkilling mixture, she did not sleep soundly as her knee throbbed constantly. She awoke early, feeling tired before the day commenced.

At breakfast the minister said, "My daughter works for the Post Office, and she offered to take you as far south as her delivery route would go when I told her about your predicament. What do you think, madam?"

"Oh, Pastor that would be marvellous indeed!" Em was very grateful for the relief it gave her.

His daughter had an old vehicle, but thankfully the bike fitted on top. About two o'clock in the afternoon, Miss van den Bosch dropped her off, wishing her well.

"Take care Em, make sure you stop before curfew." The post mistress said in a motherly kind of way.

"Thank you, thank you so much," Em said with sincerity. "I will." She had brought her about ten kilometres farther south to a town called Harderwijk close by the aqueduct Veluwemeer, one of the tributaries of the IJsselmeer. As with most of The Netherlands (meaning the lowlands), the flat land is crisscrossed with canals at every turn, and in Em's youth, windmills dotted the countryside. Without the mills, most of what is today The Netherlands would have long ago been reclaimed by the North Sea. The intricate system of dykes, which the tenacious Dutch built and maintained for hundreds of years, is indeed remarkable.

Em took off with a little haste, but she soon realized "slow and steady" was all it could be, walking, pushing her cycle alongside her.

As with the day before, she hobbled along. Throughout the rest of the day, she persevered, still in a lot of pain. Em had never visited her sister Cien, who lived in Putten, which was about five to ten kilometres farther south. Eventually she reached a little village called Ermelo, but Em determined, "I don't care what it takes. I'm going to walk until I reach Cien's house. She will gladly let me stay until I recover from this cursed knee injury—at least enough to ride the rest of the way home."

Curfew had long since gone when she at last entered the village of Putten. Everywhere laid the charred remains of houses. The policeman had been understanding of her dilemma and given her directions. At last she entered Cien's gate. Two days since she left her uncle's home and she had only covered about forty kilometres, less than half the distance home. She began to fret about her babies and Ben. Will they be all right? By now they too will be worrying about me. Oh, dear God, please help me have a safe return.

Em's emotions heightened as she knocked on Cien's front door a good half-hour after curfew.

Cien later told Em she froze at the sound of the knocking. Painful memories raced back into her mind.

Cien suddenly asked in a strong, clear voice, "Who's there?"

"Cien, Cien, it's me, Ma!" Em whispered in as loud a voice as she dared. If someone else saw she was out beyond curfew, God only knew what could happen!

"Ma, Ma, what on earth brings you here?" Cien wrenched open the door and rushed her inside. The door closed instantly, and Cien leaned against it, trying to regain her composure.

Finally, still in disbelief, she said, "Is it really you Ma?" The two sisters rushed into each other's arms.

Little Corrie seemed to be having difficulty remembering just who Em was. As they moved out of the tiny entry, he asked, "Is this one of my aunties, Mama?"

"This is your Auntie Ma from Zeist, son. Mama's younger sister, Ma." As Cien said this to her son, her eyes filled to the brim. Again, they hugged, both bursting into tears.

"And how are you coping, Cien?" Em asked, trying to get control of her emotions.

Cien hesitated before she answered Em's question. Turning to her son, she said, "Corrie, would you please get Mama some wood to put in the oven?"

Words wouldn't come out initially, but eventually she said, "I knew he would never return. It was like he died then, when they dragged my Cor off on that fateful day."

"But Cien, you could be wrong. Don't give up hope yet," Em said, patting her reassuringly. Together they wept. Corrie returned from his errand, anxious to catch every word.

"Thank you, son," Cien said, "What would Mama do without you?"

"It's okay, Mama, I love to help. You know that."

She smiled through her tears and quickly tried to change the subject. "Now, tell me, how did you get here? Let's find you something to eat and drink."

She then looked down at Em and saw her torn dress, her coat and boots covered in mud. Gradually her eyes took in the whole picture, but when they reached her belly, she stopped short. "Ma, you're not pregnant again, are you?"

Em nodded a little coyly, even though it was her fourth pregnancy. "Yes, I'm due in May or June, Cien."

"Oh, that husband of yours! I'll have to speak to him. Doesn't he know what causes it yet?" They suddenly laughed, and the heaviness of the situation was immeasurably lightened. "Now enough of this frivolity. Come and have a cup of coffee. Quick, Cor, go and boil up water for Auntie Ma."

"That would be delightful," Em said, smiling at her nephew, observing his likeness to one of her little sons at home.

"Now what brought you here, and what happened to your poor knee?" Cien asked, carefully unravelling the bandages from around her knee.

"Well, it's a long story, but it started five days ago." Em explained her story in detail to her sister, and how she came by her injury.

Cien didn't have much for supper, but she and Cor gladly shared it with Em that night, although Em offered to share what she had.

"Don't be silly, girl," Cien said. "Out here in the country we can always get food. You keep it for your family."

After a couple of days resting up, Em's knee started to settle down; she was anxious to get home to her family.

"Thank you so much, Cien, for all your help. I really needed you, and I hope my visit has helped you to know how much we care, although it is so difficult to get together in these frightening times. God willing it will soon be over."

"God speed, my dear Ma." She was unusually loving and noticeably kinder in her manner than Em recollected of her younger life on the farm. Em realized she had mellowed somewhat. Doubtless the trials she had had to bear had made her more empathetic than she was before. Losing most of the men of Putten had left a heavy pall of fear over the women and children left behind. Out of the 658 men taken only 11 men returned after the war ended. Sadly, Cien's Cor was not among them.

Cien and Cor kissed Em good-bye and stood arm in arm, waving until she was out of sight. Once again, it was a time for tears, and flow they did. The two sisters wondered, How much time will elapse before we see each other again?

Leaving Putten, Em made good progress after her few days of rest with Cien and Cor, which she and Cien had immensely enjoyed. The time spent also allowed the knee to recover quite a bit and now she was able to peddle with some discomfort but tolerably. She rode on in a southerly direction to the town of Nijkerk and from there entered the Amersfoortseweg—the road to Amersfoort and home! The final part of the trip, although much more congested with people, was at least uneventful, and she managed to stay on the bike, so the kilometres clicked away much faster than on foot. Everywhere people seemed to be on the move searching for food. Em saw sadness, despair, and heartache on all faces, and each one had his own story to tell.

The familiar sights of her hometown began to appear on the horizon as Em pressed on. Her spirits rose as she came to the last of the roadblocks outside of Zeist, and realized that probably, just probably, she was going to make it home safely and with her bike bags as laden as possible with "the impossible."

The soldier who examined her papers excused himself and went to speak to an officer who was inside the booth at the roadblock. They seemed deep in discussion for some minutes, and Em became extremely nervous, fearing the worst.

After what seemed an eternity, the two came toward her. The soldier now stood back and let his commanding officer take over.

"Madam you are free to go." He handed Em her papers. "But the bicycle must stay. The Occupying Government has made a decision to confiscate all bicycles or other means of transport." He began stepping forward to take the bicycle away from Em.

Em clutched the handlebars more tightly, refusing to relinquish the faithful bike. "But sir, I have authority, as these papers verify, to keep this bicycle, and unless you can provide a written order saying otherwise, I will not let you take it. Sir, please recall. I am a midwife and my work focuses on saving lives. It cannot be argued that it is not an essential service."

"It seems to me," he replied, "it is an essential service for you, madam." Reluctantly he let go of the bike, adding, "I will let you go this time, Mrs. Bijl, but you may not be so lucky in the future. Continue! Heil Hitler!"

Em rode off triumphantly, head held high. "I did it! I actually did it! I'm almost home."

The medieval township came into view. She experienced a surge in energy as she turned into Veldheimlaan.

As she knocked on the back door, she found herself humming softly. It was "In Holland staat een Huis..." She smiled to her self, Ben's old favourite. There was a great rush to the door. Gerda and Charles tussled on the other side of the door, both trying to open it, but with little success. At last Ben opened the door.

"Mama, Mama!" they shrieked with joy. "Mama's home, Papa!"

"Well then, children, let's let Mama in, shall we?" Em's family embraced her from all sides.

"Ben, I'm so tired …" She had summoned all her strength to ride the last forty-five kilometres, and now she was totally exhausted. She slumped sideways in Ben's arms. "Put me to bed, please," she whispered, closing her eyes.

Em didn't remember much about the next couple of days either. She slept and slept. She had been away nine days in total, but it was worth every bit of It to get that precious food. They would make it last a long time; they would eke it out, day by day, and stay alive.

When at last Em came downstairs, she was delighted to see Charles and Gerda sitting at the dining room table, having a meal that they for once ate with gusto.

"Nice dinner?" She tickled Charles playfully under his chin.

"Yes. This is the nicest dinner I can ever remember, Mama!" he cried. That was the truth if ever she had heard it!

Gerda erupted with enthusiasm as Em sat down. "The barley tastes so much better with some salt and a little butter! And we had half an egg each, Mama. I had forgotten how yummy they are."

"Mama, I'm so glad you're home. I missed you," Charles said, reaching up to hug her. "And you must look at the big bruise on my leg. It's as big as the world!"

"Oh, is it schatje? Eat up your dinner and then we'll see what you've done." Together they investigated his injury. A deep purple-red bruise jumped out at her, spreading from the little fellow's knee all the way down his leg to the ankle on the outer side of his leg.

"But it's going to be all right, Mama," Charles reassured her as he saw the expression of concern written on her strained face.

"Yes, my pet, I believe it will be fine." She kissed him again after a thorough examination. "Mama loves you! It's great to be home again!"

The next morning, Gerda bounced into the room, brandishing her dolly. "Mama, I don't like my St. Nicholas present anymore."

"And why not, Gerda?"

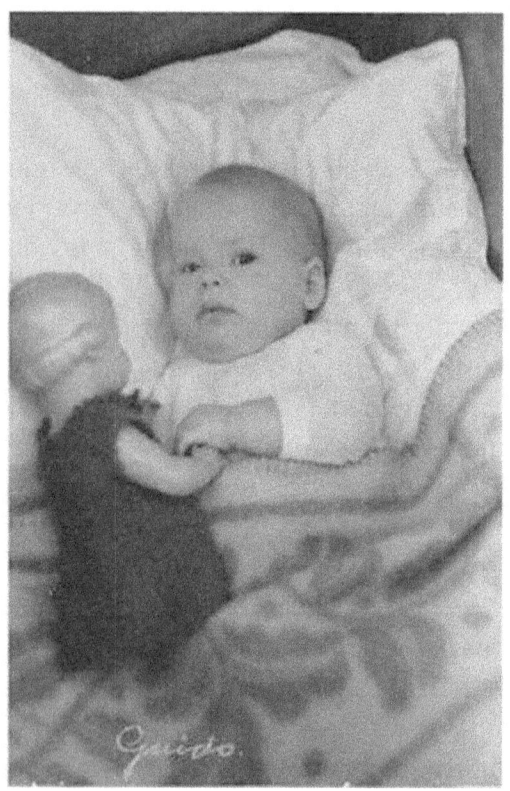

Gerda gave baby Guido Charles (in later life he preferred his second name) her only dolly to cuddle.

"Because I just remembered something. This dolly is not a real present; she's my old doll, which I thought I had lost, only she has a new dress. Look, Mama, don't you remember Annie?" she added, looking Em right in the eye. "St. Nicholas should have left me a new dolly because I have been a good girl, haven't I?"

"Well, maybe he thought that because you loved Annie so much, you would rather him find her and return her to you! What do you think?"

"Well, perhaps, perhaps." Gerda shrugged. Then looking at the doll, she said, "Yes, I am glad she came back, I suppose."

"Louis and I like our cars, Mama," Charles said, holding up a little wooden carved vehicle.

Little Louis was now running around, but he was covered in little bruises from head to foot. Although not serious, they were always a worry, since they kept his blood iron levels low. Nonetheless they were typical of active little boys with Haemophilia.

Ben came down from his upstairs darkroom. He smiled at Em, bent down, kissed her on the forehead, and said, "How's our Mama this morning? Look the sun is shining and it's not so cold. If you bundle up, maybe, just maybe if Mama feels better, she will take you children for a walk to see the Slot near Gerda's school this afternoon. Would you like that, children?"

"Ohh, yes, please, Mama!" Charles said excitedly. "We've missed our lovely walks since you went away to Uncle—what's his name? But I do like the real nice food you've brought us to eat."

"But I don't want to go to school today. Can't I stay home? Please, Mama?" Gerda protested and pleaded, eyes searching those of her mother and then hopefully into her father's.

"You won't have to go to school for a while yet, sweetheart, but guess what? When you do, you can then walk with Mama on the way home when she comes to pick you up."

Gerda sighed reluctantly. "All right, Mama."

CHAPTER 21

Em's Courage and a Man with a Kind Heart

The meagre supply the Bijl children had considered a real feast was eaten with painstaking care, little by little as they tried to make it last as long as it could. Indeed, it was reminiscent of the way Em and her sisters used to relish a biscuit as children, and the one whose biscuit lasted the longest was the winner! After five or six weeks, the proverbial cupboard was bare, save for that revolting barley. Ben was like a caged lion, only daring to go outdoors when it was absolutely necessary to conduct his "business," which by now was mainly the underground smuggling of passports. However, his meeting points were always in close proximity to home, to minimise the risk of having the bike confiscated and he himself carefully searched.

Em was now nearing her sixth month, obviously pregnant, although not so big, due to lack of proper nutrition.

"I would like to go to Cien in Putten, Ben. It's not so far, and we need more food."

"Em, you are too far along now to risk it. Think about what happened on the way out of Zwolle."

"Yes, and it frightens me too, but I have more hope of going and coming back with the bike, due to the fact that I am so pregnant. They're not all hard-hearted you know."

"Yes, but these days there is so much senseless killing. If you happen to be in the wrong place at the wrong time, you're dead!" Ben punched his fist into his open hand as he spoke. "I worried myself sick last time you were away. I had you dead and buried. I just can't let you go again, Em!" His eyes searched deeply into hers as he drew his precious wife toward himself.

"Even so, whatever the risk, I must go. For all our sakes, I must go. Cien is so depressed, and she needs to see me too, seeing I'm the closest of our family and she now has to face life without Cor."

This comment was really only a side issue—Cien was coping, although it was a terrible situation. Besides, Cien knew the locals and they were more than generous in sharing the little they grew with her and they offered to help Em if she returned. "It's not half as far as Zwolle," Em persisted.

"And anyway, I'm going Ben. What else can we do?" Ben frowned. He said nothing.

"I've been studying the map. I think I should go via the little back roads and try to avoid seeing the Nazis on the boom gates in and out of the bigger towns. For without doubt, if they see me with my bike, now things are so desperate, they'll confiscate it for sure. The bigger towns have much more officious men at the checkpoints too. Perhaps from here to De Bilt and then on to Den Dolder, but instead of riding straight on to Amersfoort, I could straddle the town and cross over Hilversumseweg just before the crossroads…"

"That's a good idea, Em. It's only about one or two kilometres north until you reach the turnoff to Nijkerk. If you get there safely, you'll only have another eight kilometres to reach Putten. So, have you thought about when you'd like to leave?"

"How about Tuesday?"

"That soon?"

"Will my waiting solve the problem?" Em retorted.

"No, I know it won't," he conceded bitterly. "How much longer will this crazy war continue?" He ran his hands across his head in anguish. "How much longer will Europe's harassed inhabitants suffer? The futility of war! A man won't have a hair on his head soon, what, with all this worry."

Tuesday came. It was a bitingly cold day, typical for the middle of winter, especially as the winter of 1944–45 was one of the most severe on record. The Nazi's action to stop all transportation of food to the western regions of The Netherlands in reprisal added to the nation's distress. This was in response to the history making Rail Strike the Dutch people staged a little earlier. Blisteringly cold winds from the North Sea added to the chill factor as usual, but the sun thankfully was shining, even though there was no warmth in its rays, as Em rode out. At the little village of De Bilt she stopped for a drink at the well in the small square. The weak sun suddenly disappeared behind billowing clouds. Em shuddered. She put on another warm jacket underneath her long woollen midwife's coat.

Em thought as she prepared to go on, the blessing of living in the lowlands is—riding is not often strenuous here. She remounted with some difficulty because of her being a little front heavy. I must be very careful this trip.

Em quickly passed through Den Dolder and before long had reached the edge of Amersfoort. She veered left toward Hilversum, riding around this large town via the many little country lanes, so as to avoid road-blocks if possible. The sky looked cold and sinister; it was around ten o'clock in the morning when the sound of planes heading closer made the hairs on Em's neck stand on end. Surely, they won't come really close to me? she wondered, but in fear she prayed once again, as she had many times before.

The plane's engine began to roar, it was so close now. How many were coming over? She breathed a sigh of relief when she saw just one plane coming toward her.

Perhaps they won't take any notice of me; perhaps they are on a mission. As the plane drew closer it came down lower. A sudden ringing of bullets whistled through the air, almost on top of her. Memories of the IJssel Bridge came flooding back into her mind. She rushed the bike over the edge of the slightly elevated laneway into a grassy ditch. There just beside the ditch was a large and billowy willow tree, which had grown profusely because here water lays everywhere.

Em fell on her face. She scrambled towards the protection of the old willow, rolling sideways, trying to protect her belly. The bullets kept whistling past her. They were very close, some actually embedding into the tree's trunk.

The plane stopped circling and moved on, suddenly roaring upwards. It was a Nazi plane. Oh God, please make them go away, Em prayed. Why are they shooting at a lonely woman? Salty tears streamed down her wind blown cheeks. For the first time in her life Em swore: "Bastards!" It was some time before she was game enough to try to stand again, she felt so weak. Em lay under the protection of the tree.

Perhaps it was half an hour or more, she wasn't sure, trying to regain her composure. The delicate fronds of the willow swayed gently in the strong breeze. The peacefulness now was completely incongruous with the violence only minutes before.

Eventually she raised herself up and climbed back on the faithful bike, thankful the bullets had missed! The rest of the journey, being about twenty kilometres in all, proved uneventful. By mid-afternoon, Em arrived in Putten. Em's head ached relentlessly by the time she arrived at her sister's little cottage.

*

Cien was out gathering the wash off the line. It had dried in just one day because of the biting wind. She was enjoying the invigorating fresh air and the intermittent sunshine. She began talking to herself while she folded the clothes, looking at each item critically, "It isn't good enough! Nothing is blue-white anymore, like Mama taught us it had to be. But no wonder - there's no soap and no "blue" these days." Those luxuries were only things to dream about. Soap had been unprocurable for many months, and most women, especially those with little babies, like Em, had fingers bleeding everyday from rubbing dirty nappies and trying to get them clean without soap. Cien was used to being on her own during the day, and she had plenty of time contemplating life.

*

Meanwhile, Em knocked on the quaint little Dutch farm-house door. The windows were so delicately framed by the white lace curtains, which merely frame the window during the day, while the heavy curtains are pulled across for warmth during the evening.

Cien has done a good job with those curtains, Em thought, making a mental note as she knocked again. Still there was no response. She walked quickly and hopefully through the side garden to the backyard.

Em prayed. Please let her be here. There was Cien, bending down, about to gather up her wicker basket full of clothes.

At the sound of Em's voice, Cien dropped the basket and ran with outstretched arms toward her sister. "Ma, Ma! I had a feeling you would come again before the baby arrived. Thank God for bringing you safely to me! Come in, dear sister."

They hugged each other tightly and then hurried inside and shared the past couple of months' events over some mint tea. Mint grew everywhere in the moist ground around the farms and made a delightful drink.

Then, while Cien walked down the lane to pick up Corrie from school, Em lay down for a well-earned rest. She slept like a baby. She awoke to the tantalizing aroma of fried eggs. Yes, mouth-watering fried eggs sizzled away in the frying pan—one for her, one for her sister, and one for her nephew Corrie. That, along with some black rye bread, was their evening meal. Em felt it was fit for a king.

"Tomorrow is Wednesday. We'll go out together and see what we can get from my kind neighbours, Ma. Although many lost homes, their veggie gardens and orchards thankfully survived."

"Mama, can I come with you tomorrow, please?" Corrie pleaded, delighted to see Auntie Em again so soon. He chattered on about school and how the big boys liked to play tricks on Mr. Reitsma. He laughed merrily, recalling how Mr. Reitsma, the school teacher, spent much of the afternoon looking everywhere for his spectacles. "Anton had hidden them in the fireplace ledge. He couldn't see well with them but without them, well…"

They all laughed.

"Well then, did he eventually find his glasses?" Em asked, imagining the situation in the classroom while this was happening.

"Oh, yes, Auntie, one of the spoil-sport girls told him where to look—and who hid them. Wow! Was Anton in trouble then."

"And, Anton got the cane, did he?"

"Did he! He got six of the best and a letter home to his parents."

Cien smiled. "Now boy, getting back to your lessons—you must go to school. Okay?"

"Aw, do I have to, Mama?"

His mother's eyes told him the answer.

"But after school, Corrie, we will come and meet you and will walk home together," Em said soothingly. "Maybe tomorrow we may even find a little treat for you."

"Oh? What is it, Auntie?" he pleaded.

"Wait until tomorrow," she said reassuringly. "Tomorrow."

"It's off to bed with you now, my boy, but clean your teeth first."

Corrie hugged his Mama and then his Auntie Em and sadly went upstairs to his bed. He hated bed times.

"Since his father was taken away, he says to me, 'Mama, I miss Papa so much. Why did it have to be my Papa?' Life is so unfair." Em nodded, tears in her eyes imagining it was one of her own children.

"But I tell him, think of all the other children who are also fatherless as well Cor—you are not alone my dear boy. But I know that doesn't take away his personal pain." Em nodded sympathetically.

The two sisters sat up late into the evening catching up.

"I thought I wasn't going to make it here today Cien," Em said.

"What happened?" Cien asked.

"Well, as I was bypassing Amersfoort on one of the country lanes, a German plane swooped down really low, and when they saw me, I don't know if it was just some young fellows trying to frighten me— but they circled around and came back and started firing bullets at me! I dove into a ditch and then they suddenly flew off. I was terrified, Cien…" She began to cry and shake all over again.

"Is that really so? What would they want with a lonely woman? They must have no conscience, Ma. What next?" Cien took Em into her arms and rocked her consolingly and stroked her dark hair. "It's all right now. You're all right. They didn't get you. How about we put you to bed? A good night's sleep will make a big difference to your spirits and your nerves, girl. You just wait and see."

The next morning was sunny enough, but by ten o'clock, clouds began to buildup, first in patches, and gradually the day became colder and menacingly overcast, much like the previous day.

"I don't think it will be too long before it begins raining, Ma. Let's get going. You ride on the bike to conserve some of your energy," Cien ordered, just as she had always ordered all her younger sisters.

"What about you, Cien?"

"I'll be walking. Like I always do, Sis. Besides, I am not pregnant." Cien was tall, solid, and very strong, and she loved to walk. Along the way, they discussed their father's untimely death.

"You said Ben was able to attend Papa's funeral. What did he say about Mama? How did he feel she was coping with the shock?" Cien asked.

"I cried all day on the day of his funeral … wishing I too could have been with everyone … but war is no respecter of people."

"Yes, I felt the same, Cien, but I had to think of my baby first, even though it hurt right to the heart. But Papa wouldn't want us to put his grandchildren in danger, would he?"

"Yes, that's right, yet I still felt guilty. And then there was my Cor. You know I'm tough, Ma, but at the time I thought I was going out of my mind. Can you believe it?"

"Yes, of course I can."

Em studied her sister's face, and empathy for her sent a shooting pain into Em's heart. "What if it was my Ben?"

"I really think the reality hadn't hit Mama at the funeral—it all happened so quickly. One day Papa was fine, the next day he was dead. In a way, I guess we all knew he could die quickly, with his ulcer troubles. I certainly did, being a nurse. Bleeding ulcers can kill very quickly! However, although I thought that's what took Papa, Mama says he died of a brain haemorrhage!"

"A brain haemorrhage! How awful! What did Mama say?"

"Well she mentioned to Ben and the others that the doctor had always said it could happen and not to muck around with his stomach bleeds. They found later that his death was not from his ulcers but a brain haemorrhage. Whether knowing the risks, can in anyway prepare someone for their mate's death … that is another story."

They lapsed into silent contemplation.

"And then she had to face Jannie's death. Our poor Mama. What pain to lose another child. Thankfully she has strong faith in God!" Cien added.

"Yes, Gerrit, Jannie's poor dear husband—he was just devastated, as you could imagine when she and her infant were snatched away." Em's eyes welled up with tears thinking of his heartache.

At that moment they were passing an old windmill. Its latticed arms rotating briskly in the wind seemed to beckon the women toward it.

Em stopped riding, contemplating the peaceful setting before their eyes. "The windmill has been a symbol of survival in the wetlands of The Netherlands over the centuries. I love the feeling of security the old mills give me when I see them there, silently working away. Kind of like The Netherlands's life blood."

"Spoken like a true nurse." Cien laughed at Em's observation.

It wasn't too long until they arrived at Mrs. van Doorn's boederij (farm) just before eleven.

"Welcome, ladies. Do come in, please," she said with such a friendly smile. She was such an echte Hollandse Meid, (genuine Dutch girl), as Em put it later, on the way home.

"So, this is your sister from Zeist, Cien. You are definitely 'sisters'— that lovely smile gives you away. Now won't you sit down please in the window seat and enjoy the view while I prepare the coffee?"

Two windmills were visible through the white lacy curtains that framed the front windows. Alongside the lane, ran a narrow canal. Almost all blocks of land in the country were surrounded with canals. These in turn, at regular intervals, ran into larger wider canals, upon which the farmers punted or used horses on a towpath to pull their barges to the nearest town, with their delicious cheeses, milk, cream, or butter. They even carried livestock to sell at the market. Seagulls flocked in abundant numbers, and their constant squawking was an audible reminder that one was never very far from the sea.

"Looks like we just made it before the downpour. The wind is certainly whipping up now. Look at the mill's arms racing around!"

The foremost windmill was quite close by, and they could see the enormous arms turning, at first slowly but now quite quickly as the force of the wind rose. Its crisscrossed timbers made it look quite delicate despite its great size.

Quickly though Em's thoughts were led elsewhere, as the aroma of coffee—albeit just chicory coffee—stimulated her senses. Mrs. van Doorn entered the living room with a tray of "chicory coffee" and some freshly made damper (a simple but delicious bread without yeast, like a large scone). Em's taste buds were running riot.

One sip, and Em said, "Thank you Mrs. van Doorn, this coffee is a real treat."

"Enjoy it Ma. A piece of brood?" The kindly neighbour held out a porcelain plate with the delightful bread. They reminisced of better days and speculated on how much longer the war would continue.

"Elevenses" is the custom of drinking coffee or chocolate along with cake or delicious biscuits at eleven o'clock each morning. It is in fact ritualistic. One must never have lunch before coffee!

Following the pleasant experience of eating and drinking, Mrs. van Doorn led them around her farm, and whatever she was able to spare she willingly handed over to the young widow and her pregnant sister. When they took their leave, they were well and truly laden with butter, eggs, and lots of fresh greens, besides a little spek. Spek is a peculiarly Dutch word, and it is the fat cut off the bacon that has been dried and when needed is fried in its own fat and ends up crisp and delicious! Ma remembered when she was growing up, her family's personal doctor, Dr. Blumsheim, saying, "The farmers eat themselves sick on the spek and then drink themselves well again with the butter milk!"

Mrs. van Doorn cupped her hands around the sisters' faces and kissed them affectionately on both cheeks. "It was lovely to meet you, Ma," she said. "Jacob will be sorry he missed seeing you today, Cien. He's gone to Nijkerk to try to sell some of our "forbidden pig"—(all pork was to be surrendered to the Nazi army)—"on the black market. But it helps us survive."

"You are very lucky Mrs. van Doorn—you still have your man. What a blessing!"

"Yes Ma, my Jacob is one of the few to remain after the reprisal on Putten. He was returning from Amsterdam. He had taken his barge on the canal to sell our cheeses and pork as he has today. Thankfully he was away that day. It was devastating to him to come home and find such a blood-bath and just about all his friends gone..." The three women suddenly became silent—tears welling up in their eyes.

Finally, Cien swallowed hard, and said, "What's done is done … but now my friend, we must say thank you and goodbye."

"How can I ever thank you, Mrs. van Doorn?" Em asked.

"Just get home safely and share what I've been able to give you with your husband and children, and I will be repaid, Ma." Her eyes twinkled with pleasure. "I am glad to be able to help. Now off you go, and Godspeed!"

"Thank you once again," they said, and then the sisters began the pleasant walk home.

It was good to spend that morning away from the usual hustle and strife of the war in Europe. It was also good to find enough food to fill the belly and stave off the gnawing pain of hunger for a few more days. As they meandered along the lane on their return, it all sounded like a terrible nightmare—a dream gone wrong! The war seemed so far away until, as they neared the village, the charred remains of many homes jolted the women into the present.

As promised, Em and Cien met Corrie at the schoolyard gate. He came running out, swinging his satchel with such excitement. Today he led the throng out of the classroom, eager to spend time with Auntie Em, and most interestingly, receive her promised present. What could it be? Corrie had been preoccupied with that question most of the previous night and all that day.

"Hello, Mama, hello, Auntie Ma! Have you brought my surprise with you?" They looked at each other and laughed at Corrie's youthful exuberance.

"Yes I have, Corrie." Em dug deeply into her coat pocket. It was her great-coat, and the pockets were accommodating. Eventually she drew out her hand.

"What is it, Auntie?" he asked, peering as closely as he could into her almost-closed hand.

"Open it and see, Corrie."

Open the brown paper bag he did, and out of the depths of the bag came a lovely piece of damper, fresh from Mrs. van Doorn's oven. And to top it off, it was covered in a scraping of berry jam and a smidgeon of cream!

"Wow, Auntie, this looks great!"

Without another thought, he attacked the generous serving of damper with enthusiasm, but alas, it was gone all too soon.

"Thank you, Auntie Ma; that was delicious. Have you any more?" His blue eyes were wide open with expectation.

"Sorry, jongen (a young boy). There's no more." Em smiled, imagining Gerda's face in a similar situation. "The things before the war that children and adults alike took for granted are now so special. If nothing else, war makes one appreciate things as we never did before."

With mixed feelings, Em prepared to leave Cien's home the next morning. As she dressed, Cien innocently enough made some remark. Em bristled, although she said nothing. I've never really got on particularly well with Cien because, whatever she said was always "right" as we, her younger sisters knew only too well. In Cien's mind, there was only one way to do things—hers! Well, Em sighed as she finished combing her hair. That still remains the same! And Em, you sure know you're no push over!

She had tenacity and determination in more than usual measure, but when it came to degrees, Cien won hands down! Em had determined to leave that Friday morning, having satisfied herself that her grieving sister and nephew were coping as well as could be expected in such difficult circumstances.

"Do take care, Sis," Em whispered as she embraced Cien for the last time before taking her leave.

"Do be careful, Ma. Please take our love to Ben and the children." Cien spoke with gentleness in her voice.

"Thank you for all your help and support." And then she reached out and embraced her fatherless nephew, saying with a lump in her throat, "May God take care of you and your mama, Corrie, until we meet again—hopefully this terrible war will end soon! Now be good for Mama, won't you, Corrie?"

The child looked at his mother. "I wouldn't dare disobey Mama, Auntie Ma!"

Em laughed in spite of herself, thinking, That would be the honest truth!

"Come on, Corrie, Mama isn't that bad," Cien said raising her eyebrows. Everyone laughed.

"I really must leave now. It's going to be a long, long day." Another hug and Cien helped Em get on the loaded-down bicycle. She gave Em a hefty push to set her off down the quiet little street in Putten. Em turned and waved briefly as best she could.

Em's mind relived the few days she had spent with her sister and nephew. She thought about Cien's generosity in sharing food with her. She really is a good woman, even if she is a bossy boots. Yes, had it not been for Cien's help, I wouldn't have received all this wonderful food. Granted there wasn't too much … but even a little delicious spek—I can't believe my luck.

Passing through the town of Nijkerk an hour or so later, Em took in with interest the comings and the goings of people. There was plenty of movement in these difficult times, mainly people walking along the narrow roads on a visit to a friend or a relative who lived out of town, one who could help with sustenance. Although some smiled wryly or even sympathetically, most looked very sad.

An old, grey-bearded man wearing threadbare, baggy trousers and cap asked Em, "How come you are still riding your bike since most of us around here have long since had ours confiscated?"

"I am a midwife, sir, and the Nazis, although reluctantly, recognise the need for a faster form of transport than foot in my work. As you doubtless know, babies do not always come on time. This in itself, is probably the only reason I still have my bike."

"You're a stranger in these parts, madam; where do you come from?"

"I live in Zeist; you've heard of it? A small town about twenty kilometres out of the city of Utrecht."

"That's a long way, madam—and for a woman in your condition!" he said as his eyes lighted on her bulging coat. "I wish you a safe return." With that parting comment, he waved as he turned down a side lane and walked slowly on.

The ride from the outskirts of Nijkerk to the main highway south was about six kilometres and Em was feeling unusually well, perhaps because of the regular meals she had eaten with Cien since her arrival in Putten. Pedalling quietly along, greeting passers-by, and listening to the sound of birds in the bushes and trees along the road was quite exhilarating, especially as the sun had broken through.

Em started humming. She hadn't hummed in ages, and soon she broke into song at intervals and then lapsed back to humming when the words eluded her, or the notes were too high. She had always loved singing. Strangely it somehow brought a release and her cares were momentarily lightened.

It was only about two kilometres after she turned south onto the highway that she saw the crossroads up ahead, and for some reason, unlike a few days earlier as she cycled through, there appeared to be a roadblock set up in both directions. Straight ahead led to Utrecht and a right turn led to

Hilversum, where Em intended to go in order to miss the road checks in Amersfoort as she travelled south toward Zeist and home.

Oh no! This is a new roadblock. A crowd of people were banking up behind the barricade. Those few with bicycles were quickly separated from their precious and only means of transportation. The bicycles were being loaded onto the back of waiting trucks. She could hear the desperation in the people's voices as they argued profusely. Those on foot were quickly checked and waved on. Her heart palpitated. "Thank God my papers are genuine—over that matter I need not be concerned." Em approached the soldiers at the block.

"Halt! Heil Hitler!" came the soldier's command.

Em got slowly down off the well-laden bicycle and stopped in front of one of the soldiers.

"Papieren, bitte," the soldier said, holding out his hand expectantly for the papers he had just demanded.

Em searched her bag and finally retrieved the mandatory identification papers. She handed them silently to him.

"These papers are in order. You, madam, may pass on; however, the bicycle is to remain, by order of the commanding officer, for the use of the Fatherland. Heil Hitler!"

"Young man, you can see I must get home to Zeist, and I could not walk that far." She held firmly to the handle bars of the bike, looking him in the eye. "I am also a midwife and am authorized to keep my bike, as I am needed to help deliver new borns in the Zeist district. You cannot have it."

"Madam, I have my orders. Give me the bicycle. Quickly now."

"I am not going to give it to you," she retorted, hanging on even more tightly.

"Let go, madam; I do not want any trouble from you. Just give me the bike and you can go." The young soldier began to grab at the handlebars.

"I demand to see your commanding officer then," Em stated, almost fiercely, still standing her ground.

At this, taken aback, the soldier turned on his heel and shouted in German, to his associate, "Go and request Commander Sickinger's presence immediately, please!"

His associate quickly rode away and in about ten minutes returned with another man following closely behind.

The commanding officer approached. He was a handsome man, made more so by the soft blue-grey of his uniform and his cap. He was of reasonably high rank. His shoulder stripes indicated that clearly. Em thought he looked about the same age as Ben, maybe a little younger, late thirties perhaps. He approached the soldier detaining Em first, and in German, discussed the situation briefly.

He then turned and said in fluent Dutch, "Heil Hitler Mevrouw!"

Em said, "Good day, Sir." She clung tenaciously to her bike as if her life depended on it.

"Madam, we are under orders to confiscate all forms of transport. My officer tells me you are a midwife. I understand your concern, but orders are orders. Please give me your bicycle. Come now! Let go!"

"Could you please step aside for a moment and I will explain why I will not allow you to take my bicycle away."

He followed Em as she moved away from the young soldiers at the boom gate.

She opened her long overcoat for him to see her belly and then added, "Besides as you can see—I am about to deliver a child of my own, and I live in Zeist, and it would be impossible for me to walk home wIth the baggage I have in this state. It is still about twenty-two kilometres to my home, and I must get home by nightfall. Would you like to be responsible for the death of an innocent woman and her newborn child, if I went into labour through the great stress you have put upon me on the way?"

Commander Sickinger looked away to the east, his thoughts appeared far away; his face softened almost into a smile, and then suddenly he called to the soldier, "Let this woman go—with her bike!"

"But Commander, your orders were—"

"Yes, yes, I know. Now let her go, verstanden?" he added in their mother tongue. He looked resolute. "Heil Hitler!"

"Heil Hitler, mein Kommandant!" the soldier responded with bowed head. With a click of the heels and salute from the soldier, the commanding officer walked quickly away while Em stood spellbound in utter amazement.

After what seemed like half a kilometre, she negotiated the rebellious bicycle and began pedalling as hard as she could muster up strength, but the bike seemed to take forever to pick up speed and leave the blockade behind.

Whatever was it that made him take pity on me? She analysed the conversation she'd had with the officer. She thought about it most of the way home. She passed around the township of Amersfoort without mishap and rode steadily toward home. Anyway, whatever the reason, Em thanked God again for his kindness. Thank God he had a heart.

The Germans as a nation were not bad. It was the dyed in the wool Nazis people feared. People cannot help but be influenced by the country of their birth. This loyalty determined in most minds what was right and wrong.

As Em progressed toward Zeist farther to the south-west, she thought she could hear the sound of cannon in the distance, perhaps south-east. Indeed, as she rode closer, the noise became clearer, although still quite distant.

In recent months, the Allies had been pressing forward through Belgium and in the south of The Netherlands. Thankfully they were forcing the German army farther and farther north. The British took Nijmegen quite quickly, almost without a hitch, but although they had landed in Arnhem in droves, they did not have equal success. Ben said they were desperate for reinforcements to prevent the Nazis supply line from getting through. The Allies were pushing them back and each day news had it that they were getting closer.

Em swallowed hard as she contemplated all the pain and heartache those five long years had wrought. Her eyes welled up with tears, which she quickly brushed aside; she had to have clear vision on the road, as evenings close in early in the Dutch winter, and visibility would be poorer.

Let it soon end. Now, Em, pull yourself together, you cannot afford to fall off this bicycle in this condition.

It was February 1945, and the resounding cannon-fire was eerie, frightening, but conversely it perhaps heralded good news. Em continued to live in hope. The end must be in sight because that very day the Allies were closing in! These observations reminded Em, "You're on the home stretch now girl, don't give up!"

Curfew was imminent as she pushed herself, fighting the extreme tiredness of her body, to force out of her muscles that last bit of strength to reach home before dark. It was really quite cold, and the wind was beginning to whip up again, as it so often does there when moving from winter into early spring.

Em stopped and added another layer before rewrapping herself in her great-coat. The last fifteen minutes of riding through the town flew. Em noticed people hurrying along the windswept streets, trying to beat the curfew hour. A smart-looking military vehicle drove past her. It slowed down, and for a moment, Em held her breath in fear. The vehicle stopped.

"Are they after my bicycle?" She gasped. Thankfully as she drew level with the vehicle, the young officers were fully preoccupied, totally oblivious of the midwife riding by, or for that matter the more sought-after bike.

"Liebchen, kommen sie hier mit mir!" ("Darling, come here with me!") One smiling, strikingly handsome young man beckoned to a tall and slender girl, whom he was helping alight from the vehicle. Then she saw two more young people getting out of the back seats of the car—another officer with another very attractive, dark-haired young woman. The officers were tempting them, holding out unmistakable little packages.

The girls were giggling and laughing, and then one said almost in disbelief, "Chocolade! I haven't had chocolate for at least five years. Thank you!"

It was plain to see the officers' attentions were wholly diverted and the young women were running the risk of being disowned by their families, should their fraternizing with German officers or soldiers of any kind become public knowledge. These two girls' secret was safe with Em; Em didn't know them, and even if she did, she was not one to interfere. Hand in hand the two couples walked into one of the few restaurants that was still allowed to operate in Zeist during the war. No doubt run by collaborators, Em thought, and solely for the comfort of the Nazi occupiers. Plenty of good food in there while we locals, who just live here, starve at leisure. Why, Em, you're beginning to sound cynical like Ben. Her frown of disapproval didn't last long, as she ceded, Their genuine distraction means, I still have my bicycle.

At last Em turned into Veldheimlaan. She breathed a sigh of relief—home was in sight—well almost. Generally, things had gone much better on this trip than on her trip to Zwolle.

Dismounting in front of number 20, Em opened the gate and walked the bicycle through and continued around the back of the house. The smell of food, albeit boiled barley, wafted around the corner from the kitchen. Ben had scrounged something from someone to concoct a simple soup. Em's stomach gurgled with hunger. She knocked on the door.

Ben opened the door, after checking via the kitchen window. He was thinking it would be Em, and this time, it was! Excitedly, he flung the door open wide and welcomed Em in.

"Em, my Em, you're home safely! You're safe!" He embraced Em with much emotion, kissing her on both cheeks. "How are you and our precious infant?" He patted her tummy.

"Ben, we're fine. It all went really well this time. I've got a lot to tell you, but first have you something hot to drink? I'm so cold."

"Yes, yes, come and sit down while I call the children in and make your drink. Dinner won't be long either."

He walked excitedly out of the kitchen and called the children who had been playing in the living room. "Mama's home!"

CHAPTER 22

Living with Haemophilia

As Ben alerted the children to their mother's return, Em slowly summoned the strength to get to the lounge in the living room. She sank into the soft cushioning and breathed a deep sigh.

"It's so nice to relax. Putten is a long way. But this time I'm not exhausted."

"Mama, Mama. We missed you! What did you bring for us?" The children bombarded Em with questions as they crowded around her.

"It's so good to be home, my precious children. How are you?"

"I'm good, Mama, but we missed you," Gerda said as she planted a kiss on her mother's cheek and then gave her a perfunctory hug. She was always too busy to give anyone a long, tight cuddle. It was either drawing or reading—the two things she really loved.

Before Em could say much in reply, Gerda took off to return to the job at hand—reading this week's favourite book. She was a good little reader even at seven and stole every opportunity she could to sneak outside and climb up the tall chestnut tree across the street in front of the vacant allotment. It was not until the neighbour opposite the Bijls, knocked on the door one day that Em realized where Gerda's secret hiding place was. The old man was most concerned that she would fall out of the tree and hurt herself. But Gerda, the "tomboy," reassured her parents that she was perfectly safe and insisted on taking them across the street to show them how she could safely climb into the leafy branches and sit in a safe fork of the tree away from the world and its cares. Even in the winter time, she could easily hide there because of the thickness of the branches, and if there was any sun to be had, up there it was at its best.

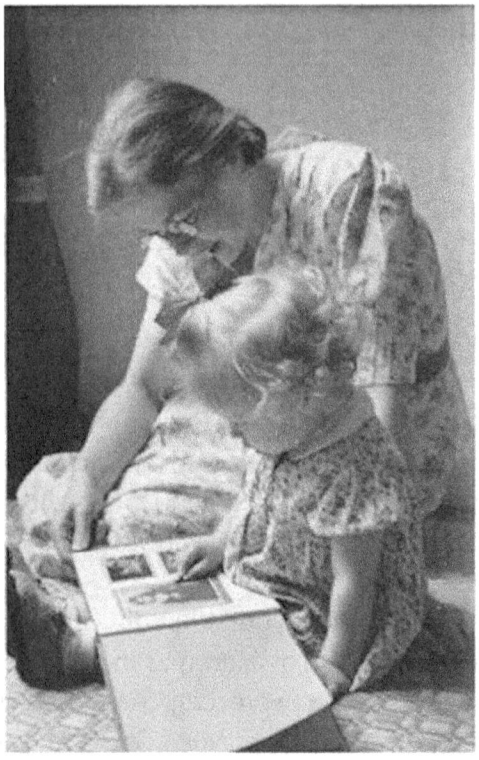

Em with Gerda enjoying another book.

On the other hand, Charles was much less studious, although he was quite bright. He would rather play with animals or look at animal books or how-to books than draw. Perhaps his illness made him more house bound, although he did enjoy sporty things when he was well. Skating on the frozen pond near the forest on the edge of town really interested him, and sleigh riding. He liked the water, but it was always so cold! Ben was intent on teaching all his children to become strong swimmers. It wasn't easy. Charles was affectionate and a shy little boy. "Mama! Mama! I'm so glad you're back. Please don't go away again! Promise?" Charles peered into his mother's eyes, searching for a positive response.

She sat forward in her seat, reached the cherubic face, and managed to kiss and hug him too. Unlike his sister, Charles hung on.

"Mama missed you both as well, but I promise this, Charles. If Mama goes away again, it will only be because our lives depend on it. Understand, dearest?"

"No, Mama, I don't! Really I don't!" His bottom lip quivered.

"You're probably right son; let's hope it isn't necessary anymore. Okay?" Em stroked his blond head, and then after pausing, looked around expectantly for her toddler. Louis, now about one and a half, had not come to welcome her.

"But where is my Loeki?" Em asked, suddenly anxious. She twisted in her lounge chair, and across the room she saw little Louis. He was laid up on the sofa, sleeping under a blanket.

"Shhh! Louis is still asleep, Mama. Papa said we are not to wake him." Charles filled her in on the afternoon's happenings.

Just then Ben arrived with a hot drink for his thirsty wife. "Here, Mama. This will revive you. So how was the trip?"

Em launched into her experience at the crossroads and how the kind commander had let her keep the bike, even against his orders. Then she saw Louis begin tossing about on the sofa. "And how is my little Loeki?"

On hearing his mama's voice, Louis began to cry. "Mama, Mama!" He lifted his blond curly head from the sofa, arms outstretched, but had not run to the chair in which she was sitting, like his siblings.

Em immediately got up to her little son, sensing all was not well. "What is wrong with Loeki, Ben? Is he all right?" Em tried to pick Louis up.

Ben said hastily, "Better not lift him, Em. You'll hurt him."

They had seen a lot of little bruises in the last eighteen months since his birth, but until then, nothing extreme. Em felt sure Louis had Haemophilia like her brother and Charles, but Ben kept saying, "You can't be sure. It may just be because of lack of proper nutrients—after all, some people bruise quite easily."

"Did something happen while I was away?"

Charles broke the silence. "Just look at his ankle, Mama! It's as big as an elephant."

Em deftly but gently pulled back the blanket covering Louis, and there was a little ankle, swollen like a tennis ball, and radiating out from the swelling, purple-black in colour, the bruising having spread into his tiny foot to the tip of the toes. One look and she knew.

"So, what happened? Do you know, Ben?"

"The day you left, I noticed it looked slightly bruised when I was putting Loeki to bed, Em. The next morning, he awoke crying, and when I picked him up, I saw the bruise had grown dramatically. I questioned Gerda and Charles, in case they knew what had happened. Gerda said he had fallen on the concrete landing at the back door a couple of days before."

Em's eyes filled with tears. Mentally she was blaming herself. What about this precious little person I'm carrying now? God, please let it be a little girl!

"He's not as bad as Charles was a couple of years ago, and he survived, no thanks to the Zeist Hospital, but your efforts. Yes, you, Em, and that lovely Dr. Meyer. Her naturopathic remedies did wonders for building up his blood and getting rid of the bleeding and bruising." Then, in an effort to lift Em's spirits and divert her attention, Ben spread out his arms to his children, beckoning them,

"Come, Em and children, let's see what Mama's brought home to add to the soup."

There was an immediate reaction; the children followed him like rats following the Pied Piper into the kitchen and the "goodies." They crowded around the kitchen table, even Gerda abandoning her story, examining the contents of Em's bags, chattering excitedly at the life-sustaining treasures within.

"What's this? Spek!" Ben chuckled in disbelief, "Where on earth did you get this delicacy? Even when farmers have it, they usually hang onto it jealously, not sharing it around."

"Oh, yuk!" Gerda said as she examined it inquisitively, "It looks disgusting! What is it, Mama?" Gerda and Charles did not even recall seeing such a thing.

"What did you say it's called, Papa?" Gerda said as she studied it apprehensively.

"It's spek. It's the rind or skin and fat off the back of the pig."

"Yuk! I don't want any of that!" Gerda quickly responded.

"Just you wait until you taste it after Mama has prepared it to eat with other things. I don't think you'll say yuk then." Ben laughed, his eyebrows dancing.

"Cien's neighbor Mrs. van Doorn was so kind." Em filled them in. "She seemed to delight in giving. She gave us spek, eggs, and butter, as well as some yogurt to add to our barley—enough to last for at least a month, the way we've learnt to ration! And of course vegetables."

"This parsley would certainly add to the flavour of the soup—oh! And here's an onion. That should make a marvellous combination. Wait for it, family, Papa is going to add this to the soup whilst Mama has another hot drink."

The children prattled on excitedly.

Em related all the events about Auntie Cien and Cousin Cor and how things were going for them in Putten. Gerda and Charles excitedly shared their experiences with the sleigh Ben had made out of bits and pieces—just a box and a rope. They had snow fights and even made a snowman. Predictably Ben took photos to show Em when she returned. They had such fun on the day it snowed while Em was away. The children's enthusiasm was especially visible. There were so few opportunities in those dark days for them to be and act like children. Ben and Em were happy to see something good happening in their lives. However, on the downside, little Loeki was certainly not well. They were sure now he also had Haemophilia.

Ben called the family to the table for the evening meal.

"Tonight's dinner was the best I can remember eating, Papa," Gerda, always very vocal, asserted. "Even the barley tasted nice in that soup! Charles actually ate it in a very short time, and can you believe he asked for more?"

Ben sighed contentedly. "A change indeed, rather than Papa standing over you for an hour or so, trying to convince you to swallow even a few mouthfuls!"

The boy smiled at his father. He knew what his Papa said was true. Em looked pale.

"Tired?" Ben asked.

She nodded. "Would you mind if I go straight to bed?" Em yawned as she spoke.

Sadly, although Em went to bed early that night, she and Ben had a fretful night with Louis. "So much for a good night's sleep," Em contemplated at half-past one in the morning as she prepared wet bandages for Louis, just as she had on Charles' injuries, and just as she had learnt from observing her own mother doing on Gerrit, her brother, so many years ago.

Ice was usually the first topical method of treating a bleed on the outside of the body. Then came the bandages. They were dipped into Arnica, a homeopathic remedy known to curtail and eventually stop the swelling. Another remedy was minute dosages of Witch Hazel in water to help stop internal bleeding. During the night, when the child woke, she would rewrap the injured ankle with fresh Arnica bandages and try to make him comfortable with Aspirin, and eventually the little fellow would drop off—until the extreme pain in the swollen joint forced him awake again. These were long nights for Louis and his parents, hovering over him like eagles watching over their fledgling. Charles and Louis, like all boys born with Haemophilia, learnt to live with much pain, from their earliest recollections. Days of pain were most common, but in more serious injuries, it could be weeks and even months of being bedridden. Pale and listless, boys with Haemophilia are often worn out by acute pain.

"I'm glad I know what to do for my sons. At least my experiences growing up with Gerrit have somewhat prepared me for this." She was just settling into bed; the hall clock on its nightly vigil was just gonging half-past two. With a long yawn and sigh, Em finally fell into a deep sleep.

Not two hours later Louis started moaning in pain. Em jumped up and applied fresh bandages and gave him another Aspirin—the only thing on the market she could give him for the pain. She of course gave him naturopathic remedies, but sometimes the pain was more than they could mask.

It was ten o'clock in the morning when Ben roused Em by pulling back the heavy drapes and blankets off the bedroom window. During the night there had been a heavy snowfall and everywhere the brilliant white lay. The Pubbens' roof was laden with a white snow shawl, and all the trees were glistening with magnificent flakes, hanging like crystal chandeliers.

He stood contemplating the peaceful and exquisite scene before his eyes. "Look, sweetheart, it snowed overnight. Come and have a look at it." Em murmured something unintelligible, instantly drifting off again, even before she could drink one mouthful of the cup of herb tea Ben had brought her.

He stood looking at his wife. "Em, you have such a kind heart— never a complaint—all the patience in the world. A wonderful mother for my children." He leant over and softly placed a whisper of a kiss on her forehead. She didn't move, and he could hear a soft snore coming from her. "She's completely spent, poor thing."

He walked away sadly to see to his little son in the cot who was whimpering with pain. "Papa's coming, Loeki. It's all right. It's Nurse Papa's turn again during the day until Mama recovers."

Charles in the wars with Haemophilia - bleeding again.

*

Another example of Em's nursing expertise and resourcefulness was demonstrated some years later when Charles was about eight years old. Like most curious and mischievous children, Charles and Louis were fascinated with the modern invention of the electrically operated washing machine that the Bijls had invested in after the war. When Mama was not in sight, he and Louis would delight in wetting their hands and sticking their fingers in the wringers, and at the strategic moment, they would withdraw their fingers and beat the wringers. This theory was all right until one day, the wringer beat them!

Charles had somehow been distracted and his arm began to be pulled through the wringer. He screamed for his mother. Louis ran to get her. Meanwhile the wringer gobbled up Charles' arm up to the elbow, and still the child was unable to release the safety knob. By the time he did release the knob, the wringer had reached almost to his armpit Em rushed in, frantic, when she saw what he had done. Em yelled as she ran to the door of the shed in the backyard where the washing machine was housed. By this time, Charles had already released his arm from the wringer.

"Mama! Mama!" Charles wailed, clutching his squashed limb. Try to imagine the old type wringers and how tightly they pressed the clothes between the two rubber-covered steel presses. Remarkably, the arm was only slightly flattened but nevertheless bruised from fingers to armpit.

Picking up her son, she raced frantically into the house and immediately gave Charles the Witch Hazel drops, known for slowing bleeding, and applied cold compresses to try to stop the external bruising as quickly as possible. Next the wet bandages were applied with Arnica. After six months, Charles was still wearing a sling and his left arm was still partially paralysed, as there was a lot of nerve damage. Even back in the late 1940s, Em was aware of the need for exercise to promote healing of the body. She made a game out of an exercise to promote and restore the mobility of the hand and finger muscles and tendons. It was a bowl of warm water into which she placed about twenty lovely marbles with bright, rippling colors. She urged Charles to dive into the water and retrieve one marble at a time, and with each marble he was given a reward. He complained bitterly, but after each marble he got a "zoutedrop" (a double salted liquorice treat). Needless to say, by the end of the afternoon, Charles had succeeded in picking up each and every marble.

Over time, day after day, Em encouraged her son to do these gentle stretching exercises. Charles and Em saw the great things that had happened since he had done the exercises. Although he was never completely able to use that arm or hand again as one normally should, he was able to get by. To encourage Charles to use that arm even more, on his ninth birthday Ben and Em bought him a half-size guitar and encouraged him to learn to play it, as this also gave the arms, hands, and fingers great stimulation. That started a lifelong love affair with guitars.

CHAPTER 23

The Desperate Winter 1944-45

Despite the precious foodstuffs that Em had brought home from Putten, which by comparisons was a feast, the Bijls were like the majority of people in The Netherlands since 1944 had been, literally starving or at least extremely malnourished.

Ben was really concerned. "Em, I am worried about you in this malnourished state. The risk of haemorrhaging, which I don't need to tell you, is far greater when the body is in a weakened state. And this is the second pregnancy you have been deprived in, so it could be far more dangerous."

"Don't worry, Ben, I'll be all right if we can just get a little food each day. I guess I'll hardly have a tooth in my head by the time this war ends. These babies are taking a lot out of me. But I don't mind as long as they are born reasonably healthy. It's the food that can be gotten on food lines that I fear. It's so devitalized. It probably doesn't do anything except stem the hunger pangs. Stop worrying. If we lived in Amsterdam, we'd really have something to worry about."

"Yes, I guess you're right, Em. Pa wrote while you were away at Putten, did I tell you?" Ben added sadly.

"No. What did he say? Everything must be okay for them or you would have told me." Their eyes met instantly. "Yes?"

"Spot on, Em. But he did say things are so bad that schools have closed because there is no heating or electricity and of course the growing problem of no food. Children are dying in their mother's arms. Grown adults are so weak, they can only sleep all day, many of them dying from deprivation."

"Ben! What about your sons Ben and Hans, and your brothers and their families? How are they coping?"

"Well, together they are surviving, helping one another with the little they can rake together. Living in such close proximity has made this possible. Just one member of the family stands in the food lines each day, while the rest of them stay in bed to keep warm, and conserve what little energy they have. This way they only have to stand in the freezing cold winds or the snow about once a week instead of everyday."

"That's good. Okay Ben, the whole nation will perish if something isn't done soon."

"The Dutch people have been pleading with the Allies to supply some basic food items, and I read in the paper this morning that they have promised to supply food in air drops very soon. I only hope it's soon enough!"

February and March dragged on. The whole country was still waiting for relief supplies. Everyone prayed help would arrive since thousands had already perished.

One morning the people in Ben and Em's Utrecht district, as well as in other parts of The Netherlands, heard the whirring of planes overhead.

"Those planes are very low, Ben, and it's unusual for them to pass over in the morning." Em turned her head to the side, straining to hear, stopping her task at hand. "You don't think it's food drops, do you? Oh God, please let it be food!"

Ben raced to the bedroom window. "Could be. Lord, I hope it is!" He peered out in the direction of the sound. There in the close distance he saw parachutes with huge canvas parcels dangling from them, falling toward the ground.

"It is! It's food - food from heaven. It's finally arrived—the long-promised food aid."

Em joined him in awe at the window. The sky was adrift with "mushrooms," and the prospect of food excited the taste buds. It all seemed too good to be true.

"I'm so thankful! It's wonderful…" She wiped the tears from her eyes. Ben took her in his arms and danced around the bedroom. Finally, he stopped and sat Em on the side of the bed. "Everything is going to be all right, schatje. You'll see!"

"Ben, I do hope it's not too late to help our baby!"

Ben quickly put on the wig, veil, nurse's dress, and coat, brushed Em's cheek with a kiss, and raced off.

Em stood smiling at the window, still unbelieving. She heard the back door open as Ben rushed out with her faithful old bicycle. It slammed shut. Quickly down the street and around their block he rode in the direction of the parachute drop. Shortly he arrived at the playing field where several people were converging as well. The huge chutes with their enormous big parcels in tow were scattered across the spacious field. All in the neighbourhood arrived with bags in their hands, heading to the parcels. Already some were frantically trying to pull them apart.

"Can't I help you, Sir?" Ben smiled as two men looked up at the sound of his voice. The smile on their faces indicated some amusement.

"If it isn't Sister Bernadina! Great day, isn't it? Yes, it certainly will be when we get the outer covering off. Now, Antonius, I think we've just about got it open."

As they pulled the covering aside, the aroma of freshly baked bread wafted into their nostrils. "Wow! This is manna from heaven! Smell the aroma of this—heavenly isn't the name for it! Smells fantastic!" They eagerly tore the wrappers from one of the loaves, biting into it hungrily.

"Here, Sister, try this. Mmm! Mmm!" A not-so-clean hand held out a chunk of bread.

Ben gasped as he swallowed the first mouthful. "And it's white, soft, wheat bread! Marvellous!"

"Mmm! You can say that again," Antonius mumbled, saliva dripping from his mouth as he spoke. "And what else is in that box?"

"Looks like mostly bread, but wait—on the bottom there are tins, tins of …"

The other fellow opened one deftly with his penknife and peered into it. Then his eyes lit up. Next, he dipped his finger in and tasted it. He smiled. "It's dried eggs!"

"And this tin has sugar in it!" Ben added excitedly. "And this one has powdered milk! Aren't they angels, those Swedes?"

"Damned if I know who dropped it, Sister, but it sure just arrived in time. Honestly, I thought if we had to last another month without relief, half the population of The Netherlands would perish. It's arrived just in the nick of time, I say," Antonius replied gratefully.

"Yes, that's what my father wrote about life in Amsterdam too," Ben said. While they were talking, a police car arrived. A policeman from the Zeist Police Station alighted to supervise the distribution.

"Looks like Sergeant Alleman," Antonius whispered to his companion. "Do you recognise him?"

"Yes, that's him. I guess he's here to make sure the food is shared around fairly."

"A good thing too." Antonius eyed Ben off suspiciously. Then Antonius and his friend grabbed more than a fair share and raced off, arms bulging with foodstuffs. Sister Bernadina frowned disapprovingly. "Well, Sister, I'm going before he gets here to tell me how much I can have. I'm taking what I feel my family deserves. Right?"

Ben stood, shaking his head. "Some people."

The police sergeant approached them, his smiling face like a broken coconut. Then, winking at Ben, he said, "Glad to see you're here, Sister. Would you care to help me dole out this food before you get on with your work?"

"Certainly, Sergeant Alleman." Ben tried to smile delicately. By this time, quite a crowd had gathered around the sergeant, and together they broke open parcel after parcel while Sister Bernadina made sure each family got a selection of what was available.

"Tell us who are the angels who sent us this?" a woman in the crowd asked.

"Why, the Swedes of course!" Sergeant Alleman volunteered. "Who else? They have been trying to get food to us for months now, but you know bureaucracy—full of all the red tape under the sun—takes forever to organise things. But here it is at last! They have promised to supply food for the Dutch until this bloody war ends."

"If it ever ends," she answered sadly. Exhaustion was written over her gaunt face.

She's old before her time, poor soul, Ben thought as he listened. He handed her her allotted stuff as she got to him in the queue. All too soon though the food ran out. The policeman waved the remainder of the people away.

"Sorry, friends. That's all today, but there will be more tomorrow, and those who got none today will be given priority tomorrow."

"That's right. Trust me to miss out," one poor old lady whimpered.

"I've prayed to die many times this winter, but the Lord hasn't put me out of my misery."

Ben saw how frail and broken she was. "It's all right, madam. He knew we would soon have food and you will soon feel much better. Here you are. Please take one of my loaves—it will see you through tomorrow and more. Yes?"

"Oh, thank you, thank you, Sister." The tears in her eyes were all the thanks Ben needed for his compassion. "Do you really think there will be more food drops?" She was doubtful.

"Why yes, my dear. Sergeant Alleman assures us more will arrive tomorrow and will continue to be delivered until the war is ended. That's right, isn't it, Sergeant?"

"Yes, that's true. Wonderful, isn't it?" He patted the old lady on the shoulder to encourage her. She walked away with a little hopeful smile on her weary old face.

"Well, Sister, it looks like our work is done for today. Many thanks for your assistance. I don't know what it is about a uniform, but it always helps people to remain more orderly; have you noticed?"

They both laughed. Ben forgot who he was for a moment, but the sergeant, who already knew his secret and had often helped him out of danger in the past, was not going to give him away. In fact, he was responsible for many a warning call during the time the Nazis were making regular raids on civilian homes.

"See you tomorrow then." Ben's eyes had a devilish twinkle in them. "Bye for now."

As he walked slowly away, the sergeant whispered under his breath, "What a fellow indeed! Few would dare to do a 'Sister Bernadina,' that's certain."

This demonstration of humanity helped negate the seriousness of the food shortages that they had been experiencing for the past year or so, especially that fatefully cold and heartless winter, which seemed to emulate the state of the oppressor over them. How thankful they were to Sweden, one of the Allied countries, who had continued supplying food for many months after the war ended in May 1945. It was still terribly rationed, but at least it was edible, wholesome basic food stuffs—bread, dried eggs, and other primary foods. After what they had endured in recent months, it was indeed manna from heaven and tasted like it too.

News that the end of the war was imminent was filtering through. "Now is our turn," Ben said excitedly as he heard these reports. "Just wait and see, Em, the end of the war is imminent. Please let it happen before Em gives birth."

*

A few weeks passed, just five or six, with the regular food drops revitalizing the worn-out population of The Netherlands at the death-knock. Thousands of poorer people—the young and very old from the cities of Amsterdam and Rotterdam were not so lucky. Some fifteen thousand died during the winter of 1944–45.

Ben and Em and their little family were amongst the luckiest ones—food came before it was too late. They were young enough to exert themselves vigorously to get food from other sources. They also were "blessed" with Em's trusty bicycle and Ben's incredible foresight!

One evening Ben was sitting in bed with his headphones on, listening to his crystal set. The children were asleep in their make-shift beds on the floor surrounding their parents' bed like satellites. Em was just about to get into bed, with only weeks to go before her fourth child arrived.

"Em, Em! The Russians and the Americans are right this minute physically converging on Berlin! Isn't that great news?"

"If it's true then it would be wonderful, Ben." Her voice was paper thin and weak. "I am so sick and tired of struggling."

Ben nodded. "I agree. Anyway, my love, come to bed. It's so late. Let's hope it ends before our little one arrives. Fancy bringing another child into this terrible world."

"Yes, just fancy that! And yet you men insist on making love even though you know the likely consequences. Shame on you!"

"But my schatje, if you weren't so loveable—"

"I guess that's as good excuse as any." Em laughed despite her anguish.

Ben's eyebrows began dancing up and down suggestively. She leaned across the bed and kissed her husband. Naturally, he responded amorously.

"Ben, control yourself! Good night!" She turned away quickly, trying to avoid the situation looming before her. The days of the contraceptive pill or implant had not yet arrived. She felt well-founded trepidation.

"Good night, my sweet. Love you." He pursued her.

"And I love you too." Her reassurance set him off again. He stared at his wife with a look of pleading, and then, totally frustrated, blew out the candle on his bedside table.

*

A few mornings later, on May 5, 1945, Ben woke a little earlier than usual. He immediately donned his earphones to hear the latest news.

"Em! Em! The Canadians are marching into Zeist—yes, Zeist this very minute! They have come at last to liberate us!"

"Are you sure? Can it really be true?" Em suddenly sprang to life. "That means the war has ended?"

"Yes, Em, the war is over!" He jumped across the bed and hugged and kissed her. "Germany has capitulated and has been ordered to withdraw from The Netherlands."

Tears streamed down Em's face as he spoke. She looked stunned. "You'd better believe it, because the Canadians are coming into Zeist right now as we speak. Let's dress the children and walk down to the main street to celebrate with our neighbours and friends. Because I'm sure they too will be feeling just as exhilarated as we are! I think this is a day too special to miss, don't you?" She nodded enthusiastically. "And we just have to share it!"

Gerda sat up, rubbing her eyes and trying to understand her parents' sudden elation.

"Gerda, schatje!" Her father lifted her into his arms, twirling her around. "The war has ended."

CHAPTER 24

Liberation Day Arrives!

What joy filled the hearts of the people as finally they heard the news, that they had so much desired to hear for the previous almost six years—peace at last, freedom at last, the long, dark night had ended!

Ben and Em, along with their children dressed quickly and walked down to the main street of Zeist. Even before they arrived at the Town Hall, they could hear the sound of tumult everywhere.

"What's all that noise Papa?" Gerda asked as she ran forward straining to hear and see more.

"That's the sound of drums, and voices, children. Voices shouting for joy because the war has finally ended. Freedom at last!" They neared the corner leading to the main street. "Look children! You can see now for yourselves. See there! The Canadian soldiers who have liberated us from the Nazi strangle-hold."

"And what's that other funny noise? What are those men in skirts holding?" Gerda was fascinated.

"That's the Scots Band playing their bagpipes." Em replied, smiling as Louis and Charles put their hands over their ears.

"I think it's an awful sound." Charles said and Gerda totally agreed. They all laughed.

"It certainly is a unique sound." Ben added, "It really tugs at one's emotions though."

"Too mournful for me, I'm afraid." Em admitted.

"Why are the people holding up those coloured striped bits of material and waving them?" Charles asked naively.

"Don't you know silly. That's our country's flag, they're waving." Gerda said contemptuously to her little brother.

"Come on Gerda," Em interrupted before Charles could respond, "Charles doesn't go to school yet and that is probably the only reason why you know what they are. In his short life he's never seen a Dutch flag, only the Nazi Swastika."

"Oh, sorry Charles," she ceded.

Since the Nazi Occupation the red, white and cobalt blue striped flag had been banned. "Today's turnout shows the House of Orange is still where most people have their loyalties. I guess they had them hidden away during the past five years, praying for peace to return. And, today - children, today is that day!"

"I see, so that's why the people are so happy." Gerda concluded. "Actually," Ben added, "the Canadian soldiers are every bit as happy as we are. Look how they are throwing their green berets high into the air and whooping!"

"Yes of course, because the war ending, means they can go home to their loved ones too." Em added smiling.

"Look children. Here comes the Mayor of Zeist. He is going to make an announcement, I think. Shh now." The mayor waved his arms in front of the crowds and instantly there was a deafening hush.

"Ladies, gentlemen and children. Please remain silent and listen now to the radio broadcast from our Sovereign, Queen Wilhelmina on this day May 5, 1945. This is a day of rebirth and return to freedom." With deep emotion, the people of the Dutch nation listened intently to the words of their beloved monarch.

Here is Queen Wilhelmina's announcement to her subjects, translated from Dutch into English:

> "My countrymen,
>
> "The hour of our freedom has now come forth. The moment, which both you and I have waited for with such

intensity and impatience, is here. I know what bitter-tasting times you have had to experience being cut off from the rest of our Fatherland these past few months.

"The pressure has now finally come to an end. I know also that you have displayed courage beyond what is normal for humankind, and you have lived through and have carried the darkest load.

"Hands are outstretched to you to end your suffering as speedily as possible. And the speed in which that occurs depends on how calmly and cooperatively you conduct yourself in the coming days.

"Obedience from the many, whereby the Government can give rulings, which will restore us all, is needed.

"Listen to the instructions of your Netherland's military officers and overseers who will instruct you in the rulings and the leadership of The Netherland's Government, whose task is to oversee the rebuilding of our society.

"I hope to return to The Netherland's Government speedily and be with my responsible advisors, sharing in the job of governing our land again.

"May God's blessing rest upon you all. Rise up again, Netherlands. Long live the Fatherland!"

The Netherland's Anthem played as Queen Wilhelmina's restoration speech concluded. The crowds cheered and clapped and danced joyously. It seemed endless!

Then the Mayor announced: "The people of Zeist will celebrate Bevrijdingsdag (Liberation Day for The Netherlands). That is May 7, 1945. It will be a street procession with bands and soldiers and civilians all together and culminate in the town's Central Park for partying. All welcome!"

Throughout The Netherlands, the Dutch people also prepared to celebrate V-E Day held on the May 8 as well. Many of the Allied troops would still be seen, as the "mopping up" work went on during the following months. In Zeist, along with the rest of the free world, people celebrated the end of the most monstrous war in the history of mankind!

On May 7 Em rushed to get the children ready.

"Why are we wearing these big orange sashes, Mama?" Gerda was tugging at her ribbon, which her mother had just pulled over her right shoulder and tied across the left side of her waist. "Boys don't wear sashes; that's sissy!"

"The big party we are going to at the park today is to celebrate the return of peace to our country and the return of our Royal Family to our homeland."

"So now, what do these sashes have to do with them, Mama?" Gerda frowned impatiently, tugging again at the sash.

"Well, the Dutch Royal Family is from the House of Orange, and that is what the orange sash signifies, Gerda. That is also why the boys can wear one today as well. It is a special celebration. Today there will be lots of games, and special foods for everyone to enjoy! Sound exciting?"

"Yes, I can't wait to eat more of those lovely foods, especially the white, fluffy bread we have been eating since the planes dropped it in the fields."

"Come on, children. Are you ready?" Ben called. "We should go now, or we will miss the march." Ben was pushing the big old carriage with Louis sitting up in it, all eyes, while Em clasped Gerda and Charles' hands and guided them to the front door.

"We're ready now, Ben. Have you got the camera? This is an historical day? We should have some photos!"

"What do you think I am, Em?" Ben winked as she approached him at the front door. "Of course, I have! You should know that it's in my blood, passed down from three generations of photographers! I'd never miss a once in a lifetime opportunity to record history like this Em."

Bevrijdingsdag celebrations in Zeist on May 7 1945

The Bijl family arrived just in the nick of time. The town's dignitaries came along the street in cars and on foot, led by the town band, as well as the Scottish Military Band. Close on their heels followed the Canadian liberators. The Canadians, with their green berets, were the face of the Allies who had fought so long to release many from the strangle-hold of the Nazi Swastika and its tyranny in The Netherlands. Ben raced around taking photos, which he intended to sell as souvenirs to the public.

Everyone joined in singing liberation songs, and songs about their homeland rang out. Eagerly the townsfolk joined in the singing and dancing. After the victory march, they met on the street and shared wonderful meals together as well as fun-filled games—all signifying a spirit of release and freedom.

"Quick, Ben." Em nudged her husband to look behind him. "Please take a photo of Charles - look! That young Canadian has put his beret on Charles' head! Look how cute he looks!"

Ben took the photos and walked up to Charles and his newfound friend. "My name's Ben Bijl," Ben said in Dutch, smiling broadly at the friendly soldier. "This is my little boy." Ben held out his hand.

"Pleased to meet you, Ben. My name's Peter McLean." He spoke a little Dutch, intermingled with English. The Canadian shook Ben's hand. "This is indeed a happy day for everyone!"

"That it is! Thank you for your country's part in helping bring about our liberation, Peter." They managed to understand each other basically. Then Ben's eyes twinkled as looking down, his eyes lit up upon the tell-tale silver foil of chocolate paper in his son's hands.

"And Charles, my son, what is this?" Ben asked, pointing to the scrumptious, "melt in your mouth" brown slab.

"Ohhh! It's choco—what did you call it, Peter?"

"Chocolate, Charles, chocolate—got it?"

"Yes, Papa, it's chocolate! Like some?" Charles offered some of a now sticky lump to his father.

"No, no, Charles!" Peter said. "You have that one. See, I've got more. Here's one for your father too!"

Ben willingly accepted the block of chocolate. "Thank you, Peter. This will indeed be a luxury for old Ben!"

"What's this 'old' business, Ben?" Peter laughed heartily. "You're probably younger than my dad."

"Possibly, but I have two older boys—Ben, who's almost eighteen, and Hans, who's about eleven now. They live in Amsterdam with their mother. Where do you live in Canada, Peter?"

While Peter elaborated, Ben keenly demolished a few squares of the chocolate.

"I live in the state of Nova Scotia. My family are farmers on the east coast of Canada. It's beautiful country, very cold like The Netherlands, but still I love it and can't wait to go home to see my family." Em strolled across the park to where they were standing.

"By the way, Peter, this is my wife, Em, and our other children, Gerda and Louis."

"Pleased to meet you, ma'am," Peter said as Em held out her hand.

He smiled approvingly. Em was still a beautiful woman.

"I am pleased to meet you too, Peter. Ben and I have been talking about leaving The Netherlands in the next few years. Canada is one of the places we have discussed as a possible new home for our family. Do you think we would like it?"

"Why yes, ma'am! I'm sure you would. Canada is indeed a beautiful country. And the Dutch people are used to the cold climate. So yes, I believe it would be a good choice."

A chorus of shrieks of delight deafened them all, demanding their attention. The time had come for the games and races to begin. The first was the egg and spoon race. Louis, Charles, and Gerda lined up with the other children. Each child was given a spoon with a boiled egg on it. The gun fired, and off the children hurried. Oops! Gerda's egg fell off, amidst many others. There was nothing to it but to pick it up and keep running to the finish line at the far end of the park. Screams and laughter echoed throughout the park as they made their way to the end. The winner was awarded a gift, but all the other children were given their egg to eat for their efforts!

Next came the sack races. After many spills, ups, and downs, the excited young ones reached the finish line. They were enjoying themselves immensely. However, they derived the most fun out of the three-legged race. Gerda and Charles were a pair. They set off very well actually, but as their enthusiasm to win grew, their balance became tottery. Before they knew it, they were sprawling on the grass! Many of their mates came hopping along past them. Every child was favourably rewarded for his or her effort in each race, so no-one felt overlooked.

In the middle of the park were two large boxes, covered in brightly coloured paper. One was labeled "Boys" and one "Girls"—a lucky dip! Without looking into the box, each child could choose a parcel. Gerda unwrapped her little gift. Gerda gasped in excitement, "Oh! A tiny doll!" She drew her to her chest, adding, "And I love her." Charles' gift was a toy airplane.

When Louis saw his brother's gift, he asked, "One for Loeki too?" Em took him to the "Boy" box and he too was able to choose a parcel. His parcel, probably the first real present he had had in his short life.

Em asked him, "Well Loeki, what is in your parcel?"

"It's a bear Mama–a bear!" A grin spread across the delighted little child's face. "Loeki likes him very much."

"There's something in that box for everyone, isn't there?" Ben observed. "Just as well he likes the bear," Ben whispered to Em. "For a second I was afraid he would still want Charlie's plane."

Em laughed softly. "These gifts are so unusual to our kids, they are thrilled, I think, with anything new!"

The afternoon flew past all too quickly, although people lingered, not wanting the pleasure of freedom to end. Em being so close to her baby's birth offered to go home with Louis and allow Ben and the older children the opportunity to stay on, but Ben disagreed.

"No, my schatje. We'll all go home together. It's been a thrilling day, and I would like to get home reasonably early, so I can develop some of my films. We can sell the photos as mementos—postcards over the coming weeks. I think almost everyone will want some of these to recall a unique day in history, don't you?"

"Yes, I believe they will. A great idea, Ben! Good then. Let's round up the children. It's going to be hard. They are having so much fun!"

Across the park amongst dozens of other youngsters, Ben saw them. "Look at them. It warms my heart. Laughing and running and playing! Something that these children, especially the boys, have known very little about for almost all their short lives."

"It's wonderful to see." Em said. "We have lived in 'prison' for so long, we'd almost forgotten what it is like to be happy and carefree."

As they walked home, Gerda, who was in her eighth year, said, "This has been the best day of my life, Mama and Papa!" Then, reconsidering, she said, "Ah well, perhaps apart from Auntie Jannie's wedding."

"Was it, sweetheart? That's good. And you know what?" She looked into her father's magnetic eyes in avid anticipation. "You're probably right!"

The children fell asleep very early that evening. Summer was on the doorstep. Rarely if ever had they had so much excitement and exercise in one day!

Ben and Em for the first time in years sat truly relaxed on the comfy sofa.

"Well, Em, it's been a memorable day, hasn't it?"

"Yes, schatje. It's like resurfacing after waking from a long and horrible nightmare. I have to keep pinching myself to make sure it's real."

"Tell me, how are you really feeling?"

Tear drops fell from her deep-blue eyes and stained her cheeks. "I am so grateful Ben. I prayed to God that this baby would not arrive before the war ended. He didn't let me down—but I don't think it will be too long. The baby dropped quite low a couple of weeks ago, a sure sign that things are getting ready. Our baby will be born in peace! Thank God."

"That certainly is a blessing, Em. And it may surprise you to know I too have been praying—yes, me—old Ben."

Em smiled. "And what have you been praying for, Ben Bijl?"

"I am still praying that you give me another daughter! I have four sons and only one daughter."

Em's lips quivered and then tears returned. Sob after sob seemed to be rung from her heart.

"What's wrong? Isn't that what you want too?" Ben asked incredulously. Em nodded. She just wept.

"Women! I will never understand them as long as I live. Just look at you!"

After sometime she commanded control of her emotions. "Now"— Em swallowed hard, trying to retrieve her voice—"it's all right. You took the words out of my mouth. That was my second wish. A healthy little girl."

*

That first week of May 1945 was like the curtain call for a blockbuster movie that had finally ended—from darkness into light— like passing from reality into unreality. The heavy burdens of bondage for the past five years were cast off like a kite floating high in the sky after hours of being entangled and restricted.

The downstairs clock struck nine. Em opened her eyes to golden sunlight streaming in their bedroom window. She stretched like a cat, long and hard, thinking, Sunshine always lifts the spirits. It is almost always heralding better things to come. She then snuggled into her blankets and enjoyed the wonderful feeling of freedom—the feeling of being safe!

"Ben, do you realize that for the first time in years we were able to go to bed in our pyjamas last night?"

Ben wriggled around in the bed. His eyes opened wide, signalling recognition, and his lips curved into a gigantic toothy smile. "Yes, schatje. And what a luxury that is!"

He suddenly stopped smiling. He looked out the window, framed by billowing curtains, contemplating. Then looking toward Em, he added, "And I hope we never again have to spend night after night being woken by the sound of air raid sirens and planes swooping low over our homes—and bombs going off and the fear of waiting for the bomb to hit its target—will it be us? Going out the next morning to see parachutes caught up in tall trees and the parachutist dead, enshrouded in what should have preserved his life. Such irony! Great craters in the ground where a bomb has exploded and just missed a home or a shop. Or worse still, an explosion killing and maiming its innocent occupants.

It's bad enough to think of parents dragging small children up out of bed to stand in the doorways, or next to the stairwell, in case their house is hit during an air raid."

Em wiped away the seemingly endless flow of tears from her eyes as her husband's words came tumbling out, expressing her own sentiments exactly. How long they had been bottling up their fears and yearnings. She whispered, "And now at last it is over."

Ben discerned her reactions to his words. He quickly sat up and wiped away the tears that continued to fall. Washing away the pains and tensions of one of the darkest time periods in history just as a sudden downpour in a parched land revitalizes and refreshes.

Ben finally spoke about his vision for the future. "I don't want my family to suffer as we just have and try to live through this again."

Em asked, "So you are still determined to emigrate to Canada or South Africa?"

"Yes, or we could even consider New Zealand. Young Bert next door has a friend who already lives there, and he says, "It's a beautiful country, green and lush with magnificent lakes and mountains and lots of other wonderful things! Perhaps Australia is like that too. You know, although I love our homeland, it isn't the most diverse landscape, is it?"

"Mostly lowhills and polders in the south and tall dykes and polders keeping out the sea all the way north, with reclaimed land as flat as a pancake! But I still call it home, Ben," she replied a little pensively.

"Only until we adjust, dear; only until we settle down. Well I have much work to do. What time is brekkie?"

"Do you mind if I make it an early lunch today? I'd like to savour the wonderful feeling I have at present. I don't want it to end. You know?"

"That I do. Ah well, I guess old Ben won't starve before eleven o'clock after what we have come through. How about eleven for brunch?"

Em rolled over, closing her eyes once again. "Yes, eleven would be fine. And what would you like to eat today?"

"Something I have salivated over for three years at least. A piece of fresh white bread, with wads of butter, covered with slices of tomato, and sprinkled with sugar."

"Well that I can make for you—as unusual a request as it is. I was amazed that they actually offered each family a couple of tomatoes in the last food drop. I guess they know it's been years since most of us have had any salad vegetables at all. Most people like tomatoes with salt, but you always were an enigma, weren't you?"

Ben stopped at the end of the hall, about to disappear down the stairwell. He retraced his steps, sniggering softly, ignoring Em's comment. "What's wrong with the world anyway? Didn't you know that tomato sprinkled with sugar is the poor man's strawberry? What more delightful taste could there be?"

But Em didn't answer. She was already asleep; he studied her for some time.

"Ben," he said aloud, "you are a lucky man. And I have a feeling that somehow brunch will be later than eleven o'clock." He tiptoed out.

*

From V-E Day onward, whenever Ben rode down the main street of Zeist, he was amazed to see how quickly things had changed. Many thriving businesses were immediately closed down, with their owners shamed. Meanwhile other brand-new businesses were bursting forth, opened by the Dutch loyalists.

Over dinner Ben related the latest news from the local paper.

"The Government has ordered that any who have been disloyal to the House of Orange be arrested. For the NSBer's, humble pie will be on the menu."

They were arrested and publicly condemned by the loyalists, who happened to be a majority. Also, any girls who were known to fraternise with the Nazis were publicly shamed. They were humiliated—the Dutch patriots shaved off all their hair, and they were forced to wear black scarves, with the swastika emblazoned on them, to identify them publicly as collaborators. The Dutch people were finally feeling a sense of justice taking place, with the tyrants being forcibly removed.

The Allied armies continued to stay on to help re-establish the rightful government of The Netherlands and ensure that at least essential services could be quickly restored—electricity, gas, and water being foremost. The Swedes kept up food supplies for many months until the polders were pumped out and new farms re-established where the Nazis had flooded them in the south. It was going to be a long haul, but peace, along with united effort, opened the way for success.

Less than three weeks after the Victory Day celebrations, in the early hours of the morning of May 25, 1945, Marjolein Anna was born. Marjolein was a tiny little bundle weighing just a little more than four and a half pounds. She was healthy and very pretty despite the malnourished state of her mother during those long and perilous nine months.

"It's a girl!" Ben said, rubbing his hands together.

Em kissed and cuddled the tiny pink little being so marvellously protected throughout her development in the womb. She smiled more than she had in years.

"While you get to know this little angel, I'll race downstairs and make a cup of real English tea—Peter the Canadian gave it to me. Won't be long!" Ben dashed out the door. Em could hear him whistling on the stairs. A few minutes later, he returned with the rich brown brew.

The next morning Em heard shrieks of excitement as Ben shared the lovely news with Gerda, Charles, and Louis and their faithful neighbour Mrs. de Rue who had become the adoptive Oma since she was so close by and so happy to be involved in their lives. They were soon tripping over each other, trying to be first up the stairs to meet their tiny baby sister.

Even Louis, who had had recurring bleeds in the ankle, was able to hobble up the stairs, saying, "Zelf Doen" ("I'll do it myself") with even more determination than Gerda. He climbed the stairs, refusing anyone's help for the first time in a couple of weeks to go along with his older siblings to welcome into the Bijl family a new little sister!

"Oh, Mama! She really is beautiful!" Charles said as he examined the new arrival, clutching her tiny fingers and feeling them grip tightly around his in return.

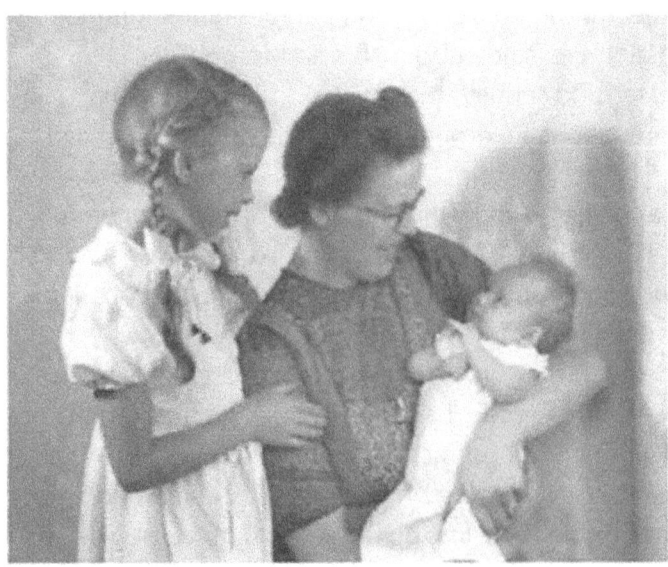

Baby Marjolein arrives three weeks after war ends.

The bonding had begun.

"She's like a real life-size doll!" Gerda said, gently stroking the downy head. "And what is her name, Mama?"

"Papa and I think we shall call this little girl Marjolein Anna. Do you like that name?"

"Yes, it's a very pretty name," Gerda said, leaning her head to one side when evaluating things. "Yes, I like it!"

"I like it too. Come, Loeki!" Charles held out his hand to his younger brother. "Come here and meet your new baby sister."

The little curly head bobbed up beside the spacious double bed. "Here Loeki, I will help you up." Charles offered, but the spirited toddler struggled to climb up on the bed alone, saying as usual, "Zelfdoen!" Louis' determination won out. He was soon snuggling up to Mama and taking his first look at baby Marjolein. Gently kissing the tiny head, "Loeki's baby," he said in awe.

"Yes, Loeki, she's a little playmate for you when Charles goes to school in July." The little curly head was suddenly tossed back, and the tiny hands were clapping in sheer delight. "Loeki's baby!"

Mrs. de Rue was delighted to share in the family's joy too. "Congratulations Em. She's a lovely little thing. I'm so relieved she arrived safely." At that moment Ben appeared at the door of the bedroom. Turning to him, she added, "Congratulations Ben, she's small but healthy."

"Thank you, Mrs. de Rue, she is. Now, children, make way for Papa. I have a hot cup of tea for Mama and Mrs. de Rue. Move aside please."

Ben laid the tray on the table, and as he handed the tea to Em, he added, "There's a treat here for you children too—chocolate!"

"Chocolate! Chocolate!" chorused the three excited siblings. A race ensued to reach the tray first.

Ben winked at Em. "Now, now! Share like good children. That's it!" He nodded as Gerda made what was in her estimation a fair distribution. She studied her handful after her father's gentle censure and offered another piece each to her younger brothers.

"Now enjoy your real English tea, schatje," Ben smiled.

Em responded, "And how about some chocolate for the hardworking Mama and Oma de Rue?"

"Why of course! How could we forget Mama?" Ben pulled a full block out of his pocket. "For you, dear Mama!"

"You know chocolate is my favourite food!" Em admitted.

"And here is some for you Oma." She said handing her a generous chunk.

Mrs. de Rue smiled, adding, "And thank you Em for sharing with me."

Ben laughed. "I doubt you'd be alone on that subject. Now enjoy! I am going to take some photos of our baby and tomorrow when you've rested up a little, we'll dress up this little gem and the kids and then take some family photos. Then we'll organize the printers and send the printed photos out to the family."

Three weeks later they put the final addresses on the envelopes to send the announcement of Marjolein's safe arrival to friends and relatives, as had been their tradition, even during the war.

Ben was about to place the last photo in the last envelope when he stopped and studied it before sealing it up.

"I'm not biased, Em, but you and I make beautiful children. Just look at them!"

At that moment baby Marjolein stirred in her bassinet. Em contemplated her husband's observations as she walked across to the baby, and lovingly picked her up. "I couldn't agree more. You know the saying though, Ben, 'Every mother crow thinks her baby is the blackest.' Some things are miracles!" She kissed the downy little head. "And this little beauty is one of them!" Em looked from the children in the photo before her to Ben. Their eyes met, there was laughter in them, and the joy of being a family was never more evident.

He leaned forward and kissed Em's forehead tenderly. "Old Ben loves you, Em."

"I know you do, Ben. You kept your promise."

"My promise?"

"Yes, you promised me when the war began you would never leave me or our children." Grasping his hand in her own, speaking from the very depths of her heart, she said, "Through all the troubles, pains, hunger, cold, and fears we faced, you did your very best for all of us. Ben Bijl, you proved your love for us. Yes, schatje, you kept your promise! And I'll always love you."

Ben studied his wife's face. With a smile of triumph, he replied, "It was nothing, my sweet, nothing."

"Ben Bijl, will there ever be a time when you are serious?"

Ben stared at the floor, pondering Em's comment. Seconds ticked by. He said nothing. Finally, Em said, "Why Ben, you are never lost for words. What's wrong?"

He slowly raised his head. Their eyes met. He breathed deeply ready to reveal what was in his heart.

"There was, my dear wife. You are the best thing that ever happened to me. The day I looked at you and said, "I do! I was serious." Yes. This time Ben was serious.

War's end. Peace and happiness reigns again.

EPILOGUE

Many of my readers have asked for the sequel to "Focus on Survival" Would you perhaps be interested in reading what happened to the Bijl Family?

Please keep checking my Facebook, Instagram and Website: www.focusonsurvivalbook.com

For news of what's coming up. Come with me on the journey as the Bijl family rebuild their lives after the war ended. The heartache of losing one of their precious children that acted as a catalyst to leaving the place of their birth. What prompted their decision to emigrate to Australia? Also how they finally set sail for Australia, coming via the Panama Canal. Feel the apprehension Ben and Em face as they disembarked, along with its many new challenges as well."

Look out for the sequel: Chasing Rainbows

AUTHOR'S BIO

Julie Annette Bayl

Julie Bayl was born in 1950 in Sydney, Australia, the second child of Bruce and Betty Judd. Both her parents' families came from farming Backgrounds, having properties in Victoria and New South Wales.

Circumstances after World War II led to her family settling outside Parramatta, where she and her siblings grew up. She has always had an intense interest in history.

In 1971 she married Charles Bayl (originally spelt Bijl) whose family had emigrated from The Netherlands in 1953 seeking a better life. They settled at Marmong Point on beautiful Lake Macquarie, north of Sydney.

After her marriage, Julie also lived there for three years until she and Charles moved to Cowra in Central New South Wales in 1974 and later had three children, Anita, Paul and David. They now have two delightful grandsons, Lennon and Banjo.

Soon after her marriage to Charles, her mother-in-law, Marlene (Em) shared with her stories of their family's experiences during World War II, which really intrigued Julie. Sadly Ben, Em's husband died just eighteen months after Julie's marriage.

Em expressed pleasure in Julie's suggestion that she would like to write their story. After many long conversations, note-taking and much research, Julie began to pen their exciting and heart-warming story –a story that needs to be told, not simply as an historical record but as an inspiring true story of courage, resilience and ingenuity.

Exterior cover of book by Mental Block Design Co.
Copyright Paul Bayl 2016

www.ingramcontent.com/pod-product-compliance
Lightning Source LLC
Chambersburg PA
CBHW052017070526
44584CB00016B/1790